941.1

CANCELLED

# SCOTLAND'S HISTORY

## APPROACHES AND REFLECTIONS

'Someone recently made, I think, the nicest remark ever made about me; I do treasure that. He said that I combined the enthusiasm of youth with the wisdom of age. Now, what better a judgment could you wish for than that? If anybody would put that as my epitaph, I'd be very happy.'

Gordon Donaldson
(Radio Shetland broadcast, 1992)

# SCOTLAND'S HISTORY
## APPROACHES AND REFLECTIONS

GORDON DONALDSON

edited by

JAMES KIRK

1995
SCOTTISH ACADEMIC PRESS
EDINBURGH

Published by
Scottish Academic Press Ltd.
56 Hanover Street, Edinburgh EH2 2DX

ISBN 0 7073 0728 7

**British Library Cataloguing in Publication Data**

A catalogue record for this book is available from
the British Library

Typeset by Trinity Typesetting

Printed in Great Britain by Martins the Printers Ltd, Berwick upon Tweed, bound
by Hunter & Foulis, Edinburgh

# Contents

# *Preface*

My association with this volume arose in the summer of 1992, on a visit to Dysart, when Gordon Donaldson inquired if I should be willing to read his text when he had finished revising it. His work on the volume, interrupted when he entered hospital in Kirkcaldy for surgery in the autumn, was speedily resumed during the winter. On a subsequent visit to Dysart in January, I learned that his text was nearing completion. I next met Gordon Donaldson in hospital at Windygates in late February where he imparted word of the gravity of his illness and requested me to see his book through the press.

In this volume, Gordon Donaldson, who has been said to combine 'the enthusiasm of youth with the wisdom of age', presents, in twelve hitherto unpublished essays, the mature fruits of sixty-years' study of Scottish history. The book reflects – and sometimes recounts – his experiences in teaching, researching, writing and even in giving evidence before the House of Lords in peerage cases. Above all, it reflects a familiarity with Scotland's older records which few can equal (and he throws in a tantalising note, 'John Knox on Queen Mary's payroll'). Donaldson's wide-ranging knowledge has made him a formidable reviewer, who as a matter of course counts fifty factual errors in a single book. He makes hay of oral tradition, rejects any logic in Jacobitism, revises common views on surnames and Christian names, and on some cherished myths he does a demolition job which, in his own words, Attila the Hun might have envied. He is most serious when he contests the image of Scotland as 'backward', explores Scotland's international links, discusses the Anglicisation of Scotland, and questions the logic of turning a battlefield into a tourist attraction. He muses on how 'the same old errors are constantly being trotted out by new writers', and makes confession of errors of his own, at which – like much else in this witty book – the reader will chuckle.

In preparing the Index for a work embracing such a variety of topics (from General Mihajlovic to the Garvelloch Isles), I have sought to be as comprehensive as is practicable. I would express my gratitude to Dr Douglas Grant of the Scottish Academic Press for his particular interest in the work. Finally, the intention of preparing an invited Memoir of the author as a preface to the collection of essays in this volume has been modified, and the fifty-pages of Memoir will form part of an enlarged biography of Gordon Donaldson to appear as a separate publication.

The University of Glasgow                                    JAMES KIRK

# *Foreword*

This Foreword opens with part of an address given at the launching party of *The Sunday Mail Story of Scotland* on 14 April 1988 and reported in *The Sunday Mail* on 17 April following.

It continues and concludes with remarks which I often made in an introductory talk to my Ordinary Class.

I don't know whether any of you have ever stood, as I have so often done, on the bridge of a ship leaving Aberdeen harbour. If so, you may have wondered why the skipper, as well as looking ahead to the open waters of the North Sea, from time to time looks back over the stern. He does this because the line of the navigable channel is marked by two white beacons among the buildings of the town and, in order to keep in the channel, he must have those two beacons lined up. Somewhat similarly, the skipper of a ship heading north out of Kirkwall looks astern to keep the tower of the 850-year old cathedral of St Magnus in line with the westmost point of Shapinsay, because only so can he take the ship safely through the narrow Sound of Vassa.

What is true of the master of a ship is even more true of anyone practised in rowing a boat in his home waters. He has familiarised himself with points on the shore and he keeps on his course by what he can see astern and not by looking ahead over his shoulder.

In each case, it is only by looking back that the skipper or the oarsman can be sure of his way forward. I wonder if this is the argument for knowing history. Can we know where we are going without knowing where we have come from? Do we need to look back sometimes to make sure we are on the right course ahead?

I remember once hearing a man say, 'I'm not interested in the past, I'm only interested in the future.' I have often thought that a peculiarly silly remark. The man who made it is now a Member of Parliament. The truth is that the past has shaped the present, and the past and the present will shape the future.

Some of the marks in Scotland's past where we should find guidance about where we are going may have been entirely lost by erosion, but it is easier to see that many of them have been displaced and to perceive how and why they have been displaced. Scots are apt to learn what is called British history but is really English history. At an elementary level they may hear of Alfred and the Cakes rather than of Bruce and the Spider. At more advanced levels, in universities as well as in schools, they are taught more about Magna Carta than about the Declaration of Arbroath, about the Petition of Right than about the National Covenant and about the Court of King's Bench than about the Court of Session. Scots will look in vain to English history to learn where they have come from or where they are going.

What gives me more concern is what takes place not in formal education, but at a more popular level and in the impressions conveyed by what people see, hear and read in their daily lives. In 1987 the Prince and Princess of Wales took part in the commemoration of the ninth centenary of the death of the Prince's ancestor William the Conqueror; but they took no part in the commemoration in the same year of the fourth centenary of the death of Mary, Queen of Scots, who was no less his ancestor and indeed through whom he derives his descent from the Conqueror.

In the publicity given to the raising of Henry VIII's warship the *Mary Rose* in 1982 we were constantly told that Henry was the ancestor of the Prince of Wales. No one seemed to stop to ask how this had come about, considering that Henry had only three children, none of whom had issue. The Prince is in truth descended not from Henry but from Henry's sister Margaret, who married James IV of Scotland. Her present Majesty herself referred to Elizabeth Tudor as 'my great forebear', a term which properly means ancestor and not predecessor. That reminds one of the schoolboy who wrote that Elizabeth Tudor, the Virgin Queen, was a great success as a Queen. Such verbal slips, relating to the royal family, are to be regretted because what they do and say is constantly in the public eye. I sometimes wonder who advises the royal family on historical matters.

The press has much to answer for too. Last year 'Scotland's National Newspaper' informed its readers that 'the British Monarchy' was restored in 1660; but there was no single 'British monarchy' in 1660, and in Scotland King Charles II had been crowned on 1 January 1651. The same journal mentioned a treaty 'between Britain and the Low Countries' in 1528 and it again ignored Scottish history by referring to 'the first Freemason Lodge', being inaugurated in London in 1717. We had become almost accustomed to being told that Henry VIII was an ancestor of Prince Charles; but *The Scotsman* went one better on 15 February 1993 when it intimated that the childless William III was an ancestor of Prince Charles.

The anglocentric character of our culture is all the more pervasive because of the domination of the southern-based mass media. The great bulk of what people hear reflects English attitudes. The BBC has a perfect genius for mispronouncing Scottish names, and its Pronunciation Unit expressly rejects the origin and meaning of a name as criteria for determining its pronunciation. 'What's in a name?' I hear you say. But names often encapsulate history, and mispronunciation may obscure their historical associations. If you say La*mont* you suggest that the name is French — bad French — whereas if you correctly say *Lam*ont you show that it is good Norwegian. Or if you say Menzies in the manner the spelling suggests you disguise the fact that it is the French de Menières. By such mispronunciations important marks in the past are mis-placed or rendered misleading, so it is in vain to look to such marks for guidance about where we are going.

Yet there are plenty of marks to be seen if we keep our eyes open to the survivals of the past which still exist around us.

I have sometimes heard the remark, 'I always think that the trouble with history is that it starts at the wrong end.' What this means is that we ought to start our history with the present day and work our way back to earlier times. That would amount to writing history backwards. But the remark indicates the possible relation of past, present and future. It also makes me wonder whether those who study history are always aware that what they are studying is the explanation of the present, the explanation of phenomena which they can see around them today. I should like to enlarge on that, even at a very elementary level, to indicate some of the things which Scottish history can teach, whether to Scots themselves or to non-Scots who are perhaps seeing the country for the first time.

Some of the phenomena, as I have called them, which you see around you spring very readily to mind. There are many old castles and churches, many old houses large and small, there are disused industrial premises and equipment like old coal-mines, ironworks, quarries and so on. As you move around the country you cannot fail to notice disused piers and harbours, disused roads and bridges. Among the things you learn from history are the reasons why those things came into being, why they were used, by whom they were used and why they are now disused. A chapter in this book titled 'Presenting Scotland's Historic Heritage' has something to say about this topic.[1]

Some of you may have travelled up Glenogle by train before the railway closed several years ago. If so, you might have noticed as you looked out of the carriage window that on the other side of the valley there can be seen the modern road and traces of two earlier roads, each with its little bridges across the many streams. That is just one example of a glimpse of something which provides material for a good deal of history. Not many miles away from Glenogle, on the north side of Loch Tay, you may be enterprising enough, if you leave the road at the place now called Lawers, to find down by the lochside a deserted village, with remains of a church, a laird's house, a mill and some other ruins — and a pier. The now deserted village was abandoned because communications, once

---

[1]See below, p. 136.

by water along the loch, later moved uphill to the road. You have at Glenogle and Lawers tangible, visible phenomena which demand some historical explanation, which demand such a thing as a history of transport.

Another phenomenon, of a very different kind, which one cannot help noticing is the linguistic divisions within Scotland. There are, to begin with — and here I start with the present — a great many languages now spoken in the country, several of them by fairly recent immigrants from outside Europe. But two of the languages now spoken have been spoken for a very long time, though neither is indigenous, for one came from Ireland and the other from England. The former is 'Gaelic', or 'Irish' as it used to be accurately called because it came from Ireland, which is now spoken by less than one and a half per cent of the population and is to some extent kept alive by a costly life-support machine. The other, which originated with immigrants from the continent who also settled in England, is spoken, or at least understood, by very nearly everyone in Scotland and is called English. But of that language there are a very great many variants and dialects, some of them with elements which originally came from tongues other than English, and these dialects constitute the vigorous 'Scots' of everyday speech. The linguistic differences suggest that there were at one time in Scotland various races, so we are led on to study the coming of diverse peoples to Scotland, their settlements in different areas and the process whereby they came to form a single kingdom, if not a single nation.

Again, look at a map of Scotland — not the physical features, which result from geology, not from history — but the names which men have put on the map. A very little investigation reveals some significant points. A single physical feature may be known by different words in different parts of the country. In some areas you find the word 'inch' meaning an island, in other areas the word 'eilean' with the same meaning, while in other areas the names of islands end in '-a' or '-ay'. Likewise, in some areas an inlet of the sea is called a 'firth' or a 'voe' or a 'wick', in others it is called a 'loch', in others a 'bay'.

There are more phenomena connected with place-names which raise interesting questions. If you plot on a map all the place-names beginning with 'Pit-' or 'Pet-', you will find that they are confined to a certain area of the centre and east, admittedly a very large area. In the same way you could plot all the place-names beginning with 'Bal-' and all the place-names ending in '-ton'. No doubt you would find that those groups overlap to a considerable extent, but you would also find that each type of name is particularly prevalent in certain parts of the country. In a more restricted area you would find names ending in '-ham' or 'hame'. It appears that all those four names — pit, bal, ton and hame — have much the same meaning, of a settlement, a holding of land, a farm or a homestead.

The existence of different names for the same thing — whether a geographical feature, a settlement or an artefact — always suggests that the people who bestowed those names spoke different languages and were of different races.

The study of place-names should be especially revealing, but it is dangerous to deduce anything from a place-name until one knows how old it is. There are a great many instances where a house, a farm or an estate has been given some fancy name in quite recent times, a name which may have been copied from one in a different part of the country, a name which may reflect nothing whatsoever except the idiosyncracy of the proprietor who bestowed it. Some proprietors have taken a name with them from one property to another in a region where such a name would not be 'native'. Nowadays, when national or local administrators are active in the most trivial of decisions, local authorities have often bestowed quite inappropriate names or would have done so had they not been checked. Some years ago a local authority insisted on calling a new housing scheme 'Westwood' although it was observed that, in view of topography, the appropriate name would have been 'Southdub'. In council housing we find randomly-chosen names like 'Carlton Terrace' and 'Meadowbank Road'. I was instrumental in preventing a group of houses in Argyll being denominated 'Lochnell View'. A bad example was set by central government when it gave the name 'Glenrothes' to a new town which is not in a glen and is about a hundred miles from Rothes.

But, without entering on the technicalities of that complex study of place-names, there is still a lot to be learned from the map. Look, for instance, at the names of the old divisions of the country which were later known as counties. There is one group in which the name consisted of the name of a town followed by '-shire' — Perthshire, Aberdeenshire and so on. But there is another group of quite different character — Caithness (correctly accented on the first syllable, by the way), Sutherland, Fife, Argyll, Moray. All those areas became sheriffdoms and then counties, but their names suggest that they had different origins.

An interest in those names might easily lead one on to notice the names of some of the older Scottish peerages, like Argyll, Buchan, Caithness, Moray and Sutherland, which clearly are of similar character to the second of the two groups of county names and indeed are sometimes identical with them. But you will find among the peerage titles a number of names of regions which are not now in use as administrative units but may have been so used in earlier time, as well as geographical names of a more fanciful nature: Lord Breadalbane is not only Earl of Breadalbane but also Viscount of Tay and Pentland and Lord Glenorchy, Benderloch, Ormelie and Wick — the Caithness names being a reminder that his ancestor claimed the earldom of Caithness. It should not be forgotten that the heir apparent to the throne is not only Prince of Wales but Prince of Scotland: he is Duke of Rothesay, Earl of Carrick, Baron Renfrew, Prince and High Stewart of Scotland and Lord of the Isles, titles which could collectively provide material for a lecture.

The study of the names of districts and regions is obviously linked, at least potentially, to the study of institutions of local government. We must learn how shires originated, about the office of sheriff; and also about how counties

originated — very much more recently than sheriffdoms. It may be deducible
that some of the names — like Atholl, Badenoch and Lochaber — which are
now names of neither counties nor sheriffdoms may represent some older
system of administration which existed before sheriffdoms or counties were
thought of. On the other hand, in the twentieth century administrative units
have been saddled with names which make neither historical nor geographical
sense and can lead only to confusion: Gordon, the name of a village in
Berwickshire, has been conferred on a district in Aberdeenshire. There has also
been very proper indignation at the substitution of anglicised versions of names
for native versions, notably Spey Valley for Strathspey and Clyde Valley for
Clydesdale — as well as the tautological 'Inchcolm Island'.

The names of towns can be as illuminating as those of counties and districts.
There are nowadays a considerable number of towns whose names end in the
element '-burgh'. But many of them are not of very great antiquity and date
from periods long after the burgh had become a recognised institution. There
are, indeed, only three burghs which were so named in the period when burghs
are first heard of — Edinburgh, Roxburgh and (oddly enough) Winchburgh.
We must ask whether such names are pointers to the original meaning of 'burgh'
as a fortified place rather than an institution. (Jedburgh was indeed an ancient
burgh, but its name is a bit of a masquerade, for the original form was Jedworth.)
Colinsburgh, Maryburgh, Williamsburgh and so on bear unmistakeable marks
of their later origins.

To find more examples of history around us I turn from place-names to
material objects which furnish illustrations of old Scottish institutions.

The visitor to Edinburgh Castle sees a crown — the crown of Scotland. That
crown is not worn by anyone nowadays and has not been worn — officially at
least — since 1 January 1651, when, in the unique circumstances of the only
presbyterian coronation of a king, it was placed on the head of Charles II by the
Marquis of Argyll. But clearly it was at one time in regular use and it is part of
the history of Scottish institutions to learn when and by whom that crown was
worn and when it ceased to be worn. The crown represents an argument from
survival — the argument that there must once have been a Scottish king and a
Scottish kingdom.

Another example of the argument from survival is closely connected with
the crown. There is in Edinburgh a 'Parliament House', but no parliament sits
in it. However, the presumption is that there was once a Scottish parliament
which sat in that hall and gave it its name.

The crown and the Parliament House are in a sense museum pieces, for they
are not now used for the purposes for which they were made. But there are
plenty of buildings and institutions which, far from being museum pieces, are
very much alive today and which, in their activities, present many questions to
the enquiring mind — questions which can be answered only from history. The
whole structure of the Courts of Law, for example, and the whole fabric of the

Church of Scotland. A visit to the General Assembly of the Church of Scotland, especially on its opening day, is almost a lesson in history; it certainly would raise in the visitor's mind a lot of questions which could be answered from history.

Besides, even among the material remains there are buildings which are apt to seem museum pieces to the tourist but are much less museum pieces than many people think — are not, in fact, museum pieces at all. The tourist visiting the church of St Giles, for example, may be apt to think of it as a museum piece. But if you happen to be present in that church on a great national occasion like the St Andrew's Day service or the service on General Assembly Sunday, you will see a lot of the history of Edinburgh and of Scotland coming to life in the old building. You will see representatives of various organisations ranging from the Knights of the Thistle to the National Coal Board and including Universities, the City, the legal and medical associations. A few years ago among the Knights of the Order of the Thistle in their splendid robes of thistle-green you would have seen the twenty-seventh Earl of Crawford, holder of a title which has continued in the male line of the same family since 1360, and in the same group that self-made professional man the late Harald Leslie, Lord Birsay. You see the Lord Lyon King of Arms and his heralds, looking rather like the characters in a pack of playing-cards come to life. You might be most impressed by the Senators of the College of Justice, otherwise the Judges of the Court of Session. As they pace slowly up the church, in their scarlet robes and full-bottomed wigs, they look almost incredibly ancient, they look in fact as if they had been there since 1532, which is precisely what they have been.

Another building which seems to the tourist a museum piece is the Palace of Holyroodhouse. And it is indeed a museum piece for about forty-nine weeks of the year. But from time to time it comes to life, especially when the Queen is in residence or when the Queen's representative, the Lord High Commissioner, is in residence and the old building becomes full of people who are not tourists but are enjoying royal hospitality. The Lord High Commissioner and his Lady progress slowly through the various apartments, accompanied by their suite, greeting their guests as they pass, exactly as Prince Charlie did in 1745, as Charles I did in 1633 or as Queen Mary did in 1561, and indeed this is something which has been going on ever since the oldest part of the palace was built by James IV about 1500.

These are all examples of history around us, no doubt in its more picturesque forms. Another little illustration was this. Until very recently, if you had seen the Magistrates of Edinburgh, led by the Lord Provost in scarlet and ermine, they were accompanied by four men in antique costume and carrying antique weapons which, you may reflect, are not likely to be used against delinquents nowadays. But the Provost's bodyguard was not just invented by someone looking for a piece of mock antiquity; they were there because in 1520 the town council decided that the provost should have a bodyguard of four halbardiers 'because the warld is brukle and trublous'.

When I invited you to have a look at the people who turn up in St Giles on great occasions I mentioned the judges of the Court of Session. You might discover that the chief of those judges is the Lord President. But if you were to see the same man in different robes you would find that he is no longer Lord President; he is Lord Justice General. How this came about is again a matter of history. Speaking of that office leads me on to mention some other Scottish offices which have a good deal of history behind them. You might be interested to learn exactly how long the office of Lord Advocate has existed, or how long the office of Lord Clerk Register has existed. Both have existed for a good many centuries. But in the day-to-day life of Scotland now you may not very often hear of the Lord Advocate, and unless your interests lie in certain rather specialised fields you are unlikely ever to have heard of the Lord Clerk Register, who lost his last significant function in 1963 and of whom it is almost as true as it is of the Historiographer that he has neither duties nor emoluments nowadays. The man in modern Scotland of whom you must assuredly hear a great deal is the Secretary of State for Scotland. And you may well wonder if the Secretary of State possesses an antiquity comparable to that of the Lord President or Lord Advocate or Clerk Register. You find, however, that the Secretary of State is a mere parvenu, whose office in precisely its present form goes no further back than 1926. The reason why the Lord President has been around for nearly five hundred years and the Secretary for less than one hundred has roots in a lot of Scottish history.

These remarks should show that the past is around us all the time, even here, in this room. It may surprise you now when I tell you that my presence on this platform today is a breach of the treaty of Union between England and Scotland, made in 1707. It may surprise you now, but it will not surprise you after you have studied the appropriate tract of history.

# 1

## *Introduction: Scotland in Europe*

[This paper originated from an invitation in October 1990 by the Saltire Society to write an Introduction to a volume to be called *Why Scottish History Matters*. I was assured that 'how it would be handled' would be left to me. I explained to the editor that I was not likely to produce sentimental gush and present either romanticism or 'Here's tae us, wha's like us?' However, the editor replied that my comparative detachment would be particularly valuable and that she was 'extremely keen' to have my contribution in a volume which would present 'different voices'. I gave way, and when I began to consider the possible scope of the paper it occurred to me that, as other contributors to the volume had little to say about Scotland's place in Europe, I might usefully make that theme one of the strands in my work. This proposal was warmly welcomed by the editor, who said that without my contribution the book would be inadequate on the European dimension. When I submitted a draft the editor wrote, 'I'm delighted to get your piece, which I found most entertaining,' and she added later that she valued my 'more than usual detached approach to the paraphernalia of Scottish identity.'

I was not surprised, however, when I learned of criticism from Celtomaniacs, who accused me of being 'hostile to the Highlands' (when in fact what I was doing was only protesting against the extension of a largely fictitious Highland 'image' to the whole of Scotland). I agreed to a number of amendments which were suggested, though the one thing I would not withdraw was my reference to the 'raucous skirl' of the bagpipes (unless indeed I was allowed to substitute 'cacophony'), for I protested that I was presumably expected to be expressing my own views and not having words put into my mouth. My concessions, however, did not suffice, and I was next asked if my paper could be removed from the beginning of the volume to the end, with no change except the omission of 'Introduction' from its title. I was prepared to agree even to this, though I thought that I should be allowed to revert to my original version, purged of the amendments which I had conceded. Then I happened to learn, indirectly, that there was to be a new Introduction. This I asked to see and when

I discovered that it contained what I called a 'vituperative attack' on me I decided to withdraw my contribution. The whole concept of producing a volume which would contain 'a variety of voices' to give it 'freshness and value' had evidently been jettisoned.

That 'Introduction', prepared for the Saltire Society, is printed below, with the addition of a few sentences which appear within square brackets.]

> Boswell: 'I do indeed come from Scotland, but I cannot help it.'
> Johnson: 'That, Sir, I find, is what a very great many of your country-men cannot help.'

When a Scot, in the company of other nationals, makes the admission which Boswell made, his revelation is apt to be met by either a suppressed snigger or a pitying smile. He is not taken seriously, and perhaps Scots, by that simple admission, lose the opportunity to be taken seriously. The reason is that the prevailing image of Scots is ridiculous, and as long as they make themselves ridiculous they need not expect to be taken seriously.

Ridicule. A few years ago I received the Minute of a meeting of the Section of the British Academy of which I am a member but at which I had not been present, and read a reference to 'James Clark (*sic*) Maxwell, arguably the greatest English (*sic*) scientist of the nineteenth century'. I protested to Sir Geoffrey Elton, the Chairman of the Section, and he replied, correctly, that Minutes recorded what had been said, not what should have been said. However, at the next meeting of the Section, when I was present, my protest was read out and it was greeted with something like a hoot of derision — in the *British* Academy. Even there the Scot was not taken seriously.

Ridicule. A few years ago, on one of my visits to Denmark, I accepted an invitation from an old friend to give an informal talk on Scottish history to a gathering of school teachers. I took pains to compress an outline of Scottish history into about half an hour, laying stress on the links between Scotland and Denmark. But at the end, when questions were asked, all of them were about Mary, Queen of Scots, and Bonnie Prince Charlie.

A recent writer remarked: 'One of the paradoxes about Scotland is that it is apparently well-known world-wide because of the innumerable false images and half truths (sometimes just apocrypha). Little gobbets of our history ... are swallowed all over the world and people in the strangest places have heard about Mary, Queen of Scots, Rob Roy, Rabbie Burns, Bonnie Prince Charlie and Greyfriars Bobby (the shortbread-tin syndrome) but not much of all the good and worthy and great things and people we have produced'.[1] [Dr Nicholas Phillipson, approaching the subject from a different angle, blamed 'the Enlightenment' for providing 'the contemporary world with a literary image of Scotland as a land of romance, caught between a feudal and a commercial

---

[1] Jack Firth, in a review in *Books in Scotland*, no. 35, p. 20.

civilisation'. He went on, 'It is an image which has stuck, turning Scotland into the tourist attraction she has been ever since, a Brigadoon of a country, a country of clans, tartans and all the rest of it. And for many Scots this image has proved to be the most enduring legacy of the Enlightenment, an albatross that has been hung round the neck of its national culture ever since.'[2] Another writer, himself a Highlander, reflected on 'the great wave of romanticism' which has engulfed Highland history, 'from Ossian Macpherson to the Scottish Tourist Board via Sir Walter Scott, King George IV and Queen Victoria. Our past is presented in a series of gaudily coloured vignettes with scant regard for what actually took place. There seems to be something in the Scottish character, whether at home or in those of Scottish descent abroad, which is irresistibly attracted to the oversimplified, overstated and too often plain wrong view of the past. It seems all too often that these misconceptions are taken as gospel; when they and their like are allowed to become foundations on which to base a view of the future of Scotland, no less, as seems to be the case at present, there is scant cause for comfort'.[3]] It has been remarked more succinctly that the Scots are proud of their past but are proud of all the wrong things.

If the process of inviting ridicule did not originate, it certainly took a great step forward, on Friday, 23 August 1822. The occasion was a great ball in the Assembly Rooms in Edinburgh attended by George IV, an event which probably marked the moment when the kilt was first foisted on Scotland as 'the national dress'. From that event the succession — or rather the descent — led straight to Harry Lauder and other stage comedians: the image of the Scot became a figure, not infrequently inebriated, speaking what passes as Lowland Scots but arrayed in a dress which at one time would have caused its wearer to be shot on sight if he had ventured into the Lowlands. The musical accompaniment is the raucous skirl of the bagpipes, an instrument once in widespread use throughout western and central Europe but now generally laid aside except in Scotland. The image is not confined to the stage: I have heard the phrase 'A kind of academic Harry Lauder'.

Along with this apparatus goes the fond belief — untenable by anyone who has given the most elementary thought to the origins and development of surnames — that there is a bond of blood-relationship among bearers of a name, who all form a 'clan'. It has been observed, by a scholar who has made a special study of family history, that 'the clan system of today is primarily an invention of nineteenth-century romantics and astute business men'.[4] It is certainly true that 'ancient', 'clan', 'family' and other names were mostly given in the nineteenth and twentieth centuries, to patterns of their own invention, by astute business men who lined their pockets — and benefited Scotland's

---

[2]'The Scottish Enlightenment, in *The Sunday Mail Story of Scotland*, ii, p. 676.

[3]Alastair Campbell of Airds, 'Glencoe: the casualty of history', in *The Scotsman*, 8 February 1992.

[4]David Moody, *Scottish Family History* (London, 1989), p. 99.

economy — at the expense of historical truth. It is salutary for a present-day visitor to Scotland to find that in the Highlands kilts are rarely seen except on lairds and their imitators (often speaking with strong English accents). He then realises how bogus the image is.

[In the metamorphosis of the Highlander from a half-savage outsider to an accepted national figure parts were played by many individuals: 'Ossian' Macpherson, Walter Scott, Mendelssohn, the 'Sobieski Stuarts', Queen Victoria, Landseer, John Stuart Blackie and Mrs Kennedy-Fraser. They made their various contributions, some by literary, musical or artistic genius, nearly all by eccentricity and at least two — 'translators without texts' — by fraud. The process has not gone unchallenged. George Rosie once wrote in some detail in *The Scotsman* about his own pet hates. 'Highlandism ran riot. The colourful trappings of Gaeldom became *de rigueur*. Every Lancashire industrialist, city financier and Glasgow ship-builder had to have his shooting lodge in the Highlands. Every family name in Scotland was converted into a "clan", complete with its own tartan. Border dynasties like Armstrongs, Elliots and Kerrs became transmuted into inferior versions of the Highland tribes. The products of Eton and Oxbridge announced themselves Highland "chiefs" and expected the fealty of their tacksmen.... By 1881 the English establishment was so besotted with the Garb of Old Gaul that the War Office ordered all Lowland regiments into tartan trousers and short, Highland-style doublets. All their protests were ignored. Regiments like the Royal Scots and the Royal Scots Fusiliers — whose ancestors had broken many a wild Gaelic charge — were obliged to assume the colours of their ancient enemies. Since then things have gone from bad to worst. Every local gala or sports day has become a "Highland Games". No protest march is complete without its bagpiper. Every police force has to have its pipe band.']

The perpetuation of false images, or at any rate false emphases, extends to little things as well as great. One of the most conspicuous, and by any standards distinguished, buildings in Edinburgh is a massive and ornate hotel at the east end of Princes Street. It was long known by the eminently solid and respectable name of 'North British', commemorating the great railway to which it owed its origin. But when, after nearly a century, it was refurbished and renamed nothing so sensible would do: it had to be something 'romantick' and preferably 'Celtick', and it became 'Balmoral'. The porter was garbed in a kilt. Scottish Gas turned this to account in an advertisement explaining 'Why the doorman at the Balmoral doesn't wear any trousers.... Every time the great mahogany doors open, a luxurious breath of Gas central heating wafts out, swirling gently around your knees, then rising to warm your entire body. Little wonder, then, that the doorman dresses to make the most of this phenomenon. By wearing a kilt.' The hotel's image is singularly at variance with its proximity to the Register House, the home of the Scottish national records, where the truth about Scottish history is to be found.

It has been shrewdly observed by Professor Edward Cowan that when the Norwegians ceded the Hebrides to Alexander III in 1266 they inflicted more damage on Scotland than many hostile campaigns would have done. Of course it is obvious that a frontier on the sounds — often very narrow sounds — which separate the islands from the mainland was probably untenable in the long run, for the fringe of the west mainland had far easier access to the islands than it had to the seat of government in the east. But the political amalgamation of islands and mainland in 1266 brought into the Scottish kingdom territories which had not been accustomed to obey the king of Norway and were not disposed to obey the king of Scots. The wars of independence began only a generation later, before the Scottish king's new subjects could become habituated to a new allegiance. Separatism was strengthened, and generation by generation Highlanders and Islanders joined forces with the English against the Scottish crown. 'In acquiring the Hebrides', Cowan trenchantly concluded, 'Scotland had created her Afghanistan'.[5]

Down to the 1290s the machinery of royal government was being extended, until sheriffdoms were planned for Skye, Lorne and Kintyre, which might have opened the way to the integration of the west into the kingdom, but the wars interrupted the process. The problem of the Highlands was simply a problem of arrested development. Nothing more was said about sheriffdoms for the west until the reign of James IV two hundred years later, when it was proposed that sheriffs should sit at Dingwall or Inverness for the north isles and Tarbert or Campbeltown for the south isles, and that there should be a sheriff of Ross at Tain or Dingwall and a sheriff of Caithness at Dornoch or Wick — all of them, it will be observed, places discreetly remote from the areas most noted for disorder. Similarly, the headquarters of Highland dioceses were judiciously situated at towns in, or as near as possible to, the Lowlands — Dunblane, Dunkeld, Aberdeen, Elgin, Fortrose and Dornoch — except in the west, where security was sought on islands. Even Elgin and Dunkeld proved untenable at times. It may not have been entirely true that there was a governed part of Scotland in the east and an ungoverned part in the west, but it is certainly true that all of Scotland, so far as it was governed at all, was governed from centres in or very near the Lowlands.

Whatever positive influence the Highlands had in reality on the culture of Scotland, their contribution to its image was an element of violence. The Highlander is commonly presented as a warrior with targe and broadsword at the ready, Highland dress of sorts is a recognised military uniform and the wearer of even the most decorative 'Highland outfit' is equipped with a *sgian*

---

[5] *Scotland in the Reign of Alexander III*, ed. N. Reid (Edinburgh, 1990), p. 126.

*dubh*, which some call a dirk and which does not look very like an instrument for eating his porridge or haggis.

But the Highlands must not have all the blame for the 'blood and thunder' emphasis in what commonly passes for Scottish history. [My own phrase has been 'blood and thunder', but when I recently met a Professor of Physics from Oregon and disclosed my own specialisation he exclaimed 'Blood and guts'.] I have often asked, 'In what other country would the founder of the National Library live in the popular memory as "the bluidy Mackenzie"?' That founder, Sir George Mackenzie, a cultivated man of letters and a legal scholar, happened, as Lord Advocate, to be responsible for prosecuting ecclesiastical dissidents who engaged in armed rebellion, who repudiated allegiance to the king and who wanted to impose presbyterianism on England and Ireland. All the immense cultural and intellectual achievements of the seventeenth century, in architecture, painting, literature and science — a true 'Enlightenment' — are ignored, while attention focuses on the violence arising from debates whether the Church should be administered by individuals (bishops) or by committees (presbyteries) and whether authority in the Church should lie with a clerical oligarchy of ministers and ordained elders or with the general body of the laity either directly or through their representatives in parliament. In the eighteenth century, somewhat similarly, the significance of substantial economic developments has often been suppressed, this time in favour of the supposed glamour of Jacobitism. The really important thing that happened in 1745-6 was not that a 'Popish Italian prince' (as a contemporary Lowlander called him) emulated the Grand Old Duke of York by marching ten thousand men down to Derby and back again but that the number of yards of linen produced in Scotland reached a record level. Instead of wasting time on the 5,000 or so Highlanders who were at Culloden on 16 April 1746, why not investigate how the quarter of a million or so Highlanders were occupied who did not 'quit their looms to dance after the Highland pipes' and were nowhere near Culloden that day?[6] The image of Scottish history as a tale of bloodshed and disorder still prevails and the historian who seeks to correct it finds among the Scots an invincible preference for the agreeable or picturesque fiction rather than the truth. [The advertisements of the Authority responsible for the care of Historic Monuments present Scotland's 'rich and colourful history' as (in large capitals) MURDER, PILLAGE, LOOTING, BURNING, TREACHERY, ARSON, TREASON, and then add (in similar type) BRING THE FAMILY — to encourage juvenile delinquency? Another advertisement, I suppose from the same source, drew attention to THE EDINBURGH DUNGEON: EDINBURGH'S NEWEST TORTURE MUSEUM, and invited us to 'Experience the horror of Scotland's past'.]

The Scots have earned a reputation for complaining. The English, with their

[6]See below, p. 148-9.

disregard of aspirates, accuse them of 'wingeing' and 'wining', but the Scots' own word, 'girning', is expressive without being ambiguous. Such girning about 'puir auld Scotland' comes from those whom Professor Hannay called 'greeting patriots'. On the other hand, Scots can be boastful ('Here's tae us, wha's like us'). But whether expressing self-pity or arrogance, Scots are obsessed by their uniqueness, their real or imagined peculiarities. It was national conceit rather than theology which convinced so many of them, at least from the thirteenth century to the seventeenth, that they were a Chosen People.[7]

One element in their pride in all the wrong things is a tendency to present a picture of isolation rather than of integration in Europe. In a stirring 'Declaration of Independence' some Scots alluded to their home as a 'place of exile, beyond which there is no habitation' — an exaggeration, of course, but not wholly indefensible geographically, for Caithness is nearer to Iceland than to France. But independence does not involve isolation: the history of Scotland, not least its cultural history, is a story of integration in western Europe; and the fate of Scotland was often determined by what was happening in other lands.

The character of the present has been largely shaped by migrants who introduced their own languages and cultures. Nothing at all is identifiably indigenous. Two thousand years ago the south was occupied by Britons whose language was the ancestor of Welsh; most if not all of the north was occupied by Caledonians or Picts, of whose material culture there are ample remains but of their language hardly a trace. Both of those races were incomers: the Britons are believed to have come from the south and the Picts to have reached Scotland by a northerly route from a homeland in eastern Europe. In or about 500 A.D. more identifiable migrants arrived. Irish, called 'Scots', settled in the west, bringing their own tongue, and English or Angles came over the North Sea to the south-east with their Germanic speech. Each of those languages had a great future: Irish spread for a time to the centre and most of the north and east, though it never achieved the kind of official status which made it the vehicle of legal deeds or administrative archives; the tongue of the Angles, from which came both English and Lowland Scots, spread rapidly up the east coast and ultimately all over Scotland, where it superseded French and Latin as the language of deeds and records. Migrants from Scandinavia arrived not long after the Irish and English, to reinforce the Germanic element, and they were followed by those second-hand Scandinavians, the Normans, with whom came a contingent from Flanders. There were no more significant immigrations until the nineteenth century, which brought hordes of Irish and some Italians, Poles and Lithuanians, and in the twentieth century came more Poles and, later, settlers from furth of Europe, who may yet provide Scotland with a language to make a good second to the speech derived from the Angles of fifteen hundred years ago.

[7]G. Donaldson, *Scotland: James V to James VII* (Edinburgh, 1965), pp. 315-16.

Some Scots like to claim that their country was defended by armies of volunteers drawn from the lower levels of society and was never conquered. In truth there was conscription of able-bodied men from sixteen to sixty, prosecutions for failure to turn up for service were commonplace, and those who did turn up probably did so at the bidding (to put it no stronger) of their lairds. It may be that there was only once a complete military conquest and occupation, by the English under Cromwell. But there had been earlier conquests of a kind, one of them a Norman Conquest: in 1097 an army sent by the Norman king of England imposed on the Scots a dynasty which was already seventy-five per cent non-native. One wonders whether, in 1997, the Scots will follow the example of what the English did in 1966 and demand a stamp to commemorate their own defeat. If they do, the Post Office, which has so often rejected Scottish demands for stamps — for example for Queen Mary in 1987 — may this time accede. The dynasty imposed in 1097 became increasingly non-native generation by generation until Alexander III, who is apt to be acclaimed 'the last of Scotland's Celtic kings', could number no more than two or three Celts in his thirty-two ancestors of the five latest generations. Contemporaries had no hesitation about seeing and describing that royal family as 'French'.

The Normans gave Scotland a kind of stiffening and discipline which saved it from the fate of Ireland, and they also brought it into line with western Europe. The cultural achievements of this integration are still abundantly visible today, in great churches from Kirkwall to Jedburgh, in parish churches like Dalmeny and Leuchars and in castles such as Bothwell and Caerlaverock, none of which would be out of place anywhere in western Europe. It may be that, as the peace and plenty of the thirteenth century were followed by the constraints and poverty resulting from the English wars, it was not until the eighteenth century that Scotland could ever again afford to be so closely bonded with Europe. The inter-relation of the individuals who mattered politically during the period of Norman influence was very close. King David I, before he came to the throne in 1124, was at the same time brother of the king of Scots and brother of the queen of England. Alexander II and Alexander III were the brothers-in-law of their English contemporaries, Henry III and Edward I. At an earlier stage, the earls of Orkney and the dukes of Normandy were of the same stock, so that William of Normandy, who conquered England, and Thorfinn of Orkney, who, some think, nearly conquered Scotland, had a common ancestor four generations back. The Northmen and their descendants the Normans were cosmopolitan adventurers, and one wonders how often men who met by chance when in the Mediterranean on armed pilgrimage or crusade discovered that they were distant cousins.

Although Scotland was remote and was poor in resources, it did not consider itself to be in a position of dependence in relation to western Europe as a whole or to any particular continental power. It never fell formally into dependence as some kingdoms did: England under John, for instance, became a vassal of the papacy. Poland, Denmark, Spain and England were all at one time or another, in varying degrees and fleetingly, nominally in a position of subordination to the Holy Roman Empire. Scotland never was, unless it was thought to be subsumed under England. It might well have been so subsumed, as it was for centuries unquestionably in a position inferior to that country. Scottish kings before David II were not anointed and therefore lacked that step of hallowing which signified full sovereignty. True, they might protest that when they did homage to the English monarch the homage was for their English estates alone, but the fact was that from time to time they were to be seen on their knees before their English contemporaries.

The only link Scotland had which implied recognition of the universal authority of the Holy Roman Empire was through the appointment of notaries public, for notaries created by the Emperor or on his mandate operated in Scotland. Even this was curbed when James III proclaimed that he had 'full jurisdiction and free empire within his realm', thereby asserting that his crown was 'imperial' — an assertion in which, it has been claimed, he anticipated England by two generations — and repudiating any shadow of the authority of the Emperor. So far as the other international authority, the papacy, was concerned, the Scottish Church had acknowledged the primacy of the Roman see from the eleventh century if not earlier. In the early twelfth century the Pope was addressing Scottish bishops as his subjects, and a papal legate appeared in Scotland in 1125. Whether the relationship with Rome was direct or through an English intermediary was long debated, and the formula whereby the Scottish Church became a 'special daughter' of Rome, with no intermediary, did not compromise Scottish autonomy, for the individuality of *Ecclesia Scoticana*, as an ecclesiastical unit based roughly on the concept of the identity of church with nation, was acknowledged. Scotland, though a daughter, was not always an obedient daughter, and she not infrequently disregarded papal policy, but escaped being regarded as schismatic. Besides, most of the religious houses in Scotland belonged to orders with headquarters on the continent. The canon law of the western church was accepted more fully in Scotland than in England, and lawsuits from Scotland regularly went to the papal curia. All in all, ecclesiastical business of one kind and another involved constant communication with the continent and there was no more doubt about Scotland's integration than about her autonomy.

Just as ordinations conferred in one province of the western church were valid everywhere, and just as the commissions of imperial and papal notaries were universally valid, so knighthood was not limited by national frontiers. The same applied to university degrees, and in an era when in Church and learning alike there was a universal language — Latin — scholarship was international and there was remarkable mobility. Until Scotland's first university appeared, at St Andrews in 1411, Scots seeking higher education had gone in considerable numbers to England and the continent. Over 1,000 names of such men can be found down to 1410. It was not national conceit that led to the foundation of universities in Scotland. Even difficulty of access to England in time of war was not decisive. St Andrews was founded when Scotland and England supported rival popes and when for a time even Scotland and France did not agree in their papal allegiance. Glasgow may have followed St Andrews because of internal rivalries in Scotland, but by the time Aberdeen came along universities were proliferating everywhere. Even after, the Scots continued to study at Paris, Orleans, Avignon, Copenhagen, Tübingen, Bologna, Padua and elsewhere. Finding everywhere much the same conditions and institutions and a common language, churchmen and scholars could and did find employment almost as easily in other lands as in their own. The tradition of the wandering scholar did not cease with the Reformation, for the Reformation itself was an international movement which linked Scotland initially with Lutheran, and later predominantly with Calvinist, countries and thus did something to stimulate migration and exchange. Medical and legal students went much to Leyden, and divines continued to go to various German universities.

But, whatever political or legal theory might dictate and whatever Scotland's independence within the European community might suggest, Scotland could not hope to escape the risk of being dominated by her wealthier neighbour in Britain, any more than Portugal could escape the risk of domination by Spain, or Norway the risk of domination by Denmark or Sweden. In her anxiety to escape becoming a satellite of England, she became for a time a somewhat reluctant satellite of France. The background of that development was nothing more peculiar than an association on a classical model, based on the aphorism, 'Stand well with your neighbour, but better with your neighbour's neighbour', for France and Scotland had a common enemy in England, a power which in the middle ages persistently followed an acquisitive policy which in the end was a complete failure. The 'Auld Alliance' with France, which was the one continental link Scots never forgot, began in 1295 and lasted until 1560. Its history and its effects on Scottish language and architecture were summarised in a pamphlet published by the Saltire Society in 1985.[8] It was in its later phase that it reduced Scotland to being a reluctant satellite — reluctant because the Scots learned that serving as a tool of French policy led to disastrous defeats (Flodden, Solway Moss and Pinkie), and a satellite because of the role of dynastic policy and chance.

Such a role was common in international relations. Had the 'Maid of Norway', heir of Alexander III and prospective bride of the future Edward II, lived, there would have been a 'union of the crowns' of England and Scotland in 1307, three centuries before one was actually achieved in 1603. When, in 1558, Mary, Queen of Scots, was married to the heir to the French throne, and when, in 1559, under 'Francis and Mary, King and Queen of France and

[8]G. Donaldson, *The Auld Alliance* (Edinburgh, 1985).

Scotland', a union of crowns was an accomplished fact, Scots were not unaware of the risks of absorption through marriage. One of them specifically 'made the example of Britanny', where Duchess Anne had married a French king and the consequence had been a decree by Francis I in 1532 integrating the duchy into France. Castile and Aragon were joined from 1490 in a dynastic union which has endured, Spain and Portugal in one which lasted only sixty years. A union of Norway and Denmark, originating in dynastic accident, lasted for over four hundred years. Norway's personal union with Sweden, not arising through intermarriage but imposed by diktat of the great powers, lasted less than a century. The case of Norway and Denmark shows how long such a union can endure and yet in the end be broken.

The Auld Alliance postulated Franco-Scottish military collaboration, and among its best known consequences were the activities of Scottish soldiers alongside the French in resisting English armies in France, especially in the 1420s. But service as mercenaries in other continental armies was long the chief outlet for surplus Scottish vitality, and its attractions possibly increased in the seventeenth century, when growing stability and order at home left less scope there for the restless. The way had been prepared, for Scottish soldiers served Denmark against Sweden as early as 1520, and later in the century it was a common occurrence for the Scottish government to grant licences for the raising of specific numbers of men for service in Denmark, Sweden and the Low Countries. After 1600 the traffic increased, and the Thirty Years' War (1618-1648) raised the demand. One of the most noted Scots of the time was John Hepburn, who had commanded the Scots Brigade under the Swedish King Adolphus and later, after transferring to the French service, died with the rank of Marshal of France, which at least two Scots had attained in medieval times. Others went farther afield, to Russia, where Thomas Dalyell of the Binns served and where Patrick Gordon had a distinguished career under Peter the Great. In the eighteenth century James Keith, a brother of the Earl Marischal, served in Spain and Russia before becoming Field Marshal under Frederick the Great of Prussia, and Samuel Greig was the creator of the Russian navy, which he manned largely with Scottish officers. Whatever their record elsewhere, one image which the Scot had on the continent was assuredly that of a fighting man.

Several Scots settled in lands they had served as mercenaries, notably in Sweden. But far more Scots made their homes in lands to which they had gone as peaceful traders. In the Low Countries commercial links were established at latest by the thirteenth century, and in the fourteenth we hear of the 'staple port', ultimately at Veere, around which Scottish commercial activities in that area centred. Of equal importance were the territories on both sides of the entrance to the Baltic, which at that time pertained almost wholly to Denmark. All ships passing in and out of the Baltic had to pay tolls to the Danish crown, and the Registers of those tolls, kept for many centuries, provide a kind of index of the economic health of Scotland. Scots who went to trade remained as settlers and formed colonies in towns like Malmö, Hälsingborg and Helsingör (where three Scots became burgomasters) as well as at Danzig, inside the Baltic.

From the east coast a Lowlander saw an open horizon which seemed to beckon him to adventure on a ready-made highway to the continent. On the west coast, when the open sea was at last reached — beyond a multitude of offshore islands — medieval man was not certain of what lay beyond, and it was only slowly that even commerce, let alone colonisation, across the Atlantic, began. But when it did it was the first stage in a tremendous diaspora which carried Scots to all parts of the world, where, it is said — by a wild guess — 25,000,000 people of Scottish descent now live. The frontier of the Scottish kingdom has remained unchanged since 1482 (when England finally acquired Berwick), but the frontiers of the Scottish nation have extended to the ends of the earth. Some have seen this movement as a reflection of pessimism, of despondency, of despair about the future of Scotland itself. That is not my view. I see the great exodus, as I see the venture of medieval Scots on the continent of Europe, as a reflection of the vitality of the nation. An acute observer (not himself a Scot) wrote that 'The Scotch emigrant is a man who leaves Scotland because he wishes to rise faster and higher than he can at home.... From Canada to Ceylon, from Dunedin to Bombay, for every Englishman that you meet who has worked himself up to wealth from small beginnings without external aid, you find ten Scotchmen.... Half the most prominent among the statesmen of the Canadian Confederation, of Victoria and of Queensland, are born Scots, and all the great merchants of India are of the same nation.'[9] These words were written a hundred years ago, but nothing has happened since then to impoverish the record of the Scots overseas.

It was not only by practising their vocations in other lands, but also by their achievements at home, that Scots made their country an integral part of the European scene. They not only put it in the main stream of development but not infrequently helped to shape such development. This is true of almost every field of intellectual and cultural activity except (perhaps oddly) theology, where Scots nearly always followed rather than led and none attained international pre-eminence, and music, for no Scottish composer reached anything like first rank. To illustrate this theme fully it would be easy to present a tedious catalogue of names, but some indication may be given by a compressed survey. In the seventeenth century — the century of Galileo and Newton — astronomy and physics were to the front, and both those sciences demanded a high level of mathematics. All astronomers and physicists were indebted to John Napier of Merchiston (1550-1617), whose logarithms dominated processes of calculation for over three centuries; and members of the Gregory family, especially James (1638-75) and David (1661-1708), were mathematicians and astronomers who corresponded on equal terms with the Dutch mathematician Huygens and

---

[9]Sir Charles Dilke, *Greater Britain* (1888), p. 525.

with Newton. Exact calculation was necessary also for superior standards in architecture, and in this period Scots departed from their native — and latterly often extremely elegant — traditions to follow classical models. The work of Sir William Bruce (1630-1710) at Holyroodhouse and Kinross House pointed straight to the achievements of the Adam dynasty, especially Robert (1728-1792), who studied ancient architecture in Italy and led a fashion which extended beyond Scotland and England: one does not spend much time in St Petersburg without being reminded of Charles Cameron, architect to Catherine the Great.

The eighteenth century also opened or at any rate widened fields of study little explored before: Adam Smith (1723-90), 'the father of political economy', is one of the most widely known of all Scots, James Hutton (1726-97) was equally the father of modern geology, and no account of European philosophy would be complete without including David Hume (1711-76), who follows in the sequence of Descartes, Locke and Berkeley. The prominence of Scots in medicine has been almost constant since the same period. Edinburgh's place as a leading centre of medical studies goes back to the dynasty of three generations of Monros in the chair of anatomy (1697-1859) but the Hunter brothers, John (1728-93) and (William 1718-93) were the leading surgeons in London. Later generations produced James Young Simpson, the inventor of chloroform, Joseph Lister, who developed the antiseptic work of Louis Pasteur, and Alexander Fleming, the discoverer of penicillin.

With industrialisation, Scottish brains turned more to practical inventions (for which they had always had a penchant) rather than theory. Watt's steam engine (1769), Nasmyth's steam-hammer (1839), Neilson's hot blast for iron-smelting (1828), Bell's steamship the *Comet* (1812) all came along — almost incredibly — in the same period as works of genius like MacAdam's roads, Rennie's bridges and Telford's canals (not only in Britain but in Sweden). And all those major creations, some of them of great beauty as well as utility, were contemporary with the work of artists and writers. Scotland's great tradition of portrait-painting begins with George Jamesone (1590-1644), since whom the succession has never failed, and it reached its peak with Allan Ramsay (1713-84) and Henry Raeburn (1756-1823). One of Raeburn's contemporaries was Sir Walter Scott (1771-1832), whose works attained almost unparalleled European popularity, often as the foundation of plays and operas. It is rather characteristic of the false and fictitious strands in Scotland's image that Scott's nearest competitor in European popularity was the largely bogus 'Celtick' productions of 'Ossian' by James Macpherson (1738-96).

Addressing the Scottish History Society in 1986, on the occasion of its centenary, I recalled that six years before its foundation Lord Rosebery, who became its first President, said, 'I think there should be a Professorship of Scottish history in Scotland', in order, so he added, that the connection of the youth of the country with its traditions should be strengthened. Before

Rosebery died, in 1929, there were professors of Scottish history in both Edinburgh and Glasgow, but after another sixty years the youth of the country is as far as ever from knowing much about its past. This has not been for want of protest and agitation. In 1926 Evan Barron, who happened to be in the chair at a Scottish History Society meeting, besides plugging his own somewhat eccentric views and demanding whether the Society had done 'justice to the Highlands', deplored the status of Scottish history in schools and universities. In 1933 R. S. Rait, who held the chair of Scottish history at Glasgow, reproached English historians for their 'contemptuous attitude' to Scottish history and instanced the treatment of Scotland in the *Cambridge Medieval History*, where it was ignored until the seventh volume, in which eighteen pages were allotted to its history from the Romans to 1328. In 1935 R. K. Hannay, Rait's opposite number in Edinburgh, criticised the lack of a Scottish content in school teaching and in the Civil Service Examination.

More publicity was given to the remarks in 1949 of an unexpected ally, Lord President Cooper, who, not being a professional historian, could not be accused of having a vested interest in the popularity of the subject. He discovered that in the University of the capital city of Scotland it was possible for a young Scot to take a degree in history without learning any Scottish history, and went on: 'There was a subject called British History, which proved on examination to be English History with occasional side glances at Scotland through English spectacles at times when Scotland crossed England's path.' He added that in the Honours curriculum Scotland was on a par with East Africa. I remarked in 1986 that thirty-five years had seen no improvement and added: 'One wonders if a present-day Lord Cooper would be sympathetic to proceedings, under the Trade Descriptions Act or the Sale of Goods Act, against a publisher' — I might have added 'a university' — 'who labels as British History something which is actually English history.' The press at the time fastened on Cooper's pointed remarks and his words had some influence in bringing about an experiment — alas! only short-lived — of making some Scottish history compulsory for Honours History students at Edinburgh.

Those who now plead the cause of Scottish history are saying what has often been said before. They may be no more successful than Rosebery, Rait, Hannay and Cooper were, but the situation has been changing and the case for Scottish history has been significantly strengthened. Scotland's international links resulted in an assimilation of Scots law and Scottish institutions to those of continental Europe, and Scotland, though the more remote country in Britain, became far less peculiar, far less insular than England, where law, universities and late medieval architecture all took their own lines. That fact alone should stimulate a fresh look at the value of Scottish history. The days when all history teaching in Britain was shaped by the assumption that the English model of parliamentary democracy was going to prevail throughout the whole world have long gone, and it is no longer valid to believe that English institutions alone are worthy of study.

# 2

## Human Memory and Oral Tradition

*Presidential address to the Scottish Record Society, 13 December 1984*

To anyone who has been in the habit of basing his findings on documentary evidence, oral tradition is apt to be no more than a very poor and unreliable second which for most purposes can be disregarded. Yet, however dismissive one may be of current or live oral tradition, history is, after all, concerned not only with what happened but with what men believed, and it is important never to lose sight of the fact that oral tradition — however false it may have been — was sometimes influential in shaping attitudes in earlier generations. Besides, there have always been inventions, fictions, erroneous notions about the recent past, and to them active human memory has always been at least a potential challenger. Indeed, all along there must have been a certain amount of interaction or tension between faulty impressions which circulated and more accurate recollections which ran contrary to them.

This must always be kept in mind in evaluating the reliability of sub-contemporary evidence and in assessing the efforts of demythologisers who are too apt to dismiss as worthless some traditional views of characters and events simply because there is no strictly contemporary evidence to support them: if those views were brought forward within at least a generation of the period when the characters lived and the events occurred they could easily have been ridiculed by individuals who remembered what had happened. In one way and another I have been brought back again and again to the question of the reliability or otherwise of oral tradition and the processes by which it was created and transmitted. One must start, in short, with the general question of human memory and its possible value as historical evidence.

There is in the first place what may be called personal, direct, primary or first-hand memory in the mind of a living person. How far this goes back of course depends largely on the individual's age, but it can be quite extensive. This is important in assessing sub-contemporary evidence, and the consideration has often recurred to me when silly people come on the air to discuss, for example, the authenticity of the Gospels. They tell us, with an affectation of something like horror, that the Gospels were not written until thirty or forty years after the events they describe. Thirty of forty years! But even people who would hardly admit to being middle-aged have memories which go back as far as that; and as the years go on the span of memory extends until, still before reaching senility, there are recollections going back sixty or seventy years. It almost seems that a special degree of scepticism is reserved for use when the Gospels are in question: it seldom seems to occur to the sceptics to apply similar standards to other similar sources, and they swallow without question an account of Robert Bruce made up largely from the verses of John Barbour, who was a mere child when Bruce died and who did not write his poem until forty or more years later. The Epistles, at any rate, and even the earlier Gospel material, were nearer to Our Lord's time than *The Brus* was to King Robert's. Barbour, like the Gospels, could have been challenged by men who had first-hand knowledge of the events he related.

Such direct memory, at least within short periods, is admissible as evidence in courts of law, and indeed most legal proceedings are conducted on the basis of such memory. One does not go far in records of legal proceedings without finding use being made of the recollections of the elderly. A Haddington Protocol Book recounts a hearing in 1537 relating to the rights of the nuns of Haddington in the lands of Permanscleuche Rig. Evidence was given by Nicol Symsoun in the Parkheid of Yester, a man of eighty-six: 'It is na tym for me to lee, for I am of greit age and knawis nocht how sone God will call on me.... I kepit catell on Permanscleuche Ryg ... and sene I left that steid it is xli yeris; and never hard pley [dispute or challenge] of any man quhill now laitle Richart Maitland of Leidinton ... maikis a pley'. There is no understood limit of time beyond which such evidence is inadmissible. But when such evidence from memory is produced in court it is usually subject to cross-examination, and it is sometimes the business of historians to cross-examine in a similar manner.

It is not only in court proceedings that formal appeal is often made to human memory as decisive. Every time a chairman asks for approval of Minutes he is appealing to the memories of members. How dangerous! Some time ago I received Minutes of a meeting which had taken place some months before and was astonished to learn that I had been in the chair. Going back to December 1563 and looking at the proceedings of the General Assembly, we find John Knox asking for verification of the instruction he claimed the assembly had given him to convene a meeting in any crisis threatening the reformed church. In response, a number of lairds, superintendents and ministers and 'the maist pairt of the haill assembley maid thair declaratioun that thai remembrytt verray weill' that it was as Knox alleged. It seems odd that there was no appeal to written Minutes, though a register of the assembly's proceedings existed. A few years later, it happened, an archbishop of St Andrews, who disliked some of the assembly's proceedings, tore some pages out of the record, but whether he so easily effaced the memory of what had happened is another matter. On the other hand, a few years later again, James VI was shrewd enough to realise that memory might be less reliable — or would be thought less reliable — than the written word: so by publicising Assembly Minutes only after a lapse of time during which memory about details was fading he was able to present a decision in favour of 'constant moderators' of presbyteries as extending to synods as well. He repeated something like his stroke about moderators when acts of parliament in 1612 went farther than the acts of assembly of 1610 which they professed to ratify. It is a commentary on James's actions and also on the effective length or endurance of memory that when a General Assembly met in 1638 it had been generally forgotten that away back in 1580 an assembly had condemned the office of bishop, and it was only the production of old registers which persuaded the majority to repeat that condemnation.

Even in the case of an individual, there are degrees of confidence in earlier memories. Looking back to my own earliest days, I am inclined to think that some memories have been lost and that there are events which I once remembered but no longer do. Of such events, including some during World War I, I can say, 'I remember that I used to remember'. Thus I used to remember, but I am not confident that I now remember, the solitary air raid on Edinburgh, in 1916, when I was three, and a slightly later occasion when we had a warning but no raid, and Armistice day in 1918; I have more confidence about immediate recall of Peace Day in 1919, by which date I was six. A good many of my memories of later years have been put into print, but, as I shall indicate later, some of them have turned out to be unreliable.

Some of the events of my earliest years were frequently recalled by my parents' clearer recollections of them and references to them. This brings me to indirect, secondary or second-hand memory — that is, the knowledge of the past which has been transmitted by older people who themselves had direct memories going farther back than one's own. We all have our personal links with the past in this way. I remember — just — my maternal great-grandmother, who was born in 1827 in the reign of George IV and died in 1919, but I was far too young to get any reminiscences from her. The earliest-born person I recall getting reminiscences from was a great-uncle who was born in 1844 and died in 1937. These were both connections with the past at only one remove. But one can proceed to a second stage, where a third person comes in. I used to tell my students, when I was talking about human memory, that I once met a lady whose father had been born in 1795, now nearly two centuries ago; the students goggled at that, for they must have thought me positively medieval, but there was nothing exceptional about it for anyone of my generation. The lady was the once well-known authoress Jessie M. E. Saxby (daughter of Dr Laurence Edmondston), whom I met in 1932 when I was nineteen and she was ninety-two and who put into print a lot of her own memories.

Outside my own limited experience, I have occasionally noted instances of memory extending over even longer periods, and instances of contacts which span the generations and even the centuries. Baroness Elliott, who is still attending the House of Lords when I write this, was born in 1903 when her father was 79; she can hardly have remembered him, but he had been born in 1823 and his father had been born in 1786. Those who note such things were startled in 1989 when the death (at the age of 96) was reported of the Empress Zita of Austria, who knew the Emperor Francis Joseph, whom her husband had succeeded in 1916 and who was born in 1830. Going a little farther back, there was Sir Fitzroy Maclean of Duart, who was born in 1835, joined the army in 1852 and did not die until 1936. He had received his commission from the great Duke of Wellington, who was born in 1769, and he was decorated for gallantry in the Crimean War. We go a stage farther back with Sir David Hunter Blair, who was born in 1853 and died in 1939. He recalled that when he was a small boy his grandfather had told him how he had once seen Bonnie Prince Charlie shortly before his death in 1788. There we have a link between Hunter Blair in the 1930s and Prince Charlie, who was born in 1720. It has been noted that Alexander Campbell Fraser, professor of Logic at Edinburgh, knew a lady whose brother had been killed at Culloden but he himself lived to be almost a hundred and see the opening of the War of 1914. In view of such examples, it hardly seems worth mentioning that one Shetland acquaintance of mine, who was born in 1891 and died in 1985, had information, through only one intermediary (1836-1916), about a member of the family who fought at Waterloo. I can draw on another case where I had personal knowledge of the informant. The late Dr I. F. Grant, who died a few years ago at the age of 96, remembered both of her grandfathers: one of them had been at the funeral of Sir Aeneas Mackintosh, who became chief of Clan Mackintosh in 1770; the other, Patrick Grant (1804-95), remembered that his great-uncle, George Grant, provost of Inverness, recalled that as a boy he had seen the crops standing unharvested in 1745-6 because so many men were in arms on the occasion of the Jacobite rebellion. Thus a lady whom I knew had spoken to someone who knew someone who remembered the '45. It is not difficult to span two centuries and more of possible transmission of evidence.

Nor is that the limit. The instance I always like to cite relates to the Empress Eugenie, who married Napoleon III in 1853. When she held her first court she was astounded to hear an old lady remark, 'As my husband said to Louis XIV'. The old lady, as a young girl, had been married to an old man who, when a boy, had served Louis XIV as a page. That, at two removes, spans the period from Louis XIV, who was born in 1638, to the Empress Eugenie, who died in 1920. But I can carry that particular example a stage farther. A near neighbour of mine in Fife is Lady Victoria Wemyss, who was born in 1890, a godchild of Queen Victoria. Lady Victoria once mentioned that she had had lunch with the Empress Eugenie, and I have had lunch with Lady Victoria. Clearly, this is a *reductio ad absurdum* and recalls the girl who said 'I've danced with a man who

danced with a girl who danced with the Prince of Wales'; it does not mean that
I have a private line to Louis XIV.

Claims have sometimes been made to startling links through exceptional
longevity. There was the case of Henry Jenkins, who was said to have been 169
when he died on 4 December 1670 and remembered having been present, as
a boy, at the battle of Flodden in 1513. And Peter Garden of Auchterless, who
died in 1775 at an age variously reported as 120, 130 or 140, had once, on a visit
to England, met the said Henry Jenkins. This, if true, would link, in only two
lives, the year 1513 with the year 1775. An even more astonishing tale was told
by a Mr Alister Mathews, of Bournemouth, about a gentleman who was 97 in
1912 and claimed that 'my grandfather's uncle was held in the arms of a lady
who had been baptised by a priest whose great-grandfather came over with
William the Conqueror'. The details, it emerged, were as follows: 'In 1066 a
family came over with the Conqueror, with a child born the previous year. He
married late in life and had a son born in 1147, whose son was born in 1230.
The latter's son (born 1311) in 1406, as a priest aged ninety-five, baptised a
daughter of the family to whom he was chaplain. She lived to a great age and
in 1506, aged 100, held in her arms an infant whose father, then aged twenty,
married a second time and at the age of 80 had another son born 1567, whose
son, born in 1650, was nephew of the child born in 1506. His child was born
in' the 1730s, 'and the latter's in 1815. In 1912 he was aged ninety-seven'. My
attention was drawn to this story by the Rev. A. Ian Dunlop, who told me in
1984 that he had a photograph, taken in 1891, of his mother in the arms of her
great-grandmother, who was 95 when she died. His mother, who died in 1982
aged 92, showed that photograph to Ian's grand-daughter, born in 1977, and
said, 'If you live as long as that old lady — your great-great-great-grandmother
— that will cover a period of 275 years.' A combination, within one family, of
a run of longevity and a run of paternity in old age can produce remarkable
results.

While there is, it seems, no limit, or hardly any, to the possibilities of what
may perhaps be called tactual or visual links throughout the generations, it
would clearly be nonsense to consider that at any rate the more extravagant of
them were of any significance for the transmission of reliable or useful
information. It is, however, worth while considering how far even direct or
immediate memory can be relied on, not least because, if it is not trustworthy,
then any information transmitted by word of mouth — or even by
unauthenticated writing — can be challenged.

That the human memory is notoriously fallible is shown by experience. I can
at least say this of my own memory, which may or may not have been
conspicuously above or below average, and I propose to give examples of my
own proven fallibility before I proceed to demonstrate the fallibility of others.
I make no apology for taking several of them from my hobby interest in the
northern isles and the ships which served them, for I should think on the whole

that a field which has absorbed me throughout my life should be one in which my memory might be particularly reliable.

My first examples, however, are not drawn from that field. I turn to an episode which was so startling that it did a lot to shake my confidence in my own memory and the memories of others and probably alerted me to the need to be critical and so started me on my collection of examples of fallibility. The episode arose from my involvement, when I was on the staff of the Register House, with the steps taken to protect the Scottish national archives during World War II. On 1 September 1939, in accordance with plans made in advance, the German invasion of Poland was the signal for the despatch to the sheriff courthouse in Oban of a box of what were thought to be items of special value — including the Declaration of Arbroath or Declaration of Independence of 1320. Nearly a year later, in August 1940, some 7,000 volumes, comprising the bulk of the unprinted material of dates before 1707, were sent to Morenish Lodge, about three miles from Killin on the north side of Loch Tay. Mr David Anderson and I were the members of staff chosen to accompany those refugee records and live with them in their wartime home. Some time after we had settled at Morenish, we heard reports of action by enemy aircraft in the Oban area, which Anderson (who naturally saw in this a case for bringing the Oban material to join what was in Morenish) reported to Mr William Angus, the Keeper. Angus, after making enquiries in Oban and finding that the air-raid sirens had been sounded only once, when a convoy assembling off Lismore was bombed, was inclined to play down the danger. However, I somehow came to believe that Anderson had gone to Oban and brought the precious items to Morenish, I formed such a positive impression that I would have gone to the stake on the conviction that this was so, and I had in particular the clearest impression that I handled the Declaration of Arbroath at Morenish. It was only when, many years later, I was writing an account of 'The Second World War: Further Adventures of the Records', that I discovered that, quite contrary to what I had imagined, the material which had gone to Oban remained there until after the end of the war in 1945 and was never near Morenish.

That was a case of totally erroneous memory. Here is a case of a mere — or should it be sheer? — lapse. Two or three years after I retired, when I was in conversation with a man who had done his PhD with me, he mentioned that he had been a candidate for a lectureship in my Department at Edinburgh in the year I retired. I expressed some surprise, and declared that I remembered nothing about it, but to my amazement he was able to tell me that I had actually interviewed him for the job before I retired. I had no recollection at all of this.

A different kind of lapse, this time a temporary aberration rather than a genuine error. When I was preparing my Petition to Lyon with a view to acquiring armorial bearings, I had to submit a pedigree, most of which was of course based on and supported by record evidence. But I had to supply the surname of my maternal grandmother, whom I had known very well — she did not die until I was over twenty. For this I relied on my memory and that her surname was Whitehead, not Innes. I immediately phoned Lyon Clerk to have the error amended. It did not much matter, for maternal ancestry was not recited in the Letters Patent granting my arms, but this mere passing lapse — inexplicable except for the fact that somewhere among my mother's kinsfolk I think there was an Alice Innes — could have found its way into permanent record.

Another instance is one of conflicting memories. For many years I was Secretary of the Scottish Record Society when Mr Monteath Grant (later Sir James, Lyon King of Arms) was Treasurer. After the Annual Meeting, held in the Lyon Office, which was then in the old Register House, Monteath Grant and I used to go over to Crawford's at the foot of the North Bridge for a cup of tea. My recollection was that on those occasions a certain lady member of the Society usually joined us for tea, but when I mentioned this it turned out that the lady concerned had no recollection of this happening though she conceded it might have happened once. In this case, who can say which of the two memories was right?

I move on to examples from fields outside my professional life, and not for the last time into maritime matters. In the first edition of my *Northwards by Sea* I related an incident from the early 1930s — probably 1932. At that time a small motor vessel, the *Islander*, was running in competition with the steamer, the *Earl of Zetland*, between Lerwick and the North Isles. I wrote that one Sunday afternoon the *Islander*, coming out of the tortuous north mouth of Lerwick harbour, ran on the rocks called the Brethren and suffered the humiliation of being towed off by the steamer when the latter came along behind her. But the late Captain Inkster, Lerwick harbourmaster, who happened to have been on the *Earl* that Sunday, was able to tell me that the *Islander* did not run on the Brethren but broke down off the Brethren and was then taken in tow by the steamer. When I wrote, in the 1960s, I was going by what I remembered from a press report I had read thirty years earlier. It was only an error of detail, but it is perhaps worth noting that I had made the incident a shade more dramatic than it really was.

Another lapse also related to the North Isles steamer. I remembered that at the end of August 1934 there was a particularly bad Saturday, when the *Earl* was unable to call at my local port, Burravoe, on her way south: I was right about that. But I thought I remembered that a friend of ours, a Mrs Johnson, who had joined the steamer at her previous port, Mid Yell, had found conditions at sea so unpleasant that her mind was made up to leave the ship at Burravoe if she did call there. Alas! for my memory. Not only was Mrs Johnson not on the steamer that day, but she had been dead for two years by that time — I was reminded of that when I checked with her daughter. Another error of detail. I think all I had got wrong was the identification of the hapless lady passenger: she may have been another acquaintance of ours, a Mrs Houston.

These are all examples of failures of my own memory. I now look, by contrast, at examples of failures in the memories of others, some of which I was able to correct from authentic evidence.

The first example is not a faulty memory in a single mind but rather a lapse which had passed into something like folklore. I have more than once mentioned it when I have been lecturing about patronymic names in the northern isles, but I escaped — narrowly — from putting it into print. In my early days there was in Hamnavoe, South Yell, an old lady whose official name was Joan Robertson but who was always known as Joan Gertson — 'Auld Joan Gertson' — because, so it was said and universally believed, her father had been Garth Robertson. It occurred to me that it would be interesting to check this, and one day I asked my friend the local Registrar to look it up. We found that Joan's father was actually *John* Robertson. Garth was not an unknown Christian name, and Garthson was not unknown as a surname, and I can only assume that the Garth from whom Joan derived her name had existed in her family in an earlier generation.

Another example is of a lapse which, at the time I learned of it, seemed to be on the verge of passing into folklore, and perhaps by this time has done so. Until I came on it I thought I was immune to shock from mythology, but this example was startling beyond belief. For many years, including those of World War II, my home was at 24 East Hermitage Place, beside Leith Links. I left there in 1975, but retained an association with the area to the extent of continuing to go for dental attention to a dentist in 6 East Hermitage Place. One day in the 1980s, seated in his surgery and looking out through the back window, I remarked on a site which had recently been cleared or rebuilt, and the dentist (a relative newcomer to the district) observed, 'Oh, it was bombed during the War'. This was simply breath-taking to someone like myself who had lived during the War only a matter of a hundred yards from the spot and was well aware that there had never been a bomb near it. Indeed the only bombs anywhere in Leith or adjoining areas had been at Craigentinny House, Restalrig, at and near Leith Town Hall and at Lindsay Road. No doubt there was a phase when all demolition was apt to be attributed to war damage, and the incident reminded me of the story that a visitor to another part of Leith, commenting on what he thought the effect of bombing, was told, 'That wasn't Hitler, that was the Town Council.'

Another incident, also maritime, has many points of interest. A book on *Wick Harbour*, published in the 1980s, which was sent to me for review, contained a picture of a ship with the caption 'The North of Scotland Steam Ship Company vessel *St Ola* at the quay heads in Wick. Her captain was "Bonnie Willie" Swanson'. A glance showed that the vessel was not the *St Ola* (which was in any event a rather rare visitor to Wick, for her almost invariable run was between Thurso and Stromness), but the first *St Clair*, which was in Wick almost weekly for substantial periods of her long career (1868-1937). Not only had the two ships nothing in common except that both had one funnel and two masts, but the *St Clair* (641 tons) was more than twice the size of the *St Ola* (231). I was somewhat less sure, but nonetheless fairly confident, that '"Bonnie Willie" Swanson' was an error too, for the only 'Bonnie Willie' I had ever heard of was a contemporary of Swanson's called '"Bonnie Willie" Williamson'. I looked further into it, and discovered that Swanson's Christian name had in fact been George. I speculated that the confusion and the garbled story had arisen because, during the first World War, Captain Williamson had been running the *St Ninian* across the Pentland Firth for the Admiralty and so in a sense running in tandem with the *St Ola*, commanded by Captain Swanson, carrying the Orkney mails over the same stretch of water.

I took the matter up with the author of the book on *Wick Harbour*, and he assured me that the captain of the *St Ola* had been Bonnie Willie Swanson, noted for his waxed moustache and otherwise smart appearance and also for being accompanied on board by a little dog. Now, the waxed moustache unquestionably belonged to Williamson, who was something of a dandy, whereas Swanson's moustache was rather of the toothbrush variety. The dog I had never heard of, and suspected it might be Swanson's. I phoned the late Lady Birsay, a native of Orkney who had travelled regularly on the first *St Ola*, and she did not remember the dog either, but she said she would ask Swanson's daughter, who was still alive. In due course I received confirmation that the dog was Swanson's. So the myth in Wick was correct about the dog — the least important factor — but wrong about everything else. The characteristics of one man had been transferred to another, or perhaps two personalities had been conflated.

Now to maritime matters again, this time for an example of how the truth can be distorted or embroidered. There was a curious accident one Sunday evening in 1934. The steamer *St Sunniva* (II) was on her way, as usual each week in summer, from Aberdeen to Leith and, incredibly, she went aground on the island of Fidra, far out of her usual sailing track, which would have taken her from the May Island to the north side of Inchkeith. What had happened was that the chief officer, who was on watch, simply forgot to change his course at the May to bring her up the Firth and instead let her drive on until she got across to the East Lothian side. That was the explanation universally accepted at the time. Many years, I suppose at least thirty years, later a different version was circulating. This was that the chief officer had given the order 'South by West', that the man at the wheel had protested, 'Should it not be West by South?' and had been told to mind his own business. Of course an experienced A.B. knew the courses as well as the officers, and there is an oft-told tale that on one occasion when an officer ordered 'Starboard' he met the objection, 'Na, sir, no yit'. It is almost surprising if the officer on the *St Sunniva* was not similarly challenged that evening, when even passengers wondered what he was up to. I was curious about the version relating that the wrong order was given, and thought I should check the facts. It so happened that the widow of William

Gifford, who had been skipper at the time, was still active, so I rang her up and her answer was unhesitating: 'He forgot to change course'. I do not think there can be any doubt that this, which was what she had heard from her husband the Captain, and which everyone believed at the time, was correct. What happened, presumably, was that someone later, puzzling over this curious incident, had invented a feasible explanation. So legends originate.

That same book on *Wick Harbour* has a photograph captioned 'The *St Nicolas* ashore on Proudfoot. She was a total loss.' Now, a North of Scotland ship, the *St Nicholas* with an 'h', was wrecked at Wick in 1914. She was a clipper-bowed vessel of about 700 tons, whereas the straight-stemmed ship in the picture is a vessel of perhaps 10,000 tons. It was not impossible that a *St Nicholas* with an 'h' and a *St Nicolas* without an 'h' both met their ends at Wick, but in view of this book's other errors I suspected that the caption was wrong and I learned from Mr David M. Ferguson that the photograph is of the *Gerona* and that she stranded not at Proudfoot but at Skirza.

I begin at this stage to wonder if memory is particularly apt to fail where ships are concerned. I certainly have more examples to offer. The magazine *Shetland Life* in June 1986 carried an article which purported to describe a voyage to Shetland in September 1923 by a medical man taking up a post as a *locum* in the islands. I wrote a letter to the editor in which I stated:

'There was no *St Magnus* in 1923, for the second *St Magnus* was lost in the first World War and the third did not come into service until 1924. The ship then on the West Side was the second *St Margaret*, which was billed to sail from Leith each Sunday in September 1923 for Aberdeen, Stromness and Scalloway. She would leave Aberdeen about mid-day on the Monday and arrive in Stromness about 11 p.m. Thus to write that he went to sleep on leaving Aberdeen may be misleading. It is hard to believe that this ship went to Kirkwall and then through Scapa Flow, with no mention of her scheduled call at Stromness. The account also seems to imply that the *Hampshire* was lost in Scapa Flow and not off Marwick Head. I am aware that ships occasionally made unscheduled calls, but Kirkwall followed by Stromness (or rather, Kirkwall and through Scapa Flow without calling at Stromness) is hard to swallow. Of course anyone who did a *locum* in Shetland in 1923 must now be nearer ninety than eighty, and could easily have made mistakes, but the account given of this voyage looks more like an imaginary reconstruction.'

When the editor wrote back he said apologetically that the author of the article was writing about 'a long time ago', which was no doubt true; but the point remains that he put into print the fruits of a defective memory.

That writer might have pleaded in extenuation that he was not an historian. The next writer in whom I detect a faulty memory is, however, a man who has written several books on Scottish history — the well-known John Prebble. In his *John Prebble's Scotland*, published in 1984, he wrote thus: 'When I did visit

Scotland for the first time ... I sailed from Wapping to Leith on a ship of the old Dundee, Perth and Edinburgh line, thirty-six shillings for as many hours afloat.... The little vessel was the *Royal Scot* and I had known her black hull and red-barred funnel since my childhood, from a coloured print my father kept in a tin with his medals, his naval record and discharge papers. As a Petty Officer Guns he had served aboard her in the Great War'. And on the page where those words are printed there is a picture of a ship named the *Royal Scot.* I subsequently elicited from Prebble that his voyage from London to Leith was made in 1936. He is wrong in almost every particular. The first *Royal Scot*, on which his father had served and of which he reproduced a picture, had been withdrawn from service in 1928 and was superseded in 1930 by a second *Royal Scot.* Prebble is wrong with the name of the shipping company; there never was a Dundee, Perth and Edinburgh; there was a Dundee, Perth and London, but the *Royal Scot* — both the first and the second *Royal Scot* — belonged to the London and Edinburgh Company. He is wrong about the fare. In 1936 the second-class fare was 40s. return in summer, 32s. 6d. from October to April. But his reference to a fare of 36s., as well as certain other details, show that he travelled second-class, and the second *Royal Scot* carried only twelve first-class passengers. I suspect he really travelled on either the *Royal Archer* or the *Royal Fusilier,* which were the passenger ships. All else apart, neither those ships nor the second *Royal Scot* had much in common with the first *Royal Scot* except that each of the four had two masts and a black funnel with a red band. However, Prebble did get the funnel colours right and he was correct that the London berth was at Wapping — the first point unimportant and the second not vital to the story. When I wrote to Prebble pointing all this out, he replied that 'The clarity of your memory makes a fog of my recollections'. He did not appear to draw the lesson that oral traditions, based on defective memory, should not be credulously reproduced.

My own knowledge of particulars which enabled me to make those corrections was not mere paper knowledge, but one based on acquaintance with the ships themselves — another factor which in a sense extends the memory. I used to startle the students by telling them that I had travelled on a ship which was built in 1868.

I can add a maritime example of which I had no personal knowledge. In June 1990 there was some commemoration of the evacuation from Dunkirk fifty years earlier. A letter in *The Scotsman* had stated that HMS Hood had taken part in the operation, and on 27 June another letter stated: 'At no time during this evacuation was HMS Hood anywhere near there. She was, in fact, completing a two-month refit and was in drydock at Liverpool' until 12 June, when the writer joined her there, and she then left for the Atlantic to join a large convoy, which arrived in the Clyde on 16 July — a date he later amended to 16 June.

Recalling World War II brings to mind a faulty impression of my own. I thought that Captain Maule Ramsay, who was reputed to be Hitler's Gauleiter-designate for Scotland, was arrested just two or three days after the outbreak of war in 1939. It was said that he had been detected when he was heard rejoicing over the sinking of the *Athenia* only hours after the war started. Many years later I saw — or heard — it stated that he was not arrested until the war 'hotted up' in April or May 1940. By the time I learned of this I was in a state of mind which led me to conclude immediately that I had been wrong.

I add two instances of what I can only call the growth of myth. I once heard it said — probably overheard it in Edinburgh's High Street — that 'St Giles' Cathedral used to be shaped like a cross, but the reformers cut the arms off and made it a simple rectangle'. A nice piece of anti-protestant propaganda. But one can see how this tale arose — confusion with the Tron Church lower down the street, which was originally on a T-plan and was deprived of its arms when the South Bridge and Hunter Square were created.

Very possibly persons acting as guides, not least when they are asked questions which they cannot answer, are under a special temptation to invent. Some years ago I brought from Shetland the upper stone of a handmill, which I had picked up adjacent to the ruins of the house where my father's uncle and aunt used to live. I had it on display in my garden at Prestonpans and when I moved to Dysart I carted it off there and set it up behind the house alongside a knocking-stone which I had acquired at Prestonpans. The two exhibits are visible, through a pend, from the footpath in front of the houses. One of my neighbour's told me that he heard someone conducting a party of visitors around and this guide pointed to my millstone and told them, 'I remember when that was dug up here'.

These various examples show how errors can be propagated even within a lifetime. How many similar errors have been propagated over the centuries? For a generation or two, people are still alive who can challenge errors. In the cases I have just given I was able, from my own memory, to challenge false stories and then verify the truth, which, as it happened, I had remembered correctly. But in other instances which I gave earlier — the Declaration of Arbroath business and the *Islander* affair — my own memory was at fault and I was corrected. One sees the interplay between false and correct memories and wonders how often invention or fiction has been corrected by those who remember the facts. Mythology, incipient mythology, can be challenged and one must assume that it has always been vulnerable to challenge for a generation or two. If there is this serious brake on mythology in the short term there must be more truth in certain tales than the demythologisers would allow.

The tension between faulty impressions and more accurate recollections could be applied in relation to many episodes in what passes as history, and enduring human memory used as a check on both mythology and demythologising. James III provides a good example. The conventional picture of his character and its influence on affairs was repeated generation by generation without receiving much critical examination. The king was given over to the company of 'low-born favourites', he neglected the nobility and was unfit, by his tastes or his temperament, to face with resolution the task of governing Scotland. It is also alleged that he was shifty, unstable and perhaps treacherous in his dealings with his brothers, Albany and Mar, who possessed the energy, leadership and ability which the king lacked but which the people needed. James accumulated a treasure in a 'black box' and, after the death of his queen in 1486, lived a secluded life at Stirling until in 1488 he was defeated by a confederacy of nobles at Sauchieburn and murdered.

The truth is probably more complex. It might emerge that James was a man in advance of his time and possessed of considerable shrewdness but that circumstances proved too strong for him. He was, at any rate, a man of artistic and cultured interests. Among his alleged favourites, those for whom it seems most difficult to offer a defence are Hommyl, a tailor, and Leonard, a shoemaker; but men of substance then spent lavishly on personal adornment, and James may have shown his good taste in his clothing as in other things. Cochrane, contemptuously referred to as a stonemason, was in fact an architect, at a time when buildings of very high quality were being erected in Scotland. Rogers, an English musician, was no mere 'fiddler', when there was a new stress on choral and instrumental music in churches. Other 'favourites' were John Ireland, a learned doctor of the Sorbonne, and William Schevez, a physician learned in astronomy who was also a bibliophile and became Archbishop of St Andrews. This reinterpretation went some way to make the favourites respectable.

There next arose demythologisers, whose novel theory was that the favourites did not exist at all but were figments of the imagination, created by writers a generation or two after the time.[1] They pointed out the possible influence of episodes in the careers of James III's contemporaries, Louis XI and Edward IV, both of whom had associates not of noble rank, and it was suggested that tales about the king's brother Mar owed something to the tales about Edward IV's brother Clarence; both were said to be associated with sorcery and both came to strange ends — Clarence done to death in a butt of malmsey and Mar bled to death in a vat or it may have been a bath.

The demythologisers went on from dismissing the tales about 'low favourites' to reject the concept of a struggle between king and nobility, to declare — despite the fates of James I and James III — that the monarchy was 'unchallenged' and to preach that the West Highlands were a stable, ordered society and haven of culture — ignoring that Highlanders saw themselves as 'enemies of the realm of Scotland' and allied with English kings. Those who 'are apt to be tossed to and fro, carried about by every wind of doctrine', were captivated by this novelty, but others reserved judgment and wondered if all previous historians could have been so completely wrong. The demythologisers made much of the

[1] *Scottish Society in the Fifteenth Century*, ed. J. M. Brown (London, 1977); *The Scottish Nation*, ed. G. Menzies (London, 1972), chapter 3; N. Macdougall, *James III* (Edinburgh, 1982).

fact that there is little or no record evidence for some of the favourites. But the records in which they would be most likely to be mentioned were the Treasurer's Accounts, which are extant for only sixteen months of this reign, and the Register of the Privy Seal, which does not exist at all at that time. The argument from silence is irrelevant if the appropriate sources do not exist. Records do, however, show that James sent a lute-player overseas to learn his craft, that he presented an organ to Trinity College Church and that he granted pensions to poets. And Schevez, the physician and astrologer who became Archbishop of St Andrews, is amply documented. The scanty contemporary evidence, far from being irreconcilable with the 'myths', tends at points to confirm some of their essentials.

It is more cogent that the elaboration — or invention — of stories about James III began quite early, within a period when invention could have been challenged by many who had direct (or even second-hand) knowledge of the events of the reign. Some of the elements of the 'myth' appeared in James's lifetime and others no more than two or three years after his death. But even those who wrote as late as the 1530s are not to be dismissed. Admittedly, men died younger then, but even so there were men alive in the 1530s whose memories went back fifty years and others who had listened to their parents and other seniors. Anyone writing within half a century of James's death would know that blatant falsehoods could be challenged, just as I challenged the myth of 'Bonnie Willie Swanson'.

# 3

*Errors Old and New — Including My Own*

*Presidential Address to the Scottish Record Society, 12 December 1991*

About ten years ago I gave a talk with this title to an Extra-Mural Class which I then conducted each year and whose students I thought it my duty to provide with a kind of up-date on Scottish historical writing. Whatever else I gave them, therefore, they usually received a kind of digest of the reviews I had written during the preceding year. I began the talk I referred to with these words: 'I sometimes think I could give a new lecture on errors every day. It is not so much that new errors are invented: the depressing fact is that the same old errors are constantly being trotted out by new writers — it is the books that are new, not the errors. Like the Bourbons, writers on Scottish history have learned nothing and forgotten nothing.'

In that particular year — it must have been 1983 or 1984 — I was referring to a single review which had dealt with two books, Monica Clough's *The Field of Thistles: Scotland's Past and Scotland's People* and Tom Steele's *Scotland's Story*. In the former I counted over fifty obvious inaccuracies. Mentioning that figure of 'over fifty', I am reminded of another, slightly earlier, case. In 1982 I had reviewed a book called arrogantly *The History of Scotland*. The authors' names were Plantagenet and Fiona Somerset Fry, but I refrained from remarking that a combination of a Plantagenet and a Somerset was not a very promising start for writing Scottish history. I did, however, say that in their book 'there are over four dozen straightforward factual errors'. They practically threatened to sue me unless I could produce at least forty-eight errors. I retorted that if I did so I would expect a consultancy fee, but I sent them a total of fifty-two errors and heard nothing more about either a lawsuit or a fee. However, that experience had taught me that it is not enough to say that there is such-and-such a number of errors; one must give some examples. Incidentally, one wonders if it is only a coincidence that the Clough book and the Fry book both have approximately fifty errors — is this an average?

Of Clough I wrote: 'There are many prime howlers. We are told that there were "scribes writing charters in Norman-French in the eleventh century", that

Edward Balliol, who died in 1364, was still a "legitimate alternative" thirty years later and that James I's parliaments were the earliest to include burgesses.' Steele, it turned out, was very much better. His boast that 'the facts, if not the opinions, in this book are correct' was almost justified. Almost, but not quite. I counted between two and three dozen inaccuracies, most of them in the earlier periods where the author was clearly not at home. Many of them arose from failure to grasp technicalities, especially ecclesiastical technicalities, but that does not make them venial. We are told that the Celtic church was run 'by monks, not priests', as if the two were mutually exclusive, and that 'Camerons, Macnabs and MacGregors owned no land at all'. A 'fermtoun' was not a village, Charles I was crowned not in St Giles but in Holyrood, and he did not compel the nobles to give up their ecclesiastical properties. Mr Steele is somewhat credulous if he believes that some Hay families are exempt from the normal laws of inheritance. But his biggest error, surely, is that 'from birth the Kirk and the school drum Scotland's rich and remarkable history into her children'. Would that it were so!

I wound up the joint review of Clough and Steele thus: 'It is interesting to compare the errors in the two books. Both writers state wrongly that David I founded the burghs of Edinburgh, Roxburgh, Berwick and Stirling, of which there is no proof; both declare that Edward I was *invited to arbitrate* in 1290, although there is no evidence of an invitation and he came to *adjudicate*, not *arbitrate*; both believe that parliament commissioned the First Book of Discipline. Both go astray about James V's bastards: Steele believes that Robert of Holyrood was the only one who had issue, Clough forgets Robert as ruler of the northern isles and places his son Patrick there in Mary's reign — which was before he was born. Rather oddly, Clough credits Knox with two Blasts of his Trumpet against the Monstrous Regiment of Women, while Steele has the witticism that Knox was surrounded by 'an adoring regiment of women'.

Not all the culprits can even plead — though it would not extenuate their faults — that they were merely repeating what had been written before. Some do, after all, manage to devise new errors, and this can be almost refreshing: Lady Longford, in *The Oxford Book of Royal Anecdotes*, p. 414, scores a hat-trick by identifying David Rizzio as 'the man who murdered Lord Darnley and married his wife Mary Queen of Scots'. When I reviewed J. D. Mackie's (Pelican) *History of Scotland* I made this comment: 'The one outstanding novelty of this book is a series of quite original errors of fact' — the kind of savage remark I sometimes regret having made. But Mackie, a man well versed in a lot of the *minutiae* of Scottish history, did surprise. He gave the sum paid in terms of the Quitclaim of Canterbury as 4,000, not 10,000, merks; he assigned the celebrated exploit of Magnus Barelegs to Crinan, not Tarbert; most incredibly, Robert I was 'set upon the stone' in 1306; Edward III 'signed' the Treaty of Edinburgh-Northampton in 1328 — but that error was hardly a novelty.

More recently, reviewing a book which was really very good, Alison

Plowden's *Two Queens in One Isle*, my last paragraph was to the effect that it contained about an average crop of rather venial errors: the Church of St Giles was not a cathedral in 1503; the nunnery at Haddington was not an abbey; James V was thirty, not thirty-three, when he died; it was Bothwell's — Mary's Bothwell's — great-grandfather, not his father, who had been proxy for James IV at his marriage in 1503. I drew attention to other lapses. It was not easy to recognise the commendator of a religious house in 'John Hay of Balmerino' or the Earl of Argyll in 'Campbell of Argyll'; and Queen Mary's attendant was Mary Livingston, not *Lady* Livingstone. I observed that it would be difficult to prove that Darnley was 'reputed to be a Catholic' when he married Mary' or that James VI was brought up on 'strict presbyterian principles'.

I constantly trounce those writers who, usually because they are English, are unfamiliar with Scottish institutions and terminology, and I repeatedly ask why they or their publishers do not ask someone who is better informed to read the work and remove blemishes from what may otherwise be a very useful book. I suppose they think they always know best. When I reviewed James Lees-Milne's interesting book on *The Last Stuarts* I wrote that the author 'makes the mistakes one has come to expect from writers who are not at home in the Scottish scene'. To the usual mis-spelling of Huntly as Huntley he added Fassfern and Dalwhinny. The presentation of Sheriffmuir as a contest of 'English' against 'Scots' obscures the fact that the opposing armies were led by a Scottish earl and a Scottish duke. The statement that at Scone the Old Pretender 'took up residence in the palace', while not strictly wrong, is sure to confirm the popular but erroneous belief that there was a royal palace at Scone. This writer's inability to distinguish between England and Britain, their sovereigns and their navies, led to the nonsense that 'James II did as much for the welfare of the British navy as any man', for there was no British navy in the reign of either the Scottish or the English James II. Most regrettably of all, this writer, after stating that the jewels left by Cardinal Henry, the last Stewart, and received by the future George IV 'are now the property of Her Majesty the Queen', Mr Lees-Milne adds in a footnote 'At least I suppose they still are, for I have not been able to find out'. Almost any Edinburgh schoolboy could have told him that they are with the Scottish regalia in Edinburgh Castle — where I suppose such an anglocentric writer would never have thought of looking. (Surely the most shattering example of anglocentric terminology was perpetrated not by an historian but by a preacher in an Edinburgh church who designated 'Jesus Christ the Righteous' as not an 'Advocate' but a 'Barrister'!)

But if an English author can do terrible things when he is writing specifically about Scotland, they fade into insignificance compared with what he can do when he is concentrating on England but has occasion to glance now and then at Scotland. I was appalled by the book on *Elizabeth I* by Jasper Ridley. Almost as I have written in the chapter on 'Scotland: A Backward Nation?', I wrote 'If English historians have learned much of late about Elizabeth, eighty years have taught them nothing about Scotland: to F. W. Maitland in 1903 it was "a backward country", to Ridley it is "poor, weak and lawless, barren, isolated and backward". It does not occur to him that whereas Elizabeth could find only one bishop (out of eighteen) to support her Reformation four or five (out of twelve) Scottish bishops accepted the Reformation.' I went on to repeat some of the examples I give in that earlier chapter of the contrasting records of brutality in England and humanity in Scotland and added, 'Mr Ridley passes over in silence those illustrations of the standards of a "backward country".' After remarking on his myopia in this field I proceeded to mention some of the book's factual inaccuracies. 'Some', I admitted, 'are trivial: James V died not a fortnight but three weeks after Solway Moss; Mary was not four, but nearly six, when she was taken to France; the Riccio murderers were pardoned in December 1566, not in January 1567; it was not Esmé Stewart, but James Stewart, who accused Morton of Darnley's murder; Gowrie was executed not in October 1583 but in May 1584.... Elsewhere Mr Ridley shows surprising ignorance of Scottish affairs and institutions. It was not "the people of Edinburgh" but the Scottish government which repudiated the treaties of Greenwich in 1543. The parliament of 1560 did not create "a Presbyterian state" (if there is such a thing, which Ridley mentions thrice on one page) or even a Presbyterian church, and anyone who believes that the general assembly was "democratically elected" will believe anything. Few will believe that John Knox had "a shrewd political instinct" or that a revolt of nobles, barons and burgesses took place "under his leadership". Ridley's remark that "most parishes had no parson, but only an underpaid curate" shows how far he is from understanding church organisation. The most incredible error is that the 4th Earl of Lennox was "a Catholic" when he became regent in the protestant administration of James VI's minority. If he was, his behaviour was distinctly odd: he took an oath "for maintenance of religion" [by which papistry was not meant] and he ordered the Archbishop of St Andrews to be hanged in his pontifical vestment.... There was no need for Leicester or any other Englishman to persuade the Scots to allow Mary to have her mass; they themselves had conceded this at the outset.... Perhaps it is appropriate that Ridley's most inexcusable lapse related to a comment on Scottish affairs by an Englishman. In Archbishop Parker's oft-quoted remark, "God keep us from such a visitation as Knox has attempted in Scotland", Mr Ridley was inspired to substitute "desolation" for "visitation". This kind of carelessness makes it hard to accept as accurate anything he says.'

People can get away with the appalling howlers I have mentioned because the average standard of knowledge about Scottish history is deplorably low, even among people who are otherwise well educated. I recall an incident on a National Trust cruise two or three years ago. Lectures and commentaries were as usual being given by 'experts' (among whom I used to be classed but am so no longer), one of them a distinguished scholar in Natural History. As we came up the Sound of Kerrera approaching Oban I inevitably recalled the death of

Alexander II on Kerrera in 1249 and I suggested to the 'expert' that when he was speaking about the end of Norwegian rule in the western isles he might mention that Alexander II was taking steps in that direction when he died and that it fell to his son, Alexander III, to conclude the Treaty of Perth by which Norway ceded the Hebrides. I repeated the message, but when he spoke he said that Alexander II died and it fell to his son, Richard III, to take action. That was sad, but it was even sadder that not a single other passenger thought that the 'expert' had said anything wrong.

Of course we all make mistakes — I am coming to some of my own presently — and it is not only anglocentric writers or journalists who perpetrate howlers. John Gibson, himself a former Scottish civil servant and the author of splendid books on the Jacobite phase, was kind enough to send me a copy of his excellent work on the history of the Scottish Office during the hundred years from 1886. When I acknowledged it and congratulated him I added that my correcting pencil, which hovers compulsively over everything I read, had found little to do. I did, however, point out to him that, writing of the 1850s, he said that Scotland had only forty-five members of the House of Commons, forgetting that the number had been increased to fifty-three by the First Reform Act of 1832; and he had stated that in 1918 only the four cities were given separate Education authorities, forgetting that Leith was equally privileged. Mr Gibson also alluded to the 'little MacBrayne steamer' which took part in the evacuation of St Kilda, but in fact the vessel was the *Dunara Castle,* then owned not by MacBrayne but by MacCallum Orme. I consider it a courtesy, when an author presents one with a book, to write civilly drawing attention to errors; to do so at least proves that one has read it (just as listing some errors in a review does). I recall two other cases where I have followed this course. Naturally one does not normally review a book of which one has received a presentation copy, but the embarrassing situation may arise that one has undertaken to do the review before the complimentary copy arrives.

I suggested earlier that in a general history of Scotland the average number of errors may be about fifty. In the most recent such history, the remarkable achievement of Dr Michael Lynch, the score is forty-one, but as his massive work is about three times as long as some single-volume general histories that figure represents an unusually high standard of accuracy. In a review in *The Scotsman*[1] I mentioned over a dozen of the errors and I wrote to Dr Lynch offering to bring other flaws to his notice. Eight pages of typescript still await his attention.

When I was appointed to the Fraser Chair in 1963 and had to plan an inaugural lecture, I did contemplate speaking on 'Sources of Error in Scottish History' and even made some notes under that heading, but I have no notion now of what I might have said. The title I chose for my lecture was 'Scottish

[1]'On the fault-lines of history', 21 September 1991.

History and the Scottish Nation', and in it I did refer to errors of a kind, some of them more serious than the relatively trivial lapses which it is only too easy to notice in publications or indeed in undergraduates' examination papers. I shall come to the latter in due course. In the meantime I do not want to defer my own errors to the end of this talk, lest you think I want to make light of them.

You may have heard of the minister who exhorted his congregation to reflect not only on their sins of commission but also on their sins of omission, and this, he explained, meant not only the sins they had committed but also the sins they had omitted to commit. I propose to confine myself to the former category. And, following the practice of the reformed church, to which I adhere, I am making my confession in public and not in private. Bring out the sackcloth and ashes!

An historian's confessions. Let me begin with simple misreadings or mistranscriptions from documents. One of them some at least of you must have heard of, for I used to mention it in my Palaeography class. When I was editing James Young's Protocol Book for the Scottish Record Society I came across a man called, I thought, Richard Fassington. He was a bailie of the Canongate and was constantly turning up. I noticed that Dr Marguerite Wood, in editing Foular's Protocol Book, had rendered the name as Faffington, but in my youthful arrogance I thought she was wrong. Black's *Surnames* had not then been published — one wonders how on earth we did without it — but if it had been I might well have appealed to Black, who favoured Fassington. However, when I was about half-way through the 2,000-odd entries in Young I decided that it was not Marguerite Wood, but Gordon Donaldson, who was wrong and that the correct reading was indeed Faffington. *James Young* was issued in parts, and the earlier parts were already out before I found the error. So about half-way through that book you will find a footnote to the effect that the name hitherto incorrectly rendered as Fassington was actually Faffington, and from that point he becomes Faffington — which I still think is a less probable name.

There was another somewhat similar error, which it was not so easy to correct and which, alas! has attained immortality in print. When I was indexing the Register of Presentations to Benefices, as part of my work in the Register House, I found a presentation to the priory of Strathfillan of an individual apparently called 'sir Maktor Quhitill'. Quhitill looked fair enough as a version of Whitehill; Maktor I had never come across as a Christian name, but after all he was in the wilds of Glendochart and it was quite possible that an official scribe had made a botch of some local name. So he went down as 'Whitehill, sir Maktor'. But later, as I was working through the Register of the Privy Seal, which duplicates so much of the information in the Presentations, I found a presentation to the priory of Strathfillan where the name of the presentee appeared with 'John' inserted after the 'sir'. I realised then that the Christian name had been omitted in the Register of Presentations and that he was really sir John Makcorquhittill or Maccorquodale. But, while I could and did alter the typewritten index, the late Dr William Stephen of Inverkeithing, then engaged in compiling the additions and corrections which went into volume viii of the *Fasti*, had included the bogus, imaginary Maktor Whitehill.

Personal and place names have their own snares, because so much depends on personal acquaintance with them. I recall another error which arose clearly from ignorance. When I was indexing the *Minutes of the Synod of Argyll*, which Duncan MacTavish edited for the Scottish History Society, I had of course several entries for Tiree, under various spellings. I included with them a reference to what the record called 'Island Tirrim', because I did not then know any other place which corresponded to such a name. Alas! when, years later, I got to know the West Highlands better, I realised that 'Island Tirrim' was Eilean Tioram, in Moidart.

I said earlier that I was not going to enter on errors which I omitted to commit, but I want to include some errors which I had a narrow escape from committing. Two of them, both in the *Thirds of Benefices*, were in proper names. In accounts relating to Angus and Mearns I came across a place called apparently S. Feres — 'S. Feres fishing'. 'S' to me suggested 'South', and I very nearly invented a place called 'south Feres'. In the nick of time I realised that it was — do you see it? — St Cyrus. Then there was the mysterious signature which appeared at the end of several accounts. It read 'Robertus' followed apparently by a surname beginning with 'Th-' or 'Ch-' and tailing off into a rough squiggle. I ransacked indexes for proper names beginning with 'Th-' or 'Ch-' before I realised that I was dealing with Robertus Richardson, the Treasurer.

Another error — this time not a proper name — into which I nearly fell but which I mercifully avoided was in the *St Andrews Formulare*. The contraction *mie* is regularly used for *minime*, a very common word in medieval Latin, meaning simply 'not'. I happened to be transcribing an indulgence, the first one I had dealt with, and I kept coming across this *mie*, which I naturally extended to *minime*. But it never made any sense. Somehow, and in time, I discovered that *mie* could be a contraction for *misericordie*, which, meaning mercy, is a common word in indulgences.

These are examples of errors which I did not in the end commit but was able to correct. One which I did not correct but which found its way into print was one over which I suffered some humiliation. In giving evidence about a document produced in the Dudhope Peerage Case in 1952 I was explaining a phrase which I had rendered — and which indeed read — as 'augi portus'. Under cross-examination I said, 'I have not found the word *augus*, or, as it might be, *angus*, in any Latin dictionary'. So I went on record. Then the late Douglas Young — himself a classicist — in a letter in which he was castigating Scottish historians and had a swipe not only at me but also at Professor Dickinson — I forget for what — pointed out, somewhat rudely, that *angiportus*, as one word, does appear in Lewis and Short, meaning — as I had guessed it meant — a narrow lane or something of that kind. I did not at that time know Douglas

Young personally; later I came to know and appreciate him well and we were on very good terms — to which an inscribed copy of his book on St Andrews is ample testimony. But at the time I was irked by the tone of his letter, and I wrote to him sharply observing that historians had some qualities, including manners, which compensated for their lack of the infallibility he claimed for classical scholars.

Those errors I have been mentioning, hinging on the reading of a word or a letter, are perhaps relatively trivial and hardly worth spending time on, though it is annoying when you make them and humiliating when you are found out. I pass on to confessions of other errors, one of which, when I was found out in it, was more humiliating and more public than what I suffered at the hands of Douglas Young. The scene was a lecture at the congress held in Kirkwall in 1968 to mark the fifth centenary of the pledging to James III by the Dano-Norwegian crown of its rights in Orkney. Scottish historians had said that, while the Scottish copy of the treaty survives, though in singularly battered condition, in the Register House, the Danish counterpart is no longer extant. I had simply accepted this, and thought I was in good company. Therefore, when at the conclusion of my lecture in Kirkwall in 1968 I had a question about the Danish copy, I made the stereotyped reply that, although we had the complete text, the document itself had been destroyed by fire in the early eighteenth century. When I uttered those words I was aware of a kind of startled gasp somewhere in the audience. It turned out afterwards that it had come from Mrs Jexlev, the Danish archivist, who knew perfectly well that the Danish treaty does in fact still survive. How Scottish historians came to believe that it had been destroyed I have no idea.

Curiously enough, when 'I put my foot in it' in that particular patch of Scoto-Danish relations I was in the company of another historian who made a similar lapse in another patch in the same field. It had been widely thought that the treaty of 1469, by which crown lands and rights in Shetland were pledged, as those in Orkney had been pledged in the previous year, had not survived at all and that its details were not known. Then, over twenty years ago, Dr Barbara Crawford, in the course of her research for her PhD thesis, came across in the British Museum a transcript of the Shetland contract. This discovery was publicised in somewhat extravagant terms on both sides of the North Sea — 'Shetland's birth certificate had been discovered' — but it emerged that the document, with only slight variations, had already been printed more than once.

In connection with those Orkney and Shetland transactions there is another of those errors which are hard to eradicate. It is often said that the treaties provide for the preservation of Norse law in the islands. There is no such clause, and this has often been pointed out, but the error persists, no doubt because some people want to believe it. It is rather similar with the petitions against the Union of 1707. It is useless to produce the figures showing that the number of petitions which came from the grass-roots — presbyteries and parishes — was pitifully small: we still hear that 'one of the most striking demonstrations of virtually unanimous opposition is the Addresses of rejection of the Union which poured into parliament from all over Scotland'.[2]

Clearly, error often arises from relying on memory and failing to check one's facts. My error about the Danish original of the Orkney treaty was an example. I suspect that when writing a one-volume history or some semi-popular article there is a particular risk that this may happen. Thus in my *Scottish Kings* I was wrong in saying that James I's ransom was to be paid in four years, not six. Ted Cowan drew my attention to this, and it was put right in the second edition. I was more ashamed of a failure of memory in a field where I had made a special study. In the course of my researches into liturgical developments in James VI's later years I came on, among the Warrender Papers in the Register House, a draft of a service-book which I attributed to 1617 and dubbed the second of a series of three. Incredibly, when I was writing the Introduction to *The Making of the Scottish Prayer Book of 1637* I forgot all about this draft although it would have fitted into the sequence of events which I was trying to trace. The document was, much later, printed in *Scottish History Society Miscellany*, x (1965), and I acknowledged my lapse in Duncan Forrester and Douglas Murray, *Studies in the History of Worship in Scotland* (1984).

I never cease to marvel at how easily one can fall into error by the simple substitution of one word for another, not infrequently the substitution of one name for another. Not only can one write 'James' when what one is copying is plainly 'Thomas', but even in reading aloud, for example in collating transcripts, one can say 'James' when 'George' is before one's eyes. I am not speaking of old MSS; it happens with modern type, when one is collating proofs. In a proof I once happened to be reading, the compositor had fallen into such error: the typescript before him had 'Duke of Albany', but what he set up was 'Duke of Hamilton'. What I suppose happens is that the brain receives messages from other sources as well as the eyes, and simultaneously with what one reads the brain receives some quite different message and makes the substitution. Equally, the mind can be distracted: perhaps Jenny Wormald's astounding dating of Flodden as 13 September may have arisen from the 'attraction' of the year 1513.[3] Anyone who has read proofs or collated transcripts knows that he can never be too careful; indeed he can never be careful enough.

I have already passed from my own errors to those of others, and I am sure that there is no idiosyncrasy in the causes of error. One, comparable to what I see as the lapse of the eye, is what perhaps constitutes the lapse of the ear, and I am sure it accounts for many errors in MSS when scribes were writing from dictation. This still happens. Several years ago I was dictating a note to the late

[2]P. H. Scott, in *Books in Scotland,* no. 34, p. 29.
[3]J. Wormald, *Mary, Queen of Scots* (London, 1988), p. 43.

Monsignor David McRoberts, among other things suggesting that he might have a meal with me before a lecture he was to give. What I dictated was 'You could have a hurried meal with me', but what Miss Geddie typed was 'a horrid meal'. Perhaps she had misread the outline in her shorthand.

Printers, I have said, make their errors, not always for reasons that are discernible. A genealogical table in *A Source Book of Scottish History*, vol. i (1st edn.), had unbelievable lapses. It shows all the kings from Edgar to Alexander II in a continuous line of succession from father to son, as if Alexander I was the son of Edgar, David the son of Alexander I, William the Lion — incredibly — as the son of Malcolm the Maiden and so on. It was not long after the book was published that my eyes lighted on this, and I distinctly remember going to Professor Dickinson, putting my finger on the offending page and saying, 'That seems rather regrettable, don't you think?'

Sometimes printers' errors have a certain charm. In the earliest Court Book of Shetland, which I edited for the Record Society, there were several references to local officials called fouds, a Scandinavian office somewhat akin to that of a parish bailie. And one of the parishes in Shetland is called Nesting. So the printer came up with 'John was fond of Nesting'. Very recently I had an example where the compositor had not misread handwriting but had clearly introduced a word which had come into his mind from some other source. At any rate, my typescript had it that Deacon Brodie organised a gang of burglars, but the printer put it that Deacon Brodie organised a bang of burglars, at which the mind boggles.

This brings me to that fertile source of error, students' examination papers. I say fertile, for students have remarkable ingenuity in inventing new errors, even although they are constantly repeating old ones. I was once informed that James VI had no father. I do not know whether the student was confusing Queen Mary with the Blessed Virgin or with her cousin Queen Elizabeth, of whom one student remarked that she was the Virgin Queen and was a great success as a queen. But it reminded me of an earlier examination paper, not in Scottish History, which stated that Alexander the Great was born in the absence of both his parents. Another gem, based on a phrase in my *James V to James VII*, was that '140 Border thieves were hanged and they became as peaceful as any other part of the kingdom'. King James's Peace. Another student achieved a remarkable truth inadvertently when he wrote that the west of Scotland is 'an area of great social depredation'. Another told me that 'Charles I was very expensive', as indeed he was. And yet another verged on unconscious truth by saying that the king was 'an intricate part of the clan system'. Out of the mouths of babes and sucklings.

Apt howlers like those can be treasured. One was handy to trot out when, on National Trust Cruises, we were entering the Firth of Forth and I was giving a commentary from the bridge. I reminded passengers of the history of the Bass Rock, mentioning that it was the place where James I waited for a ship to take him to France but became a prisoner in England instead. I added that a student wrote that James I, when a boy, was captured by the English on the high seas and kept there for eighteen years. It always makes me think of a kind of Flying Dutchman. Another examinee — this time a school pupil — did me an enduring service. Asked to write a note on Andrew Melville, this child stated that Melville lived in the twentieth century and invented the jet engine. This provided me with the crack that Melville was sufficiently explosive in the sixteenth century.

Other howlers, however, are pointless. It was no help at all to say that Macbeth was Lord Mayor of Moray or that Edward I was the paramour of John Ballliol. Nor was it helpful to write that in 1561 the people of Scotland awaited Queen Mary's return 'with baited breath' — so spelled. One wonders what kind of trap they had laid for her. The most ridiculous howler I ever found dates from the days about the end of World War II when I read Leaving Certificate Papers. A pupil, asked to comment on Sir Christopher Wren, answered that he 'was a great leader in the last war and the Wrens of this war were called after him'.

May I abandon frivolity for more serious things? Professor Hannay used to say that many errors arise because people do not read to the end of a sentence. The only example I now recall he gave was that of the unfortunate Patrick Graham, first Archbishop of St Andrews. Some writers have seen Graham as a kind of reformer before his time and have seized on a contemporary statement that he said Mass three times in a day, to assert that this shows his zeal in an age when some bishops did not say Mass once in three months. But anyone reading the source to the end of the sentence sees that Graham said Mass three times a day *when he was under sentence of excommunication,* for which he was rightly deemed insane. Another example of failure to read to the end of the sentence is one of which I have made something. Some read that David I on his accession found in Scotland 'three or four bishops only' and take it to mean that there were only three or four bishoprics in the country; but anyone who reads on will learn that *the other Scottish bishoprics were vacant.* Another example was detected, as so many errors were, by Hay Fleming. In a note to his *Mary* (p. 267) he quotes Skelton as saying in his *Maitland of Lethington* that the Confession of Faith of 1560 pronounced: 'And therefore we utterly abhor the blasphemy of them that affirm that men who live according to equity and justice shall be saved', without adding, as the Confession does, 'what religion soever they have professed'. Yet another example of not reading to the end of the sentence has produced an error which has several times been repeated. In the account of Knox's attitude to the consecration of John Douglas as Archbishop of St Andrews in 1572 the source reads that he objected that 'the Church of Scotland should not be subject to that order which then was used, considering that the lords of Scotland had long ago approved and also confirmed in parliament a better order in the Book of Discipline'. Those who want to twist the evidence stop at the words 'that order' and take the statement as proof that Knox was opposed to the order of bishops.

But the supposed objection to bishops dissolves into a mere preference for the arrangements made by the Book of Discipline for the admission of superintendents.

Old errors never die. Every teacher of Scottish history is sick and tired of being told that Charles I came to grief because he was trying to introduce episcopacy — something which had been done by his father. The Covenanters, we are always being told, were prosecuted because they did not have freedom to worship God in their own way — when how men worshipped God was not the issue at all. Anna Buchan, John Buchan's sister, in her autobiography *Unforgettable, Unforgotten*, went one better by saying that at the Disruption the founders of the Free Church went 'literally into the wilderness that they might have liberty to worship as they thought fit'. So much scholarship — or even simple accuracy — seems to have been a waste of time. Janet Glover, even in the second edition of her one-volume History, was still speculating as to why 'the original' of the Arbroath Declaration is in Scotland — a matter which had been disposed of at least a generation earlier. And a very recent book[4] ascribed to Geoffrey Barrow the explanation of the mystery of Malcolm 'the Maiden's' reference to 'my son' — which was explained by Graeme Ritchie away back in 1954.

Not only are people often unaware that corrections have been made, but sometimes when errors are pointed out to them they simply refuse to accept corrections. Many years ago the attention of the Council of the Old Edinburgh Club was drawn to the inscription on the Covenanters' Memorial in the Grassmarket, which reads, 'On this spot many Martyrs and Covenanters died for the Protestant Faith'. It was pointed out that the Covenanters of the Restoration period were dissidents not from the Roman Church but from a Church which, though not Presbyterian, was Protestant. The late Henry Meikle, then Historiographer, observed — a little unkindly — that men like the Bloody Mackenzie were bad Christians but good Protestants. Meikle and I were commissioned to go down to the Grassmarket and have a look. I took him in my car — I remember it was the first car I had, which dates the incident not later than 1949. We examined the inscription and then wrote to the Secretary of the O.E.C. suggesting that if the substitution of 'Presbyterian' for 'Protestant' was thought undesirable, the adjective might be modified and the inscription left as 'died for their faith'. As the inscription is circular, in segments, we observed that the replacement of one segment by another would be simple. Not surprisingly, no action was taken.

Quite recently, an exhibition showed a portrait of a Lord Chancellor — I think the 1st Earl of Dunfermline. He is shown with the Chancellor's appropriate concomitant, the decorated bag in which the Great Seal, of which he was keeper, was carried. The caption said that this article was a purse appropriate for the Chancellor *of the Exchequer*. I drew attention to this error, but nothing was done.

[4]M. Lynch, *A New History of Scotland* (London, 1991), p. 457n.

If good errors — or bad errors — never die, good mysteries are never allowed to die either. I doubt if a year ever passes without someone telling me, as if it is exciting news, about the alleged 'Coffin in the Wall' in Edinburgh Castle, containing, the myth relates, the skeleton of the son of Mary and Darnley. The Appin Murder is another example. The notion that there is still a well-kept secret in Appin dies hard, but that tale has been in print for most of this century. Mysteries, like glamour, are popular, and out of all the errors and the mysteries comes the curious amalgam which passes for Scottish history.

# 4

## *A Backward Nation?*

A lecture on this subject was given in the Royal Museum of Scotland on 5 October 1989 and an article adapted from it was printed in *The Scotsman* on 9 December following.

'A backward country', noted for its 'barbarous deeds' and 'customary turmoil'. With those words Scotland was introduced to readers of *The Cambridge Modern History* by F. W. Maitland in 1903. At that time historical thinking in this island was dominated by the achievements of the great English constitutional historians like Stubbs, Freeman and Maitland himself, who created the image of English history as the history of ordered progress towards a type of parliamentary democracy to which, it was confidently believed, the rest of the world would one day conform. Inevitably, therefore, the institutions of a country like Scotland, which deviated from the English model, were regarded as second-rate.

Scottish historians themselves saw things through English eyes, and capitulated to the English point of view. For example, Hume Brown, the first Professor of Scottish history, wrote rather apologetically, and could express little pride in Scotland's institutional achievements. 'We may look in vain' in Scottish history, he said in his inaugural lecture, 'for that orderly development which makes the primary interest of histories such as those of England and Rome'. It did indeed just occur to him that Scotland's record might stand comparison with those of some continental countries: 'Scotland during the fifteenth century was certainly not an Arcadia, but it is equally certain that for its crimes and oppressions it would be easy to find parallels in the contemporary histories of France and Germany. Even the performances of the Wolf of Badenoch are easily left behind by those of many a robber baron of the Rhine'. But Hume Brown did not dare to suggest that parallels might be found without even crossing the English Channel. Hume Brown's successor, Hannay, did not move very far from Hume Brown's position, for he was still under the spell of the Victorian era and the concept of English history as the embodiment of ordered progress, and he remarked that 'for intellectual enlightenment we turn first to what has been momentous, to Greece, to Rome, to England'.

This attitude has still not been shaken off by English historians, some of whom continue to write of the institutions of any country other than their own in a patronising and consciously superior manner. Sir Geoffrey Elton described the reign of James IV as a 'futile, though fascinating, story' and its events as 'these romantic but incomprehensible goings-on'. This, be it noted, of a reign which began only three years after the close of the Wars of the Roses, which might well seem futile and incomprehensible without being either fascinating or romantic. Joel Hurstfield had only one word to describe Scottish politics — squalid: 'squalid baronial warfare' and 'squalid factional warfare'. Much of the false image of Scotland's past which was projected by historians in earlier generations still lingers, for example in Patrick Riley's recent remark that Scottish history looks like 'little more than a catalogue of bloody calamities'.

Too much Scottish history which is being taught or absorbed today is still Scottish history as seen through English eyes, Scottish history interpreted from the English point of view. It is only right that every nation should have a proper pride in its own achievements, but the particular form which national conceit takes in England is the idea not only that English institutions have been and are superior to the institutions of all other countries, but also that in her historical development England was always far ahead of other countries. In English eyes anything that is not English is peculiar; worse than that, it is backward if not actually barbarous.

The assumption that Scotland was backward can be challenged. We ought to have learned by this time that it is worthwhile at least trying to understand the institutions of Scotland instead of dismissing them as unworthy of attention merely because they differ from those of England. It is not difficult to show that at many points Scotland was more mature in its outlook than England, was in many ways in advance of England, and thus to demonstrate that England was sometimes the backward country.

We may start at the top, with the monarchy. What were the attitudes of the English and the Scots to their kings and queens? There is an idea in England that the whole concept of the divine right of kings, the notion that a particular family had an inviolable right to the crown, the idea that kings cannot be lawfully deposed — all the ideas associated with Jacobitism — were ideas which the Stewart kings brought with them from Scotland. The English, with their conscious air of superiority, imply that there was no room in England for that sort of nonsense and that the sensible English people taught the Stewarts a lesson and sent them packing. But this is quite contrary to the facts. It was in England, far more than in Scotland, that all sorts of half-magical ideas surrounded the kingship. The belief that a certain disease, The King's Evil as it was called, could be cured by the king's touch, was an English idea. The Stewart kings did not 'touch for the Evil', as the phrase went, until they became kings of England, and when James VI succeeded to the English throne he was at first rather sceptical about what he regarded as a quaint English superstition.

Nor did the Scots believe in the exclusive right to the throne of one particular family. They were very proud of their long line of kings, and fondly imagined that there had been over a hundred of them — their portraits, mostly spurious, can be seen in the Long Gallery at Holyroodhouse. But — as explained more fully in a later chapter, 'Reflections on the Royal Succession'[1] — the Scots believed, far more firmly than the English, that the people could choose their king and set aside a king of whom they did not approve. The different points of view came out plainly at the revolution of 1689, when James VII was replaced by William of Orange. At that time the English declared feebly that James, by fleeing from the country, had abdicated, which was simply not true; the Scots, more forthright and more logical, declared that James, by his misdeeds, had forfeited his right to the crown and the throne had become vacant. At that point the Scottish parliament was doing nothing that it had not done, or at least asserted its right to do, in the fourteenth century. It was the Scots who had the more mature point of view.

On the other hand, the Scots did treat their kings with a good deal more consideration than did the English. For some odd reason — possibly because the English, like Alan Breck in *Kidnapped,* have a 'grand memory for forgetting', in this case forgetting things discreditable to themselves — the idea has been put about that the Scots, but not the English, were addicted to murdering their kings. Queen Victoria's complaint that in Scottish history there were 'too many Jameses, and all of them murdered', was a libel. In the fourteenth and fifteenth centuries the Scots murdered only two of their kings — James I and James III; in the same period the English managed to dispose of five of theirs, with two heirs to the throne for good measure. Edward II, Richard II, Henry VI, Edward V and Richard III were all killed by either their subjects or their rivals. Sober arithmetic is against the English claim to superior rectitude here. The English were only following their own brutal old custom when they put to death Mary, Queen of Scots, and Charles I.

During the Wars of the Roses rival kings and rival families were competing for the English crown and one king was almost habitually deposed in favour of another: Plantagenet, Lancastrian, Yorkist and Tudor fell or rose in turn in England. But in Scotland the crown passed regularly, and without a single break, from father to child; for two hundred and fifty years, no less, each Scottish king was peacefully succeeded by his son or daughter. This is a kind of contrast which the English have a grand memory for forgetting: it is nonsense to hold up England as an example of peace and order and to imply that Scotland was, by comparison, backward.

The contrast can be pushed farther. The period in Scottish history which does resemble the Wars of the Roses was away back in the tenth and eleventh centuries: at that time the Scottish throne was contested almost generation by

[1]See below, p. 103.

generation, and a king was habitually killed in favour of a rival. Scotland got this kind of thing out of her system quite early, and ceased in the eleventh century to behave towards her kings as England was still doing in the fifteenth. England was centuries behind Scotland.

It is preposterous, too, that Scotland should have a reputation for being disorderly. There were, in truth, far more rebellions in England. There was not a reign between the reign of Edward II and the reign of Elizabeth, except possibly that of Edward III, when there was not at least one rebellion in England, and usually there were more than one. England was a welter of political and social unrest. Yet G. M. Trevelyan wrote about 'a century of peace under the Tudors'. Scotland's record was incomparably superior. She even managed to get through the sixteenth century, so sanguinary in many countries, without any massacres, with very few martyrdoms, and with hardly any executions for treason. Even rebellions were rare and if there were wars of religion they were wars mainly between the English and French, wars on Scottish soil indeed but wars in which little Scottish blood was shed.

In England, too, the many rebellions were suppressed with savage brutality. The leaders were put to death with all the penalties of the barbarous English treason law, including disembowelling while still alive; the Scots very properly regarded such proceedings with scandalised horror; their own traitors were, very occasionally, put away, but it was done decently by beheading. And when it came to beheading the Scots were more humane than the English. English executioners hacked away with an axe and might take half a dozen strokes to finish the job. But in Scotland there was an efficient machine called The Maiden: its sharp blade, aided by a great lump of lead weighing 75 lbs., was guaranteed to shear off the head at one stroke.

Even when England did finally grow out of the Wars of the Roses stage she still did not show real signs of political maturity by learning self-government or political freedom; instead she was subjected to the despotism of the Tudors. Under Henry VIII the king's will was law and the king's will was enforced by something little short of a reign of terror: the executioner's axe and the hangman's rope were seldom idle and all who dared to challenge the crown were dealt with savagely.

But while England was groaning under the brutal tyranny of the Tudors, in Scotland men were at liberty to form political parties and to bring pressure to bear on the government. Sometimes the fate of the country was even decided by a free vote in parliament, though not very often. But it is also true that a decision was not very often reached by bloodshed either. More often all that happened was a kind of demonstration in force when men did gather in arms, but they seem to have been content with something like counting heads, and the minority simply withdrew, so that there was a bloodless *coup d'état* involving a change of government without much if any violence. It really worked quite well, and Scotland had party government of a kind in the sixteenth century, when England was under the Tudor despots.

But the English sneer at all this. If England has political freedom and party government, that is a good thing. But if Scotland has it, at a time when England is under a despotism, then it is a sign of backwardness. England under a tyranny was orderly and well-disciplined, whereas Scotland, where there was some liberty, was a welter of confusion. It never seems to occur to the English historian who takes this attitude that at the present day the inhabitant of a dictatorship would consider his stable system far superior to the British, in which the government is liable to be changed every few years by a general election.

The Scottish Maiden was less hard-worked than the English executioners. In England the victims of Henry VIII and Elizabeth must be numbered by the hundred, and it is hard to think of a prominent Englishman in that age who did not end his days on the scaffold. Survivors were rare. In Scotland it is hard to think of many comparable executions of notables: there was Lord Home in 1516, the Earl of Morton in 1581 and the Earl of Gowrie in 1584, and possibly one should count Kirkcaldy of Grange in 1573, but those are about all. Now this contrast is not merely a matter of arithmetic — counting heads, literally: in England a man could not oppose the government without a very great risk, almost a certainty, that he would get it in the neck; in Scotland the chances of success were greater, but, even in the event of bad luck and failure, death was not likely to be the penalty. One could cite instance after instance of men who were on the losing side in Scottish politics, who were active against the government again and again, and who yet died in their beds at a ripe old age. Survivors were common. Even when the capital penalty was not in question practice was more humane in Scotland than in England: John Knox denounced Mary's marriage plans, but all he suffered was a dressing-down from the queen in person, whereas poor John Stubbs, who similarly denounced Elizabeth's projected marriage to a French prince, had his right hand cut off. Knox knew that there was more freedom of speech in Mary Stewart's Scotland than in Elizabeth Tudor's England.

It can therefore be argued that there was some political freedom in Scotland, to the extent at least that death was not the normal penalty for being on the losing side; death was not the inevitable consequence of unsuccessful opposition. A comparison of Scotland's record with that of England suggests that sixteenth-century Scotland was rather a kindly place, and certainly a safer country to live in than many others.

A kindly place. There are, in truth, some interesting examples of humanity. When a levy was laid on the clergy, one priest was excused payment on the ground that he was 'ane auld blind man' and another on the ground that he was 'ane poor auld decrepit man'. In the 1570s the widow of a burgess of Stirling, whose house had been set on fire in the course of a street affray and who had had to jump out of the window, 'whereby she is made impotent and unable to win her sustentation', received from the government a disablement pension of £50. Perhaps one should mention in this connection the appointment in 1557 of a surgeon 'for curing of the lieges that shall happen to be hurt upon the Borders when daily invasions and incursions are made by our auld enemies of England'. There, in the sixteenth century, we see something like a national health service.

The sixteenth century was the century of the Reformation, when again there was a contrast between England and Scotland. From beginning to end, the Scottish Reformation was marked by far less dislocation and violence than is popularly believed. In England, on Elizabeth's accession the bishops who had held office under her Roman Catholic sister Mary were imprisoned, and protestants clamoured for their blood; but in Scotland after 1560 the bishops retained two-thirds of their revenues and continued to sit on the council, in apparent amity, alongside supporters of the Reformation. Despite all the stress, Scotland remained a kindly place and men could differ in opinion without any personal hard feelings. In the East Lothian parish of Tranent the pre-Reformation vicar did not conform to the new regime and retained two-thirds of his stipend, while his successor, a minister of strong protestant views, was entitled to only one-third; but when the minister made his will he acknowledged that the vicar had voluntarily made over to him certain teinds of fish and salt and as a kind of 'Thank you' he bequeathed to the vicar his black gown. The two were very likely in the habit of enjoying a drink together. Again, there was in Scotland no dissolution or suppression of the monasteries. Abbots continued to draw their revenues, or most of them, as long as they lived; the monks were entitled to their portions or salaries and their quarters in the precincts after the Reformation as before it; friars were pensioned off.[2]

Every form of persecution, bloodshed and cruelty was less conspicuous in Scotland than in England. In Scotland the Roman Catholic authorities put a mere handful of protestants to death — not more than about twenty all told, over a period of thirty years; and on the other side it is hard to think of more than two papists who suffered death for their religion. Mary, Queen of Scots, did issue a proclamation which forbade the Latin mass — something, by the way, in which she was ahead of the Pope by about four hundred years — and several priests were imprisoned for defying the ban, but not one was executed. In England the score of executions was three hundred protestants under Bloody Mary and two hundred papists under Elizabeth. On the collapse of the Northern Rebellion against Elizabeth in 1570 some 800 persons were executed; when Mary's cause was extinguished with the fall of Edinburgh castle in 1573 there were only five executions and four or five men suffered short terms of imprisonment, while arrangements were made to protect from molestation or annoyance the women who had been in the castle. And yet this was the period in which, according to English historians, Scotland was a backward country.

[2]Some of the evidence for the mildness of the Scottish Reformation is brought together in Ian B. Cowan, *Blast and Counterblast* (Edinburgh, 1960), especially pp. 28-9, 31.

But there is the question of material destruction. Did the Scots not destroy their abbeys and cathedrals, whereas the English preserved theirs? The answer to that question is a complex one which has often been debated. For one thing, some of the Scottish abbeys were destroyed by the English, not by the Scots. In the 1540s, Kelso, Melrose, Jedburgh, Dryburgh and Holyrood were all burned by the English, and they were never restored after that. A hundred years later, it is said, Cromwell's men pulled down the cathedral of Fortrose and the abbey of Kinloss to build their new fort at Inverness. So part of the responsibility lies with the English. People go down to Holyrood and look at those broken pillars and shattered vaults, and say, 'Just see what John Knox did'. The truth is that the eastern part of that abbey was destroyed by the English in 1544 and the western part remained roofed and entire until so late as 1768, two hundred years after Knox's time, when it fell down through sheer old age. Besides, anyone who goes to England and looks at, say, Bury St Edmund's, will see that Scotland has no monopoly of ruined abbeys.

Scots have been a practical race, and, while they can be very sentimental in some ways, they do not regard material objects with much sentiment. Consequently, once a building ceases to be of use, or once it falls out of date, they are apt to pull it down and replace it. There is little respect for antiquity for its own sake. In England old buildings are treated with far more affection and are not only preserved but kept in use, long after they have ceased to be suitable for their function. There are many buildings still in use in England which in Scotland would have been pulled down long ago. This is to be seen in educational establishments. Some Oxford and Cambridge colleges, though hopelessly out of date and far from up to modern standards, remained in use. Edinburgh, by contrast, pulled down its old university buildings in the eighteenth century; Glasgow did the same in the nineteenth. So it was with schools. A sightseer at Eton, shown a room which, the guide proudly proclaims, has been in use continuously since 1440, may very well reflect that it looks like it. That is characteristic. Eton is still using its fifteenth-century buildings; the High School in Edinburgh is now the fifth building it has had since the fifteenth century.

This applies to churches too. In Scotland at the Reformation many of the abbeys ceased to have any practical value; some, which had been used as parish churches, were preserved and continued to be so used, but others, which were not parish churches, fell into ruin. The same applied to some cathedrals. The hard-headed Scot saw no point in keeping up a vast cathedral in a town like St Andrews or Elgin, where the local congregation could be accommodated in the existing parish church. And so far as the ordinary parish churches were concerned, as they grew old and outworn they were usually replaced by new buildings, sometimes not until the nineteenth century. In England the old parish church has almost invariably been retained, but it is often in a state of dilapidation and mouldering decay which would not be tolerated in Scotland. Differences of character and temperament come out in the attitude of the two peoples to their old buildings. In this particular the Scottish attitude is not necessarily superior to the English; but it is not indefensible.

The degree of political freedom which Scots enjoyed in the sixteenth century did not necessarily mean parliamentary government of the English type. But the Scottish parliament, among Scottish institutions, has suffered specially severely through comparison with the English parliament. And this derogatory attitude has coloured almost all writing on it, even Sir Robert Rait's magisterial work, *The Parliaments of Scotland.* But when one looks into the subject one soon begins to suspect that even that maligned institution, the Scottish parliament, was not nearly as contemptible as used to be thought. All in all, the relations between parliament, the steering committee known as the lords of the articles, and the privy council, had some parallels to the way in which parliamentary government functions today, when a cabinet very largely controls the legislative programme and determines in advance what measures will pass. Some might even conclude that the old Scottish method of passing the government's bills with little or no discussion was more sensible than the elaborate procedure of conducting long debates the outcome of which is wholly predictable. However, before the modern charade developed the British parliament did go through a phase of some independence, and it is this which is hard to parallel in Scotland. There may be fresh assessment of the Scottish parliament, by scholars who have shaken off outmoded attitudes and have ceased to measure Scottish institutions by an English yardstick.

Apart from the parliament, there is no lack in Scotland, as Hume Brown thought there was, of evidence of orderly development and of the steady evolution of institutions. There are institutions, not least at the local level, in which stability and continuity are amply demonstrable, institutions which are to be regarded not as pale imitations of English exemplars but as institutions which evolved to fit Scottish society. Many such institutions show, too, in their history, the continuing life of the nation and of the communities within the nation, a life which went on throughout the generations with little interruption from those picturesque events which cut a large figure in the history books but which clearly were of no more than superficial importance.

That leads to an examination of Scottish society. Was the social structure in Scotland backward by comparison with England? In all western European countries in the middle ages a large number of people in the countryside were serfs; they were tied to an estate, they were bought and sold with the estate, they had no rights as citizens. Now, in England serfdom did not come to an end until so late as the sixteenth century; English historians, with their grand memory for forgetting, seldom see fit to remind us that some of the subjects of Henry VIII were still in a state of serfdom. And English historians are even less likely to point out that serfdom disappeared from backward Scotland two hundred years before it disappeared from progressive England; the last reference to serfs in Scotland was so far back as 1364. (It should be said that the peculiar statutory conditions imposed on colliers and salters in the seventeenth and eighteenth centuries, while they constituted servitude of a kind, were not a survival from medieval serfdom.)

Not only is it true that the Scottish countryman was thus freed at an early date from actual serfdom. In the fifteenth and sixteenth centuries there was a steady flow of legislation in favour of those who were called 'the poor tenants' or 'the poor labourers of the ground'. Besides, as early as 1425 the Scottish government appointed an advocate for the poor. We need not believe that all this legislation was observed, but it does indicate some concept of social equity, some concern for social justice.

It is also to be noted that these measures were not the result of violent action by a militant proletariat but were introduced by administrations dominated by the magnates. On the contrary, indeed, those measures may explain why there are indications that the mass of the people in the countryside were happier and more contented in Scotland than they were in most countries. In England there was a great Peasants' Revolt; in France there was a similar movement called the Jacquerie; and in Germany there were terrible risings of peasants against their masters. In Scotland no such risings were ever known, and this apparent absence of social unrest surely indicates that Scotland was not a backward country socially.

It is a familiar bit of history that Scottish education was for a long time in advance of English education. (At the present time Scots are still apt to think that their education is superior to the English, but that may be debatable, for England has to some extent caught up with Scotland.) It was as early as 1496 that the Scottish parliament passed an education act, to the effect that the sons of men of substance should go to grammar schools and colleges; it is not until more than sixty years later that such an act was thought of in England, and even then none was passed. Recent research indicates that certainly after the Reformation, possibly also before it, Scottish attainments were far higher and more consistent than used to be supposed. Partly as a result of legislation passed in 1616, 1633 and 1646, the parish school and schoolmaster were familiar features of the Scottish scene long before the act of 1696 from which their origin used to be traced. It is much the same story with universities. Scotland had four, indeed five, universities before 1600; England still had only two after 1800. It was often remarked that a single Scottish town, Aberdeen, had as many universities as the whole of England.

One can point with equal force to various features in the legal system of Scotland which have been superior to those of England. One thing of which Scots should be very proud is the system of the registration of transfers of property. From at latest 1617 — nearly four hundred years ago — every conveyance of a piece of land, or even of a house or a flat, was recorded in official registers. No other country possesses such a thing. Historians can trace the history of any piece of land back through its successive owners; and of course when anyone buys a house or a piece of land a search in the register shows whether the transaction is a valid one. England only recently began even to try to set up anything comparable — not identical — and whatever England may achieve she will never have the precious registers which we possess. A noteworthy feature of Scottish land law was the feuing system, whereby property was transferred in return not for a large lump sum but for a fixed annual payment. Here we had a form of hire purchase which deserved the name far better than the payment by instalments which now goes by that name. The Scot, accustomed to the feuing system, always finds it hard to appreciate the merits of the English leasehold system, which does not make a permanent transfer. And, perhaps partly because of the structure of Scottish urban dwellings, Scots have never had any difficulty about transferring property in the shape of flats as well as houses, a matter about which the English made difficulties.

Thanks to the system of registration and the feuing system, Scottish land law was simpler and clearer than that of England. That great English historian F. W. Maitland, in a moment of unusual candour, remarked, 'If our lawyers had known more of Roman law, our law — in particular our land law — would never have become the unprincipled labyrinth it became'. Perhaps things have improved in England since Maitland wrote those words in 1886, but the land law of Scotland has never been an unprincipled labyrinth at any time since our records began.

The English are justifiably proud of the great extent and continuity of their records. By comparison, the national archives which survive in Scotland are meagre, though this is partly because two English invaders — Edward I and Oliver Cromwell — each carried a lot of them away and other English invaders were responsible for some destruction. Yet in compiling their records the Scots were not backward, and there was one particular in which they were far ahead of the English. They realised away back in the fifteenth century that keeping records of crown grants on long continuous rolls of parchment was unsatisfactory and inconvenient and started entering them in bound volumes instead, whereas the English worked away with their cumbrous rolls for many centuries after we had abandoned them.

There is one very significant point in private law. If a child is born to unmarried parents and the parents later marry then the child automatically becomes legitimate — legitimated by subsequent matrimony as the phrase went. That is the law of England now, but it has been the law of England for little over sixty years. It has been the law of Scotland for more than six hundred years, so that in this particular England was centuries behind Scotland.

Another little matter, not of law so much as of practice. We are accustomed to dating our year from 1 January. Continental nations started doing that in the sixteenth century, and Scotland almost at once followed their example, for James VI ordained that the year 1600 should begin on 1 January and not, as previous years had done, on 25 March. England took another hundred and fifty years to catch up with us: it was only in 1752 that backward England followed Scotland's example in making this change.

Once the assumption that Scotland is a backward country and that everything that is not English is inferior is challenged, then Scottish history can be approached from a fresh angle. The Scottish constitution used to be dismissed as simply not worthy of notice. But the belief that the British — which meant the English — constitution was so excellent that it would spread to all other countries can no longer be held, for it has become clear that the rest of the world is not going to follow the example of England. In this new setting, in the context of the present, institutions other than the English, ways of doing things different from the English ways, are more worthy of study than they used to be.

In foreign relations, as well as in domestic affairs, the Scottish way of doing things was more happily chosen than the English. Throughout many medieval centuries England's policy was dominated by two ambitions — the conquest of France and the conquest of Scotland. Despite the expenditure, generation by generation, of blood and treasure on a scale which does not bear thinking about, that policy was a total failure. By the mid-sixteenth century the only remaining relics of all England's ambitious wars were Calais and Berwick; ultimately even Calais was lost, leaving as England's only success the solitary town of Berwick-upon-Tweed. Scotland, except in so far, as a part of the United Kingdom, she has been involved in what were wars of England's making, has not been at war with any continental power since 1263.

One final point. As the European Community threatens to become more and more of a reality, the days when Britain turned her back on the continent and looked overseas to the now deceased British Empire are gone, never to return. We are going to be more closely linked with the continent than ever before. In past centuries, Scotland was more accustomed than England to look to the continent, and England, although nearer to the continent, was more individualist, more insular, than Scotland was. Many Scottish institutions, many features of Scottish life and culture, still reflect the old continental background, and affinities of a great deal that happened in Scotland are to be found not in England but in France, the Netherlands, Denmark and Norway. Scotland may therefore find it easier than England will to accommodate herself to life within the European Community, a situation in which Britain looks to the continent. That is another reason why the study of Scottish history, in its European setting and with due regard to Scotland's ancient continental links, might not be a bad preparation for life in the twenty-first century.

# 5

## *Archives and the Historian*

On the eve of my retirement in 1979 I acquired something of a fresh angle on approaches to archives. In the process of preparing to leave the Department I had to do some tidying up. This involved, among other things, going through all the files accumulated over the sixteen years I had held the Chair — as well as a little material from my earlier work in the Department — in order to determine what was worth keeping. An enormous amount was unquestionably ephemeral, completely dead and suitable only for destruction. On the other hand, I felt I ought to hand on to my successor papers which either related to current matters or were of lasting value and possibly of use to him in the future. Other papers I wanted to keep myself, either because they related to non-official ploys of some kind or because they were of a personal nature. At no point did I consider as a criterion for preservation the possibility that someone in the future might want to write a history of the Department, or — what was even less likely — a biography of one of the holders of the Chair. Clearly in my dealing with those papers the historian became briefly a practising archivist, engaged in the task of selection or weeding. And, as I have often pointed out, we are all archivists. The first thing I say to students when I start telling them about records is that we all have our own archives — accounts, receipts, bankbooks, cheque-stubs, diaries, correspondence and so forth. We are all archivists to a greater or less degree. And I have noted that most archives of any organisation, even of the state, can be regarded as falling into the three simple categories — accounts, correspondence and minute books — which comprise the archives of a cricket club. But in the line I took with that material in the Department I was not a good archivist, for I was considering only my own interests, the ongoing administration of the Department, and current affairs, while ignoring the needs of possible — however improbable — future historians.

But I am not going to enlarge on the topic of the historian as archivist. I am simply going to use one or two items in my archives which serve as texts on which to enlarge. There was a correspondence with a postgraduate student, who in one letter delivered himself of an extraordinary challenge to the significance of what he was pleased to call 'pieces of parchment'. 'Like most Scottish historians', he pontificated, 'you attribute exaggerated powers to pieces of parchment. Do you seriously think', he asked, 'that the issue of feu charters brought about that important change' in the system of land tenure? He scoffed at my conclusion that 'the absence of a piece of parchment' stopped certain individuals from being vassals of others or from paying feu duties. A piece of parchment indeed. A scrap of paper. I need hardly say that the man I am quoting had not taken a degree in Scottish Historical Studies.

Clearly this young man, in his arrogance, was getting what he fondly imagined to be his historical evidence from sources other than pieces of parchment, sources other than archives. Where he thought he was getting it I was never quite clear. In one of my letters I drew a parallel between him and Mr Prebble, who once declared that it did not matter what was found in the Sutherland archives, for it would not alter his view of the 'Clearances'. And I also recalled that story about the group of scholars from various countries who agreed each to study the elephant in his own particular way. The Englishman went off to Africa and on his return wrote a book called 'Elephants I have shot'. The German spent several years in libraries and emerged with three volumes called 'An Introduction to the Study of the Elephant'. The Frenchman wrote a delicate little work 'L'Elephant et ses amours'. The Russian retired to his estate in the forest and evolved the concept of the elephant from his inner consciousness. And the Pole wrote on 'The Elephant and the Polish Question'. I told my correspondent that he most closely resembled the Russian, for he seemed to be evolving history from his inner consciousness, instead of relying on external evidence.

One may be appalled that a man can get a degree and even proceed to research without appreciating the significance of the pieces of parchment on which the structure of law and society was based. But it is not so rare as one might think. I turn again to my archives and quote another letter, this time from one of my graduates who had become a teacher. He wrote: 'I thought this quotation might interest you. It is from a Report on Sixth Year Studies by a group of principal teachers in [I omit the name of the region]: "Many of us who are teaching Sixth Year Studies followed Honours Degree Courses which did not necessitate the submission of a dissertation and in which interpretation of sources played a very minimal role". They then go on to ask the Examination Board to tell them what skills are required in handling documents'. That is what my former student reported about his fellow-teachers. Clearly one can see how it is quite possible for a young man to reach even postgraduate studies without appreciating the significance of pieces of parchment. My former student, after thus telling me about his colleagues and deploring their ignorance, went on to say, 'I blush with shame at my "professional" colleagues, shudder at the thought of what must be passing as history in some institutions and thank the Lord that I chose to do Scottish Historical Studies.'

The rivalry in historical work and in the materials for historical writing used to be to some extent between record sources and narrative sources, between archives and chronicles. I am not sure if the conflict now is not rather between the documentary approach and the sociological approach. The young man to whom I referred earlier seemed to think that he could answer all questions by quoting sociologists and politicians, and he actually and incredibly cited Lenin for an assessment of the economic situation in a peripheral area of Scotland in the nineteenth century. I heard a member of the Record Office staff say that the trouble about the sociologists was that they had made up their minds in advance what they were going to find. This sociological approach is every bit as bad as the theological approach. I recall one earnest Free Churchman — and this is fact too — who thought that the most important factor to keep in mind at every turn in our history was the machinations of the Pope of Rome. Indeed I suppose the Marxist has what might be called his theology, if you can have theology without a God.

If it is true that a sociological approach is at variance with the archival approach, it is tragic, because as I see it social history and archival history, or rather history based on the use of archives, should not be opposed to each other but should go hand in hand. The irony is that social historians stand to gain at least as much from archives as anyone else does, and indeed more than people in some other branches of history gain. I think I would say that, looking at the mass of our national archives as a whole, and considering one category against another, bulk for bulk so to speak, the preponderant value of the archives is for social history in a broad sense.

Clearly there are some things one does not expect to find very much in archives as I understand archives. One does not look much in archives for the startling events which hit the headlines. Indeed, I have often remarked how some of the startling events do not leave much impression in the archives. Take Flodden as an example. A notary's protocol book which covers the period has an entry dated 22 August, seventeen days before the battle, stating that two parties to a wadset were in such a hurry to join the army that they could not wait for the preparation of a charter and letter of reversion, but had to be content with a kind of declaration of intent before the notary. Then there is a gap in the series of entries for over a month, until 26 September, when the notary is carrying on business — routine business — as if nothing had happened. The Register of the Great Seal does have an entry which refers to someone who had been killed alongside the king in the battle, but the business of the chancery went on as usual. The Register of the Privy Seal has an entry dated at Norham on 31 August, nine days before the battle, but its content — and it seems almost ludicrous in the circumstances — is the granting of a remission to someone who had chopped off three of his neighbour's fingers with a peatspade. Thus the day-to-day life of the nation went on. One might think that there would be some references to Flodden in the Selkirk Burgh Court records. Well, there is indeed an act, not long after the battle, relating to watching and warding, but such an act could have been passed at any time and does not necessarily reflect any special anxiety arising from the catastrophe of 9 September 1513.

Of course the battle is reflected in the Acts of the Lords of Council, and you will find particulars of military expenditure in the Treasurer's Accounts. But you will look in vain in such sources for an account of what happened in the battle. Some information can be derived from correspondence in English archives. But in the main for that kind of information one goes to the narrative sources, which come into their own in this respect.

The point is, I think, that in the main the very significance of the archival material is precisely that, while it tells us little about the startling events, it tells us instead how the life of the nation and the institutions of the nation went on and continued to operate with little or no dislocation by the crises conspicuous in political history. Very often we can detect the results of political crises, but if we did not know from other sources that the crises had occurred we would hardly be able to deduce their occurrence from the record volumes. I have drawn attention to this more than once in my Introductions to successive volumes of the *Register of the Privy Seal.*

Perhaps one should say, in a single phrase, that the archives deal mainly with the normal, not with the exceptional. I have sometimes remarked on what I call the snare of the isolated paper. A casual enquirer, dabbling dilettante fashion in private papers, may find a stray document which excites him. He is inclined to make much of it and may even think it a suitable subject for a Document and Note in the *Scottish Historical Review.* But the archival historian may very well know that this supposed discovery is really insignificant in relation to what can be discovered by systematic work through some archives. (Such systematic work may nevertheless occasionally yield some unexpected treasure for which one was not looking, and I have appended to this article an example of such a treasure, a Note on 'John Knox on Queen Mary's Payroll?')

A book called *Scotland under Charles I* was written nearly forty years ago by David Mathew. The author, concerned though he largely was with social history, showed no sign of being aware that Scottish archives — at any rate unpublished archives — existed at all. One certainly looks in vain in his footnotes for references to them. When I reviewed that book I drew attention to Dr Mathew's statement that 'inevitably it is much more difficult to reconstruct the material background of the laird of middle rank' and I went on to say: 'far from being difficult, it is simplicity itself for anyone who will apply himself to the Records of Testaments in the Register House, containing as they do inventories of the "goods and gear" of men and women at every social level. It would be too much', I admitted, 'to expect anyone to read all the thousands of inventories for a given reign; but it is not too heavy a task to examine enough samples of each class of society to provide an illuminating analysis.' Yet that book by David Mathew, coolly ignoring the archives as it does, was warmly applauded by a leading English historian — later elevated to the peerage — who contrasted what he evidently considered David Mathew's brilliant work with the activities or inactivity of what he was pleased to call 'the torpid seminaries of the north'.

I have often said that it would be no bad thing if every historian had to do a spell as an archivist. But the next best thing is for an historian, as part of his training, to transcribe and edit a record volume or at least to engage in some piece of research which involves working systematically through a record or a series of records. I am aware that not everyone would agree with this. One of my own editing efforts was characterised by another historian — and this time it was one for whose opinions I had a great respect — as 'What a waste of time'. He felt that so much of the matter in that record was purely routine, purely normal, that it was a waste of time for an historian to deal with it all. But of course his remark showed a complete failure to appreciate the very point on which I lay stress — the importance of learning about the routine, the normal, the unexciting.

I would add that another indispensable piece of training is to work on local history. I find that when I am asked 'Was such-and-such the case in Scotland in the past?', my answer is apt to be, 'I can't generalise and speak for Scotland as a whole throughout the centuries, but I can say with confidence that in such-and-such a district, at such-and-such a period, such-and-such was the case'. That is one way of keeping one's feet on the ground.

One aspect of the normal is of course institutional history. And I need hardly say that the history of institutions and the history and characteristics of the archives which those institutions created or for which they were created — those two are so closely linked as to be almost inseparable and to form practically a single study.

But it is a great mistake — and this should have become apparent from what I have said earlier — to think that archives are only, or mainly, important for institutional history. In another paper in this collection, on 'Genealogy and the Historian' I enlarge on the importance of relating politics to society. I would just add a further reflection. The narratives give us the outline of political events: indeed it is only in the narratives that we find such an outline. But if we are going to acquire full understanding of the political events and what lay behind them we have to know, Scottish society being what it was, a good deal not only about the personalities of the individuals concerned but about their family relationships, their landholdings, the offices they held, the wealth they acquired, and so forth, and those facts can be elicited only from official records. No historian should dream of studying the manoeuvrings of Scottish factions in the fifteenth and sixteenth centuries — yes, and in the seventeenth and eighteenth — without constantly taking into account the genealogical and tenurial data which the archives supply. From examples I give in what I wrote about genealogy it is very apparent that the historian can be corrected by archival evidence and saved by it from what might have been hasty conclusions, and his feet thus kept firmly on the ground.

At this stage some readers may say, 'That's all very well, but do the archives contain the material to yield the necessary information about property, social status and kinship?' This question is apt to be asked because there is a lamentable ignorance about the riches of our archival heritage. This ignorance is partly the result of the publicity which from time to time has been given to the depredations of Edward I and Oliver Cromwell — which is apt to be brought forward as a ready-made excuse for failure to attempt research — and others embroider what they consider to be a sad tale by bringing charges against the reformers of destroying the records of the medieval church and by adding allusions to the effects of civil wars and disturbances. People have been far too apt to go around wringing their hands about the gaps and contrasting the poverty of the Register House with the unquestioned riches of the Public Record Office. It is much easier to moan about the supposed shortcomings of the records than to get down to doing some honest work upon them. Possibly we suffer also from the propaganda which used to be put out about the supposed neglect — and for a time there was indeed neglect — of the Scottish records. In the early 'thirties and even in the late 'twenties there were frequent press statements about the quantities of records which were mouldering away untended in the basement or vaults of the Old Register House — and complaints also, more reasonably in those days, about the shortage of staff to care for the records. No responsible statements along those lines could have been made in recent years, but the myth, as it now is, still crops up from time to time and the idea seems ineradicable that there are in the Register House vast quantities of unsorted, unexamined, neglected material. People who make those complaints probably have no idea what archives are and would not recognise them if they saw them.

Even compared with England, and still more compared with some continental lands which have suffered more than England in successive wars, Scotland has no need to feel any shame. On the contrary, as I mention in the chapter on 'Scotland: A Backward Nation?' there is a good deal of which we can be proud. Indeed, when I reflect on the hazards and the chances of catastrophe which there were, on the effects of fire, vermin, damp and moths, deliberate and accidental damage by human hands and the phases of genuine neglect, I marvel that so much has survived.

I used the term 'adequacy'. The adequacy of the records. While it is perfectly true that one can assess archives simply by their bulk, the historian, perhaps as opposed to the archivist, is not doing just that. He is not thinking of how many yards or miles of shelving the records occupy or of their cubic capacity. He is thinking rather of their relevance, of the uses to which they can be put.

How adequate, then, are the records? For many purposes very adequate indeed. For example, for the tracing of lands and their owners over the centuries. Certainly — and this is something one may well regret — Scotland has no equivalent of the Domesday Survey at the beginning of recorded history, which in England gives a starting point in the late eleventh century. But we have some information which carries us back nearly as far. We have burgh registers of sasines and notaries' protocol books going back to the late fifteenth century. We have the Register of the Great Seal and the Exchequer Rolls, going back, admittedly with imperfections, to the reign of Robert I. We have a great deal about land tenure and land-holding in the cartularies of the religious houses and other ecclesiastical institutions. We have charters in private hands, and the splendid volumes of the *Regesta Regum Scotorum* go far towards reconstituting the charter rolls of the Scottish kings from the twelfth century.

All this material, if carefully explored, can carry us back many hundreds of years. I could not say how often it is possible to take the story back to the twelfth century, but I recall that at least twice in my earlier years I was commissioned to trace the history of a minor estate, not for any legal purposes but just for the interest of the owner, and in one case I got back to about 1220 if I remember rightly, and in another to a point rather later in the thirteenth century. Had the *Regesta* then been available I might well have done better. That seems to me not unsatisfactory, and we need not throw up our hands helplessly just because we have no Domesday Book. We can be proud of what we have.

So much for land-holding. The ample material available for genealogy and family history is perhaps better known, and in another paper in this volume I have at least implied the existence of some of the archival riches available in that field. There I was, of course, referring mainly to prominent people. But industrious searchers can usually produce remarkably good pedigrees, going back many generations, even for families of quite modest or even humble social standing. Hard work is needed, and there is an element of luck, but there is a lot of material there if people get down to it and use it. Industry is the key word, and I do not suggest that there are easy answers.

That reference to families of modest or humble status brings me to another approach to archives, different from social history in the usual sense and not identical even with social history in relation to political history. It has sometimes been said that history is the lives of great men. I doubt if any serious historian would now accept that for a moment, and it has been evident from what I have said elsewhere that I do not accept it. But history does inevitably consist of the lives of men — and women — whether great or not great. Its substance is facts about the lives of individuals. This truth is far too often obscured by the way we speak of 'a party' or of 'a church', of 'a government' or of 'the state', or even of 'an opinion' or 'an idea'. I recall Professor Duncan once criticising a statement that 'new ideas were in the air' because, as he rightly said, ideas are not in the air. They exist in the minds of individuals, and their significance is the way they affect the actions of individuals. History is the lives not of a few great men but of a multitude of men who were far from great.

When I say that, I do not mean that we should devote all our lives to biographing unimportant individuals, or even to compiling biographical dictionaries or ecclesiastical *fasti* — incomparably valuable though such books are. And every one knows how such works of reference provide wonderful foundations for studies of various kinds. Some years ago I gave an address to the Royal Society of Edinburgh on the origins and early history of the learned professions in Scotland: such a paper could never have been prepared had I not been able to make use of Professor Donald Watt's *Biographical Dictionary of Scottish Graduates*. That was a very striking illustration of how hundreds of individual biographical notices can be used to build up a picture. I indicate in my chapter on Genealogy how I made similar use of other biographical works of reference in studying some specific professions. I repeat that I do not mean that we should all compile biographical dictionaries, but we should use facts about individuals — *facts* about *individuals* — and avoid facile generalisations.

To illustrate this, may I turn to what I have often called my favourite Register, the Register of the Privy Seal? And I am turning not to a volume I edited but to Volume IV, which covers the period 1548 to 1556, to show how facts about individuals add up to a study of the development of opinion — the spread of ideas if you like. It was a critical period. 1548 was the year of the Treaty of Haddington, the year when the Scots turned to France for help to expel the English from their zone of occupation in southern Scotland — the English Pale, as it has been called on the analogy of the English Pale in Ireland — the year when Queen Mary went to France as destined bride of the Dauphin, the year when Scotland seemed more closely tied to France than ever before. By the year 1556, when the volume closes, it was already evident that the domination of Scotland by France was producing a kind of nationalist reaction or patriotic resentment against France, and John Knox had conducted his first preaching tour in Scotland.

There are various types of entries in the Register which have a bearing on how individuals were acting in this situation. There are entries arising from prosecutions of those who had broken the law, there are pardons — remissions and respites — granted to those who had broken the law, and there are miscellaneous entries which reveal the actions — or sometimes the equally significant inaction — of individuals.

I used the phrase 'breaking the law'. What laws were being broken? One can, I think, grade the offences according to their degree of gravity. There was, in the first place, failure to turn up for the army when summoned. This was very common — there are over 1,300 names of absentees in the period — but it might be a mistake to attach too much importance to the offence or to see it as evidence of what one might call conscientious objection — though not of course in the sense of pacifism but in the sense of disapproval of the policy which had occasioned the muster. I think a lot of men concerned may simply have become sick and tired of the incessant musters — there were four or five in the two years 1548-9 — and perhaps feel that they had done their share and would not yet again dislocate their routine, for instance of sowing and harvesting. It might be reasonable to argue that the absentees were not over patriotic, but it would be going too far to argue that they were actually unpatriotic, still less that they were actively pro-English.

Secondly there were the collaborators with the English occupying forces. There were literally hundreds of them too — about 1,000 names are known — chiefly of course in the areas where the English had garrisons, from Broughty Ferry down to Eyemouth and Dunglass. Some of them merely gave aid and comfort, to quote the language of the English Treason Act, to the enemies of the realm, but others went further. They entered into formal assurance, as it was called, with the English, in effect transferring their allegiance and adopting the English badge of the 'red cross' — St George's Cross. They became known as 'sworn Englishmen', as the phrase went. Clearly there were different elements here. An occupying army could exert considerable pressure on the inhabitants of the surrounding countryside; some collaborators acted merely from motives of financial gain or in order to alleviate or avoid distress. Some took the opportunity to join with the English against families with whom they themselves were at feud; some admitted that they thought they lived in 'more wealth and quietness' under English rule. That their motives were often transient is shown by the fact that most of them reverted to their Scottish allegiance when the English withdrew. Yet, as I say, there were over 1,000 of them, and it was remarked that most of the gentlemen of Lothian, the Merse and Teviotdale had 'assured' in the technical sense, and it is hard to believe that so many would have done so if patriotism as commonly understood had been a consuming passion with them.

Thirdly, there were some who showed more positive signs of their attachment to England, by departing to that country when the English armies withdrew.

All this evidence of sympathy with England is inseparable from a degree of sympathy with the Reformation, because the England of Edward VI was moving stage by stage towards real protestantism. Sometimes a formal undertaking of 'assurance' included a renunciation of 'the usurped power of the Bishop of Rome' or a commitment to be 'setters forth of God's word'. But, in addition to the inferences one may draw from political attitudes, there is evidence now and again of actual religious disaffection. There were escheats following on convictions for heresy, there was an escheat of a man who smashed a statue of Mary Magdalene. It was significant of the apprehension which churchmen were feeling that protections were issued to the Black Friars and the Charterhouse, the very institutions which were to feel the first blast of the outbreak of 1559.

An isolated incident may not mean very much, but it is different when we have two or three incidents concerning the same individual. For example, a man who had been associated with the murder of Cardinal Beaton was also guilty of fraternising with the English garrison at Broughty. Some individuals who were guilty of staying away from musters emerge also as active collaborators with the English. James Skea, who had fled from Scotland in 1547 'for fear of burning for the Word of God', became a zealous collaborator. John Rough, later martyred in England, was in the English service as a preacher at Dumfries in 1548. Cockburn of Ormiston, who had harboured the protestants Wishart and Knox, was an active collaborator. David and George Forrest, two East Lothian men who had helped the English at Haddington in 1548, attended Knox's preachings in 1555.

At this point I have drawn a little information from sources other than the Privy Seal, and have relied for one or two of those illustrations on the findings of Dr Marcus Merriman, who has worked exhaustively in this field. But my point is that bit by bit incidents concerning individuals can be used to build up general pictures. How clear it becomes that ideas do not exist in the air but in men's minds and how the development of opinion can be demonstrated by the actions of individuals.

I said earlier that the Privy Seal is my favourite register, but I sometimes wonder if I might have been even more profitably employed elsewhere. Over many years I have from time to time had occasion to dip into the Acts and Decreets, the proceedings of the Court of Session, but I have never worked systematically on that formidable series. However, when I was preparing this paper I decided to refresh my memory of it, just by taking at random a volume for the years 1569-70. It ranges widely, over every conceivable subject on which a civil action might be raised — merchants and ships and cargoes, bishops and ministers, vicars and teinds, ministers and glebes, landlords and tenants, marriage contracts, commercial contracts, dismissal of a schoolmaster, harbour dues, inheritance and so on and so on. The whole life of Scotland is there. The thought that came to my mind when I closed that volume was 'I haven't even begun to know about Scottish history'.

One last reflection. The relationship between history and archives is a two-way process. Any stimulus given to history directs attention to archives, but it is also true that publicity about the archives directs attention to history. Another chapter in this book deals with the topic of 'Presenting Scotland's Historic Heritage', including archives. All I would say here is that the opening of local record offices has given stimulus to historical interest and that the publicity given to records generally, both central and local, has been one factor in leading to a vastly increased use of archival material and the appearance in the last generation of a flood, a torrent, of scholarly works on Scottish history.

*NOTE*

## JOHN KNOX ON QUEEN MARY'S PAYROLL?

In the early summer of 1992 a correspondent raised with me the question of Queen Mary's whereabouts in the autumn of 1564, when, after leaving Perth (where she had spent some days at the end of July) she evidently went to hunt in Glentilt, in Atholl (3-4 August), and then, apart from appearances at Inverness on 11 August, at Gartly, near Huntly, on 24 August, and perhaps in Aberdeen on 30 August, she vanishes from the scene until on 5 September she was at Dunnottar on her way to Dundee, which she reached on 8 September. That, at any rate, was the evidence used by Hay Fleming in the Itinerary printed in his *Mary, Queen of Scots*. However, the late Dr William Angus, in a note on 'The Royal Household Books and Papers',[1] observed that Hay Fleming's Itinerary would have been much more complete had he used the detailed information embodied in those records, which are a peculiarly valuable source for royal movements. Fleming did state in a note that George Chalmers, in his *Life of Mary* (1818), used those Books. I thought it worth while to consult not only Chalmers (who believed that in August 1564 Mary got as far north as the Black Isle) but also the extant Household Books and Papers themselves. There turned out to be a gap in the series of the Books for the period in question, but among the material which I did examine was an item covering the twelve months from March 1564/5 and I found that, while it had next to nothing to say about the Queen's movements, it had other points of interest.

The item (E 30/11) can hardly be dignified by the name of 'volume', for it is an unbound gathering of twenty-eight folios without clear indication of its general nature and origin. It contains the 'charge' or income of diverse revenues from various royal properties and a corresponding 'discharge'. Many of the wide-ranging outgoings are essentially household expenditure, for instance on wine, and there are payments to the Queen's guard and to many very assorted individuals who were at least loosely connected with the household, including 'David Rischo, Italiane' (who got £20 a quarter), heralds, valets, gardeners, a master porter, a falconer, John Spens of Condy (Lord Advocate) and Robert Forman (Lyon). The surprise comes on fo. 19:

> 'And upon the first day of August 1564 deliverit to Johnne Knox, minister, at my lord comptrollaris command, in part of payment of his stipend ... £100.
>
> '... [10 October 1564] to Margaret Fowlis, Johnne Knox servand ... £20.
>
> '... [17 October 1564] to Johnne Reid, servand to Johnne Knox ... £40.
>
> '... [19 January 1564/5] deliverit to Robert Watsone, burges of Edinburgh, for John Knox ... £100.

[1] *Scottish Historical Review*, xxxi, pp. 192-3.

'And to Johnne Willok 18 September 1564 ... in parte of payment of his stipend ... £40.'

This is all less startling than might seem, for the *Accounts of the Collectors of Thirds of Benefices* again and again show two relevant facts, one that the income from the thirds was used for various expenses connected with the household, including Riccio and the guard, and the other that John Knox's needs or claims had some priority. They also show that from 1564 the proportion of the thirds expended on ministers' stipends was diminishing and that diversion of them to the crown was increasing. John Willock, the other clerical beneficiary, had been described in 1560 as 'primate' of the reformed religion in Scotland and he was superintendent of the West. But he was also rector of Loughborough and if the modest £40 given him from the royal income was meant as an inducement to keep him in Scotland, it failed in its purpose, for Willock, after one spell in England in 1566, finally shook the dust of Scotland off his feet in 1569.

*The Accounts of the Collectors of Thirds* are so defective that it is quite impossible to detect when Knox's stipend was not fully paid from normal sources and when other sources had to be drawn on to supplement them. Figures for 1566 indicate that his total stipend (money and victual) was worth £566, 6s. 8d., and over the years he received payments from thirds raised in a variety of areas — small sums from Fife in 1563 and 1564, £100 from Orkney in 1567, most of his stipend (amounting to £477, 6s. 8d. yearly) from Fife in the years 1568-72 and £100 (being arrears for 1567) from Stirling in 1569. In view of this background, the revelations of E 30/11 are not wholly surprising, though the payments to Knox's servants do suggest a measure of privilege for the minister of the capital.

6

## Genealogy and the Historian

*An address given to the Shetland Family History Society on 7 October 1992*

Thirty years ago I might not have thought of genealogical work as being of great significance to the Scottish historian except in so far as it produced the genealogies of the leading families, the relationships among whom have always been of importance in political history.

I have not given up using genealogical information in that way, and indeed several of my works contain examples. One illustration — a very obvious one — figures in a chapter of my little book on *Mary, Queen of Scots* and receives more extensive treatment in *All the Queen's Men*, a book which frequently turns to genealogical facts. In considering the composition of the party which maintained the cause of Queen Mary after she had abdicated in 1567, I realised the significance of the Hamilton family and their kinsmen, stemming from the fact that the Hamiltons were heirs to Mary but risked losing their prospect of a throne if Mary were superseded by her son James, because it was debated at the time whether the succession to James would pass to the Hamiltons on his mother's side or to the Lennox family, to which his father, Darnley, belonged. The leading men in the Queen's Party were mostly related to the Hamiltons, though less by blood than by marriage. Normally links by marriage did not play an important part in shaping parties or groups, and the period shows many examples of brothers-in-law, fathers-in-law and sons-in-law on opposite sides. But in this instance marriage connections with the Hamiltons involved reversionary rights to the royal succession, and it is hard to be sure how far dreams of a crown — or dreams of a close relationship with the wearer of a crown — might go.

A relevant genealogical table shows that the Duke of Châtelherault, 2nd Earl of Arran, was head of the house of Hamilton, but in 1567 not one of his sons was yet married and this improved the prospects of his daughters. Now, Lord Fleming, the Earl of Eglinton and the Earl of Huntly, all prominent in the Queen's Party, were connected with Châtelherault through the marriages of his daughters. Going a generation farther back, Châtelherault's sister had married the 4th Earl of Argyll, and this brought the Argylls into the Hamilton connection and into the Queen's Party.

## TABLE 1

## THE HAMILTONS AND THEIR ALLIES

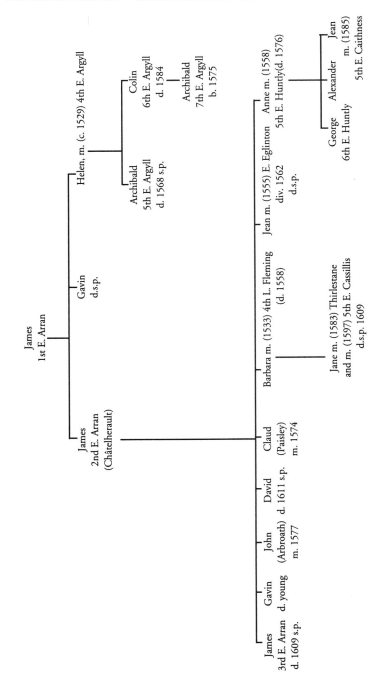

I am not suggesting that these simple genealogical facts are the whole story, but they must be taken into account, and this is only one episode among many where the historian would ignore at his peril the work of the genealogists as it is to be found in the pages of *The Scots Peerage*. Such hard facts of genealogical data may often, I would suggest, be a useful restraint on theorising about principles and ideologies when one is examining motives. In this case it would be reckless to assume that Hamilton, Fleming, Eglinton, Huntly and Argyll were in the Queen's Party simply because they shared a conviction that a sovereign should not be deposed.

Here is another example. There has been a good deal of discussion about the attitude of the clergy during the war of independence, and the question has been raised how far their attitude differed from that of the nobles, among whom, it is well known, there were deep divisions, with the result that many of them supported the English against Wallace and Bruce. Now, before we jump to rash conclusions about what shaped the attitude of the clergy, before we think that there was such a thing as a clerical attitude, we must in the first place discover how far the bishops and abbots were related to members of the nobility. If they were themselves drawn from noble families, then we should expect them to behave exactly as the nobles behaved, and, like the nobles, to be divided. But before we can do this we need genealogical information.

It is certainly clear later on in the middle ages, as the *Peerage* abundantly shows us, that the nobles and the higher clergy formed a single social group. It would therefore make nonsense to speak in simple terms about anti-clericalism as a force in the outlook of the nobles, for their anti-clericalism could have been directed only against their own brothers, uncles or nephews: it may be suggested, further, that the supposed anti-clericalism of the nobles was not an important factor except when the clergy were drawn from lower social strata — in fact, the force was class-consciousness or snobbery as much as anti-clericalism. But without the genealogist, how could the historian have written in realistic terms about the supposed anti-clericalism?

Here is another, more specific, illustration of how genealogical data help the historian to keep his feet firmly on the ground. It arose when I was preparing a paper on the post-Reformation bishops of Dunblane for the Friends of Dunblane Cathedral. The family which established its ascendancy over the property of the bishopric at the Reformation was the family of the earls of Montrose. Now, when I first came on this fact I was rather intrigued. The earls of Montrose were of course Grahams, and it was a branch of the Grahams which, early in the fifteenth century, had succeeded by marriage to a brief tenure of the earldom of Strathearn. The earldom of Strathearn, I recalled, had an ancient association with the bishopric of Dunblane. The bishopric was probably a creation of the mormaers who preceded the earls of Strathearn; it was further endowed by the earls, it was sometimes known as the bishopric of Strathearn, and the earls of Strathearn had in it some of the rights which in other bishoprics pertained to the crown. How historically apt, therefore, I thought, that the Grahams who entrenched themselves in the bishopric at the Reformation should be following in the footsteps of the earls of Strathearn with whom their family had been connected.

Alas for my fine theories! The real reason may be a more mundane and less reputable one. The fact is that Bishop William Chisholm, first of the name, apparently had as a mistress a Graham lady, daughter of the 1st Earl of Montrose. And this and no other would be sufficient reason why the Grahams of Montrose received such favourable treatment in the bishopric. How completely astray one could have gone without the knowledge furnished by the genealogist.

Speaking of Dunblane and Bishop Chisholm reminds me of another aspect of the importance of genealogy. The diocese of Dunblane furnishes some very good examples of what is usually called nepotism, that is, the practice of a holder of a benefice being succeeded by a blood relation, which not infrequently meant almost hereditary succession in office. I have given a good many examples in my *Scottish Reformation*, and any genealogist who turned his attention to the subject could find a host of additional cases, especially of course if he went beyond the succession in the male line to which the surname so readily draws attention. In Dunblane, just to give one instance, three successive bishops bore the name of Chisholm and among them held the see for just over a century. And in that period the archdeaconry, deanery, chancellory and subdeanery of Dunblane, as well as three canonries, were all held by Chisholms. That was the sixteenth-century version of Jobs for the Boys.

Nepotism or quasi-hereditary succession did not operate only in the church. It operated in secular offices as well. A table prepared by the present Lord Lyon shows how, in the seventeenth and eighteenth centuries, the office of Lyon was held in succession by three generations of the Erskines of Cambo, and in the lifetime of the second of them four of his brothers held among them the offices of Bute pursuivant, Lyon Clerk, Kintyre pursuivant, Unicorn pursuivant and Rothesay herald. This recalls that at one stage during the premiership of the Marquis of Salisbury so many offices were held by his Cecil kinsmen that it was said that the government might well be called the Hotel Cecil.

I started this paper with one of my own exercises, on the Hamiltons, and I go on now to another of my own exercises, the career of Adam Bothwell, Bishop of Orkney, which takes up a fair part of a little book called *Reformed by Bishops*. Adam's relations on his father's and mother's side are interesting enough, and a table shows how many significant people he was related to.

**TABLE 2**

ADAM BOTHWELL'S KIN

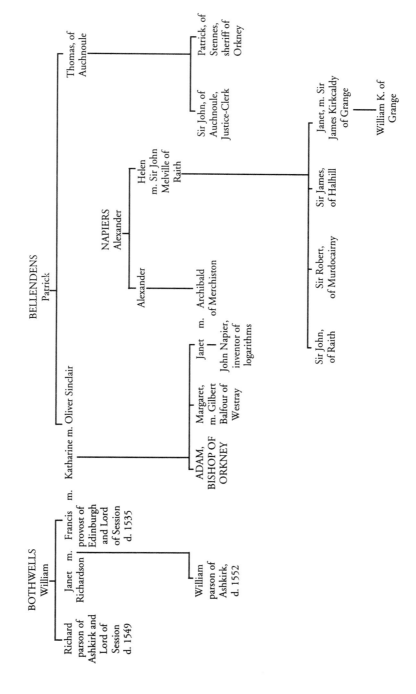

That table I prepared many many years ago. It was only quite recently that it occurred to me to look at Adam's relationships through his wife, and when I did this I was fascinated, for the man appeared in a new light. Bothwell was essentially middle-class in his own family, but through his marriage he was related to a couple of earls, he was the cousin of one of James VI's regents — Moray — and the nephew of another — Mar. This elevates Adam's social status quite considerably and it brought home to me how we can miss realities by focussing on people's formal styles. We call them Lord this and Earl of that, but to Adam Bothwell one regent was cousin Jamie and another was uncle John.

## TABLE 3

### ADAM BOTHWELL'S CONNECTIONS BY MARRIAGE

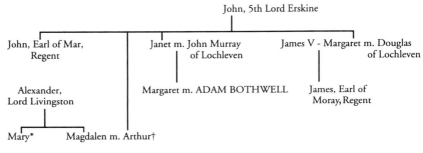

\* One of the Queen's Maries
† 'Queen Mary's favourite equerry'

That little book, *Reformed by Bishops*, deals also with Alexander Gordon, Bishop of Galloway, and Robert Stewart, Bishop of Caithness. Alexander Gordon was a first cousin of Queen Mary, and Robert Stewart was the uncle of her husband Darnley — so there you have the Queen's cousin Alec and her uncle Bob.

## TABLE 4

### ROBERT STEWART AND HIS KINSFOLK

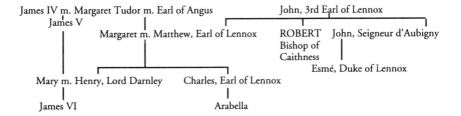

# THE QUEEN'S MARIES AND THEIR KINSFOLK

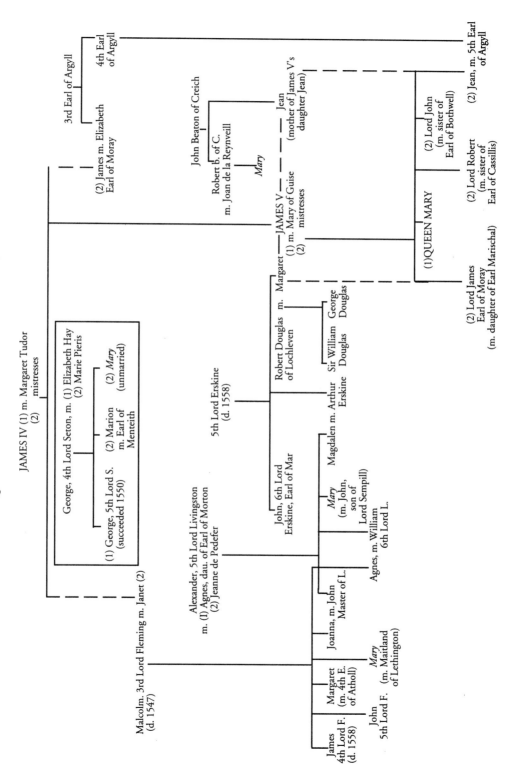

Still within Mary's reign there were the Queen's Maries, whose relationships with each other can be shown on a table. Mary Seton, indeed, was isolated, but the other three — Beaton, Fleming and Livingston — were involved in complex relationships.

Other writers have carried out exercises similar to mine. Maurice Lee, in his *Road to Revolution,* went into the connections of the 2nd Earl of Dunfermline, son of the 1st Earl, who had been the great chancellor of James VI's reign. His mother, the chancellor's third wife, was a Hay of Yester, and after the chancellor's death she married the 1st Earl of Callendar. The 2nd Earl himself married a daughter of the former Lord Treasurer Morton, which made him brother-in-law of Lord Lorne, later 1st Marquis of Argyll. His half-sisters were married to the eldest son of the Earl of Kellie, the Earl of Lauderdale, the Earl of Seaforth and Lord Lindsay of Balcarres. His first cousins were the Earl of Winton, married to the Earl of Errol's daughter, and the Earl of Eglinton, married to the Earl of Linlithgow's daughter; a female cousin married the eldest son of the Earl of Bothwell. His father's first two wives had been a Drummond and a Leslie, which connected him with the Earls of Perth and Rothes. The man was a walking *Scots Peerage.*

I move on to a rather different field and a different period — the eighteenth century and the fascinating topic of the manner in which the political 'interest' of a family or faction or party was created and maintained within the framework of the parliamentary franchise. The basic fact is that the number of men who had the right to vote in Scottish county elections was very small, and every possible consideration, direct and indirect, which might sway a voter was taken carefully into account by those who sought to secure the election of a candidate for a seat in parliament. For the year 1788 there is a list of all the county voters in Scotland — all 2,662 of them — with notes on the considerations which might influence them. Not infrequently one of the considerations was the expectations which their sons might have of preferment or promotion, in the army or navy, the legal profession or the church. That is simple enough, but how often did the considerations extend beyond a voter's sons, beyond his immediate family, to his more remote kindred? It was said that a parish might go to the tenth cousin of the tenth cousin of the possessor of a vote. Only a genealogist can tell us whether this actually happened. Indeed, perhaps only a genealogist can tell us exactly what a tenth cousin of a tenth cousin was or is. But the point is that no one studying eighteenth-century elections can, any more than anyone studying sixteenth-century political history, ignore genealogical data.

Incidentally, if I may diverge into a peculiar byway, I can illustrate what a third cousin of a third cousin is. It happens that Norman Lamont, the former Chancellor of the Exchequer, is a third cousin of a third cousin of mine. But I should hate to think that that creates any relationship between me and him.

## TABLE 6

### THIRD COUSINS OF THIRD COUSINS

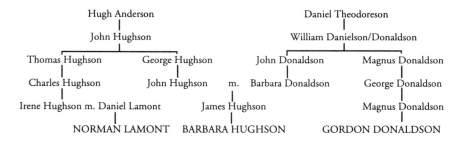

Such matters apart, the genealogist can help the historian generally in the interests of historical accuracy, by dismissing false claims to illustrious or mythical ancestors, whether it be that of the MacGregors to be descended from Gregory the Great or of the MacAlpines to be descended from Kenneth, son of Alpin, or something less extravagant. It is so often said, for example, that the Earl of Elgin is a direct descendant of Robert the Bruce. I have always answered that he is assuredly not so descended in the male line — which is what the claim usually implies — for King Robert's only lawful son, David II, was childless, and even Robert's illegitimate sons do not seem to have left descendants. Lord Elgin may well be descended from a Bruce who belonged to a generation earlier than that of the king, and he has said, 'We are not descended from King Robert, he is descended from us'. It is not impossible, indeed, that Lord Elgin might be descended from King Robert through a female line in a later generation, but that is not what the popular idea implies.

Rather similarly, the Duke of Hamilton, as he explains in the introduction to his book on Mary, Queen of Scots,[1] is descended from that lady, but only through one of Charles II's illegitimate offspring. The numerous issue of that monarch, and of William IV and others, have resulted in the existence of numberless descendants today of Mary, Queen of Scots, Robert the Bruce, William the Conqueror and nearly every monarch who has ever reigned in this island.

Incidentally, I have been amused and puzzled by the fact that claims to illustrious ancestry so often lay stress on what they call 'direct descent'. Can anyone explain to me the difference between direct descent and indirect descent? Indeed, is there such a thing as indirect descent?

That popular myth, as I think I can properly call it, about Lord Elgin presents a warning against accepting common belief or tradition. One of my favourite aversions is oral tradition, a topic on which I elaborate in another

---

[1]Duke of Hamilton, *Maria R: Mary, Queen of Scots the Crucial Years* (Edinburgh, 1991).

paper in this volume.[2] Enquirers about their pedigrees are often exhorted to begin by consulting the older members of the family — a very dangerous thing to do. Such persons may indeed make useful suggestions about places of residence or occupations, and such information may be marginally helpful by pointing the way to possible record sources, but beyond that I would not trust it a yard. There was an illuminating article with the title 'Genealogy: Romance and Reality' in *The Scottish Genealogist*.[3] The writer states charitably that few people tell outright lies about their forebears, but much is often done by selective suppression, 'forgetting', 'not knowing' and so on, especially when some distinction — or something discreditable — is being claimed for or attributed to the ancestry. But the writer went on to examine bit by bit what his father had written in a Memoir and, by recourse to relevant records, was able to prove it wrong in almost every particular. The Memoir, he generalises, was 'long on atmosphere but short on facts'. It enlarges on the Highland background of the family, but all the male ancestors who can be traced lived in Glasgow or Alloa, and the writer's mother, whom he describes as 'A shrewd old Scots lady' had been born in Somerset. The writer's father had a 'handsome figure', but when he entered the army his height was recorded as 5' 3" and his chest as 33". That father is credited with being lacerated with wounds at Tel el Kebir, but his discharge from the army contains no record of 'injuries in or by the service'. This same heroic figure, described as 'brave but foolish' — and 'foolish' was often a euphemism for 'drunkard' — died of cirrhosis of the liver, and his father — grandfather of the author of the Memoir — also died of drink. Perhaps it was not a lie that the writer of the Memoir exhorted his son not to drink.

These varied matters, and others like them, are what I would have taken up had I been asked, thirty years or so ago, what is the significance for historians of the genealogist's work. I doubt if there is much more I would have said on the positive side. But I would, I hope, have made some remarks on what I might perhaps call the negative side. I would have said that I hoped that genealogical work consisted of something wider than mere ancestor-hunting. I would still hope so, for I very much doubt the value to the general historian of the pursuit of ancestry, at least in a single line. Incidentally, perhaps genealogists would tell me how often their clients want the investigation of anything more than the 'direct' male line — a proceeding which reflects a concept on which our own society has centred and on which our own laws of succession have largely been based but which are not the basis of all societies and which some might think hopelessly out of date in the era of Women's Lib. I would say that, from the wider point of view of the general historian, following back only the senior male ancestry seems to me a somewhat barren exercise, unless it is done with some practical objective like establishing a claim to a peerage or to some property —

[2]See above, pp.
[3]Vol. xxxiv, no. 4.

barren, that is, from the academic point of view, though it may be a perfectly legitimate way of making money, and why not?

I would go farther, and say that pedigree-hunting may not merely be a somewhat barren exercise, it may be positively dangerous. To concentrate on one line of descent, or rather ascent, to the exclusion of others, tends to suggest that it has a particular importance in the make-up of the individual or in his connections. The example I gave of Bishop Adam Bothwell shows how wrong it can be to ignore the important connections through his wife. But, that apart, as we all know, the importance of any single line diminishes, in inverse geometrical progression, generation by generation. To take a very obvious example from the royal family, the kings down to Alexander III are often called 'Celtic kings'. But a little reflection shows that out of Alexander III's thirty-two great-great-great-grandparents no more than two, and perhaps only one, possessed what could be called Celtic blood — if there is such a thing as Celtic blood and if the whole notion of Celtic race is not a totally false one for a start.

Well, I suppose that is roughly what I might have said thirty years ago or so. And what I would have said then still remains valid. The historian, in his study of purely political history, still requires genealogical information to explain the kinship of leading figures and of parliamentary electors; the historian still requires to correct errors and explode myths.

But the answer I give *now* to the question, What does the genealogist contribute to history? is a different answer, or at any rate a fuller answer, because I believe that the significance of genealogy to the historian has vastly increased in recent years. Much history is now written from what it is fashionable to call a sociological approach. When I gave my Inaugural Lecture, in 1964, I doubt if the words 'sociological approach' would have meant anything to me — so quickly does jargon, so quickly do clichés, change — but even then I was groping after what is now called the sociological approach as I understand it. I said, 'The study of politics has been far too much isolated from the study of society. We need studies which would reveal the structure of society, the classes in society, the demarcation lines between classes, the location and distribution of wealth: and once a sufficient number of such studies were completed it would be possible to relate politics to society, society to politics, in a way that has as yet been barely attempted. In the same way', I went on, 'ecclesiastical history has been too much divorced from society. What is the use, for example, of knowing about the powers of the kirk session in a Scottish parish unless we know the place in society of the minister and the place in society of the elders? Scottish institutions must be studied in their social context, as the expression of Scottish society'.[4]

That is what I said in 1964. I have done what I could to encourage studies of precisely this kind, and anyone looking at the list of theses completed in my department when I was in the Chair would see some of the results. Dr James

[4] *Scottish History and the Scottish Nation* (Edinburgh, 1964), pp. 10-11.

Kirk analysed the social background of the elders in Scottish parishes in the later sixteenth century. Dr Makey analysed the social background of ministers and elders in the 1630s and 1640s. Dr John Todd studied society in the diocese of Dunblane as part of an examination of the Reformation in that diocese. Dr Graeme Young looked into the social background of the Scottish political parties in the later sixteenth century. And I need hardly say that such work is not confined to the Scottish History Department in Edinburgh University. There was an important book by Allan MacLaren on *Religion and Social Class: the Disruption years in Aberdeen*. It contained an analysis of the social background of the elders who seceded in 1843 and of those who remained within the establishment. I saw another example of the same kind of thing in one of the papers in *The Scottish Tradition*, a volume of essays presented to Dr Ronald Cant, where Mr R. N. Smart wrote 'Some observations on the provinces of the Scottish Universities 1560-1850', in which he examined the graduates to discover from what part of Scotland each of them came, and in order to do this he used the information about their parentage collected by genealogists. More recently Dr Frank Bardgett put the microscope on a single parish in the 1560s and showed the place of its elders in local society.

I found all too little time for serious and sustained work of this kind myself, but I did a little. Many years ago, when I was writing my volume of the *Edinburgh History*, I made a somewhat superficial examination of the relationships of parish ministers in the sixteenth and seventeenth centuries, and for that I was dependent on the genealogical information in the *Fasti*. Later I was engaged on a study of what I suppose might be called the sociology of the legal profession in Scotland in the sixteenth and seventeenth centuries, published in *Lawyers in their Social Setting*, edited by Professor MacCormick. What I was trying to find out was the social background and the family relationships of the legal profession, as well as its place in society when measured in terms of its wealth. In this study of a professional group I encountered at every turn relationships for my knowledge of which I was dependent on the work of the genealogists. Brunton and Haig's *Senators of the College of Justice*, Sir Francis Grant's *Faculty of Advocates* and the *History of the Society of Writers to the Signet* were seldom off my desk.

I am immensely indebted to these works, but even with their help I feel I may just be scratching the surface, since those books seldom disclose any relationship other than that of father and son or perhaps husband and wife. To do the thing properly and put all those lawyers in their social context one would need to know also about their uncles, their fathers-in-law and their brothers-in-law, perhaps even about the tenth cousins of their tenth cousins. There is really no end to it, and what this amounts to is that there is plenty of useful work for the genealogist to do.

Dr Nicholas Phillipson pursued a more detailed analysis of seventeenth-century advocates, with investigation of their parentage and the parentages of their wives, to define the social classes to which they belonged. Anyone can see that heredity has been particularly strong in the legal profession, and legal dynasties have been common from the sixteenth century to the twentieth. The present Lord Clyde is the third successive generation to sit on the bench. But heredity and dynasties can be found in university staffs as well. We all know the three successive generations of Alexander Monros in medicine at Edinburgh. And at St Andrews the Hill family had such ramifications, as a Table shows, that the advice to anyone seeking promotion was to imitate the psalmist and lift his eyes to the Hills.

## TABLE 7

### ST ANDREWS UNIVERSITY
'I to the Hills'

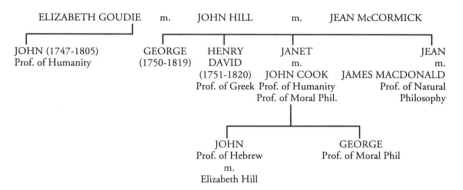

There is, however, a wider aspect to the significance of genealogical work, going far beyond such groups as I have been speaking about. It is a commonplace that blood relationship — 'the kin' — permeated Scottish society. But the whole matter requires far more investigation than it has ever yet received, and there has been far too much sheer assumption about it all. It is usually easy enough to see — thanks to the *Peerage* — how a nobleman was associated with his own immediate kinsmen and with collateral branches of the house stemming from a common ancestor. Beyond that, however, we know far too little. It is often impossible to distinguish such demonstrable relations from the potential relationship thought to be implied by a shared surname. The truth is, and we all know it, that 'the name' was as important a tie as 'the kin', but it is far too often merely assumed that bearers of the same name were in fact related to each other. Our ancestors, it must be said, made no such assumption. Indeed, I have sometimes wondered whether a supposed surname was perhaps little more than a party label, and when a man said he was a Gordon or a Hamilton or a Douglas he was saying no more about his kinship than a man does today when he says he is a Conservative or a Socialist. How far contemporaries were from thinking that the surname demonstrated kinship was illustrated in 1537, when the Angus Douglases were out of favour and it was suggested that their minor dependents should lay aside the name of Douglas and be called Stewart.

Besides 'the kin' and 'the name' there was another important link in Scottish society, and that was 'the bond'. Dr Jenny Wormald, in her book *Lords and Men in Scotland,* has quite a lot to say about the place which both kinship and a common surname had in the composition of the adherents of a bond, but clearly this is another field in which the work of the genealogist is vital to an understanding of the way in which the bond fitted into the structure of society.

However, reverting to the relation between surname and kinship, there are some other points worth making. The Borderers were often emphatic that what was involved was 'the name' and that the name rather than kinship was the primary consideration. When, therefore, one finds a feud in the 1570s between the 'surnames' — that is the term used — the surnames of Brownfield or Burnfield and Haitlie, one wonders if there was an idea of kinship at all or if these were not merely names for rival gangs. There is no doubt that men who really had the same surname often acted in concert. A classic case was that of the muster of Hamiltons to protest against the marriage of Queen Mary to Darnley in 1565: after the rebellion had been suppressed there was a pardon mentioning by name thirty-seven Hamilton lairds and 120 Hamiltons of lower rank. On a lesser scale one finds a round dozen of Cheynes respited for a murder in 1578. But it is harder to be sure what lies behind the group-names which are sometimes used. When, in 1490, six score 'Murrays' were burned to death in the church of Monzievaird by their 'Drummond' foes, I think it would be rash to assume that all concerned bore those two surnames. The same would be true of the rivalry of 'Crichtons' and 'Maxwells' which in 1508 issued in a spectacular riot in Dumfries, in much the same way as 'Douglases' and 'Hamiltons' clashed in the 'Cleanse the Causeway' affray in Edinburgh in 1520.

Clearly, we have there a central problem in Scottish social history, and a problem which is soluble only by the work of the genealogists. I know very well that one cannot expect miracles from genealogists, for, like all other historians, they can go no farther than the evidence goes, and I do not for a moment suppose that they can furnish accounts of the kinship of all the individuals, high and low in rank, who were involved in all those various rivalries. Yet I think much could be done. The matter is, of course, closely tied up with the whole question of the stabilisation of surnames, a subject on which I have more to say elsewhere in this book. Most surnames, I believe, had stabilised by about 1500, taking the place of patronymics, epithets, occupational names and so forth, and in the period before 1500 it is hard to trace the process, owing to the lack of evidence. Yet many surnames were not stabilised until after 1500 even in the Lowlands, and in the West Highlands and Islands they were not stabilised until after 1700. There should be plenty of examples which could illustrate the process, and sometimes illustrate the deliberate adoption of a name which formed some kind of label, for either political or social reasons.

Attention has been drawn to what happened on Speyside in the sixteenth century. In 1537 there was an election of a parish clerk in the parish of Duthil, and the proceedings have preserved the names of seventy-one parishioners, none of them bearing the name Grant (though both the former parish clerk and his successor bore that name). Only thirty-two years later, in 1569, over forty tenants in Strathspey are mentioned in a remission and all of them are named Grant. Sir William Fraser, commenting on this in his *Chiefs of Grant*, remarked, 'this seems to prove either that the Grants, properly so called, had multiplied greatly between 1537 and 1569, or else that the Celtic (i.e., native) tenants had, in some cases, adopted the name of their chief'. Dr Ian D. Grant, who brought this to my notice, suggested that Sir William ignored the difference between a document drawn up locally and one drawn up in Edinburgh: the writer of the latter may well have regarded the name of Grant as a suitable label for tenants who had a Grant as a landlord. However, Fraser's suggestion that possibly 'the Grants had multiplied greatly' seems to have been intended as *reductio ad absurdum*, and there can be little doubt that men could be known either by a patronymic or by a name which was, I suggest, a mere label. Of course even in the sixteenth century, on Speyside, the material is not ample, but I suggest that, as there were areas where genuine surnames did not emerge until much later, attention could profitably be turned to times and places where the situation was still fluid and try to determine how far, if at all, the surname which finally emerged really reflected or represented kinship.

It may be felt that this kind of study would be a mere piece of antiquarianism, but I could not agree. What does stand out so clearly is that 'the kin' and 'the name', together or separately, provided much of the social cohesion of Scotland. Not only so. I have often remarked on the absence from Scottish history of the kind of social unrest which issued in the peasants' revolts and similar outbreaks familiar in other countries. I have long come to the conclusion that one reason for this happy state of affairs was that there was in Scotland some concept of equity, perhaps an unusual measure of social justice, linked with the conspicuously egalitarian outlook of the Scottish people. But one wonders, too, how far other factors, in the kin and the name, contributed to this. If the genealogists could tell us more about the precise nature of those links, the precise origins of social cohesion, they might be illuminating one of the very roots of the national psychology.

# 7

# Peerage Cases and the Archivist

*Presidential Address to the Scottish Record Society, 19 December 1985*

In the nineteenth century there was something of a boom in Scottish peerage cases — over a score between about 1830 and 1890 — but, while they have been scarcer in the twentieth century, there has hardly been a slump. During the last forty years I have been engaged in one way or another in connection with eight or nine claims, not all of which ever reached a hearing before the Committee of Privileges. In one of them I did no more than examine the terms of the original creation, and after that (for no reason that was explained to me) it was decided to abandon the proceedings, and in another all I did was to check the identity of the destination of a Scottish peerage with that of the United Kingdom peerage held by the same family. I was once asked for an opinion on the succession to a certain title which is not dormant but where there was some uncertainty as to who should succeed when the present holder dies. In another instance I was asked to look over a claim to give an opinion as to whether I thought it had been made out and in yet another I was asked to give an opinion on the reliability of certain parchment deeds. Some of those deeds I found on examination not to fulfil the old standards of being 'whole and entire, not erased, not deleted nor in any part suspect, and being entirely free of defect and suspicion' (*St Andrews Formulare*, i, 392), whereupon I reported that in my view — as Sir William Fraser remarked of similar productions — 'these defects would be fatal'. One investigation hinged on research to discover whether a forfeiture of a certain peerage had ever been rescinded.

There is a popular idea, dear to the press and perhaps to novelists, that a peerage claim is usually a matter of proving descent, and indeed that is obviously an essential element, but it is one that seldom necessitates much research, and the presentation of such proof is apt to be merely formal. Naturally it is often far more difficult to prove the extinction of lines intermediate between the claimant's ancestors and those of the last holder of the title. The only claim I handled which involved serious investigation of descent — as well as of extinction — was one where what was at issue was not a peerage but the chiefship of a clan, and where, not unexpectedly, tradition was adduced as evidence and there were also doubts about the legitimacy of one of the claimant's ancestors.

Three cases with which I was involved went before the Committee of Privileges, all of them successfully. First, in 1952, was that of the viscountcy of Dudhope, claimed by Mr Scrymgeour Wedderburn. Here there was indeed a long pedigree to be proved, for the common ancestor of the Petitioner and the last holder of the title, who died in 1668, had been killed at Harlaw in 1411, so five and a half centuries of Scrymgeours had to be sorted out. Fortunately, matters of pedigree had been elucidated and presented in court before, when, in 1910, the Petitioner's grandfather established his right to be the Hereditary Bearer of the Royal Standard, so there was no need to prove once more the authenticity of a lot of the documentary evidence. As usual, more difficult of proof than the actual descent of the Petitioner from the common ancestor of 1411 was the extinction of many intermediate lines which had shared in that descent. This investigation involved a number of relatively obscure persons, like 'French James', 'John called Jak', 'Madame Sousy' and 'Alexander the writer'. It was only in 1921 that the illegitimacy of an individual in one of those branches had been proved. Some records which might have been conclusive about deaths and offspring, such as parochial records and Testaments, happened not to be extant, and it was a complication that, as Lord Normand, the Chairman of the Committee, sagely remarked, 'Dundee has always been full of Scrymgeours'. Besides, extinguishing lines is sometimes apt to mean proving a negative, and, as the Lord Advocate oddly observed, 'Logically it is probably impossible to prove a negative positively', while the Attorney General expressed a justifiable scepticism about mere probabilities and assumptions. Recourse was had to items in over a dozen categories of the national records and to Dundee Burgh archives, as well as some other sources, but even so the judgment stated cautiously that the Petitioner's case had been made out 'with as high a degree of probability as the enquiry admits of'. An interesting point arose as part of the evidence of the extinction of the line of 'French James'. Not only did he dispose of all his property to a stranger, but he also conveyed away four chaplainries founded by his ancestor 'John or Jak'. Mr Hector McKechnie, leading counsel for the claimant, observed, 'I do not think any man would have done that unless he had been the last of his line'. He placed a good deal of weight on this argument and quoted John Hubback's book on the law of evidence in peerages, to the effect that if you dispone your property to strangers that raises a strong presumption that you have no children.

However, all the research into pedigrees would have been pointless without proof of the original destination of the viscountcy, because had that destination been in favour of heirs male of the body the title would have become extinct with the death in 1668 of the 3rd Viscount, grandson of the 1st Viscount. Evidence of the creation of the viscountcy was not to be found in any of the places where it might have been expected: neither in an original 'Signature' under the royal sign manual commanding the preparation of Letters Patent under the Great Seal, nor in Letters Patent themselves, nor in the Register of the Great Seal. Such an absence of evidence, it was observed by Mr McKechnie, was 'so remarkable that one wonders whether it is due to pure accident'. It was certainly no accident that twelve folios of the relevant volume of the Register of the Great Seal, constituting the first gathering or quire, had clearly been deliberately abstracted; nor was it an accident that on the death of the 3rd viscount in 1668 his charters (which presumably included the Letters Patent of the Viscountcy) had been seized by the Duke of Lauderdale, whose brother, Maitland of Haltoun, was the chief beneficiary of the non-appearance of an heir at that point. (Those charters were not available to the Scrymgeours from 1670 until 1904.) The only proof that the destination of the viscountcy was to heirs male whomsoever was an Extract from the Register of the Privy Council narrating the production of the patent before the Council on 1 November 1641, when the destination was recited. That document was the vital production, without which, said McKechnie, 'I would have no case at all', and he had taken the precaution, as soon as he discovered it, of having it recorded for preservation in the Books of Council and Session. At the hearing, care was taken to have Mr C. T. McInnes, then Curator of Historical Records, and myself, vouch for the authenticity of the signature on the Extract as being that of Archibald Primrose, Clerk of the Council. McKechnie pointed out that the Extract which Primrose signed might have been obtained by the 1st Viscount because his precedence was challenged by Viscount Arbuthnot, and added, 'It would be a very odd thing if my client owed his chances here today to the historical accident that Viscount Arbuthnot challenged his precedence and he had to go and get this Extract'.

More than once, in the hearing of the Dudhope claim and also of the same Petitioner's subsequent claim to the earldom of Dundee, reference was made to 'the deficiencies of the Scottish records' (as not in themselves sufficient explanation of the 'remarkable' absence of certain relevant documents, but when McKechnie referred to 'some very difficult neighbours along the southern border', who 'had a habit of invading and destroying or taking away whatever they could lay their hands on' he was rebuked by Normand, who, impatient of the rhetoric, pointed out that this was irrelevant to the situation in the 1660s and the two agreed that 'Cromwell was the last of the vandals'. (It is all too common, especially among those who have not taken the trouble to investigate Scotland's voluminous archives, to attribute all their supposed shortcomings to English depredations.) When presenting such a long and complicated case, McKechnie could have been excused for occasionally 'nodding', and he was guilty of a curious lapse when he stated that a bastard could in no circumstances have heirs and in trying to maintain that position against Normand (though the latter seemed equally imprecise about the elementary point that, while a bastard cannot have heirs collaterally or by ascent he can have heirs of his own body).

The genealogy of the holders of the office of Standard Bearer inevitably touched from time to time on the national history, and McKechnie remarked aptly on their 'very colourful existence' and the 'occupational risks' which caused fatal casualties in battle (in 1306, 1332, 1411, 1513 and 1644). 'Scrymgeour' meant 'skirmisher', but, as McKechnie remarked, 'to describe them as skirmishers is an understatement' for 'they did a great deal more than skirmish'. One episode, when the Scrymgeour of the day, as hereditary Constable of Dundee, declared that if the townsfolk 'took not off their hats to him he would cleave their heads with a whinger', prompted McKechnie's remark that they were 'a very well known family, though not just exactly among the apostles of democracy'. At the other extreme from matters of national history and picturesque incident, the case involved several points of interpretation of the words and phrases of deeds and records, none more curious than the phrase in a decreet of 1671 that Alexander Scrymgeour was 'nynt from Blastilrie all by the male blood'. There was no doubt that 'Blastilrie' appeared in the record, but the suggestion was made and accepted that this was a mistranscription of 'the last erle', on the ground that 'Y' with a superscribed 'e' (giving 'Ye' for 'the') might look like a capital 'B' and the transcriber might then have attempted to rationalise by transposing the 'l' and 'r' of 'erle'.

The Dundee earldom case (1953) was a dependency of the Dudhope viscountcy, for the earldom had been created for the 3rd Viscount. McKechnie felt it necessary to apologise to their Lordships for taking 'two bites to the cherry'. However, this time there was no question at all of genealogy, which had already been amply set forth in Dudhope. But there was, in Dundee as in Dudhope, the question of the destination of the peerage, for which there was again the 'remarkable' lack of evidence to which McKechnie had alluded when he presented the claim to the viscountcy: after alluding now to the absence of Signature, Letters Patent and Register of the Great Seal entry in that case, he went on, 'And when we get to the earldom of Dundee, what do we find? No Signature, no Patent, no Great Seal Register'. None of those absences was surprising in itself: first, few Signatures from that date survive among the national records, and they ought not to have been preserved elsewhere; secondly, the Scrymgeour archives, in which the Patent should have been preserved, had been seized by Maitland of Haltoun in 1670, and the Patent was not among the Lauderdale papers in 1904; thirdly, there was nothing exceptional about the absence of an entry in the Register, for a number of grants were not registered, and there could have been tampering with the record for Dundee as for Dudhope. There is no evidence of this, but Normand remarked in the Dudhope case that 'whether it was the Lauderdales who caused the first quire of vol. 57 of the Great Seal Register to be destroyed is a matter for conjecture. But there is no reason to suppose that they would have shrunk from destroying official records as a means of getting rid of inconvenient evidence'. However, while the absence of any of the three in isolation was not surprising, collectively this dearth of evidence was indeed 'remarkable'.

There was no doubt about the creation of the earldom of Dundee on 8 September 1660, for the parliamentary records state that a relevant Patent of that date was produced in parliament on 25 January 1661, nor was there any doubt that the 1st Earl held the title from its creation until his death in 1668. The question, of course, as with the viscountcy, was the destination. The presumption in practice was heavily in favour of heirs male whomsoever, if only because about eighty per cent of the peerages created in the last two generations had had that destination, and there was also heavy presumption in reason, for first, it was unlikely that the destination of the earldom would be different from that of the viscountcy or that of the Standard Bearer, both of which were to heirs male whomsoever; and, secondly, the 1st Earl had no known sons, whereas he had two brothers, who would be his heirs male.

However, it was necessary to look beyond presumption if conclusive proof were to be found. In Dudhope, the absence of Patent, Signature and Register had been made good by an Extract from the Privy Council Register. In Dundee, the gap was filled, more surprisingly, by two volumes, one in the National Library of Scotland and the other in the British Museum, each a collection of copies of Signatures — and not just of Signatures for crown grants generally but of Signatures for crown grants which passed the great seal *per saltum*, without passing under the signet and the privy seal. McKechnie's notes on the NLS volume (MS 25.3.4) state: 'This is a collection of Signatures, ninety-three in number, covering the period 10 August 1660 to 6 October 1669, in late seventeenth-century handwriting, including that of the Patent of the Earldom of Dundee dated 8 September 1660'. A Register of Signatures is extant among the national records only down to 1642, and this collection, if genuine, supplied the want of a post-Restoration Register and supplemented the few original Signatures which had been preserved in the Register House. The first fifty-six writs comprise twenty-four appointments to offices, seventeen Patents of Dignities, eight Commissions, five gifts and two miscellaneous items. Of the fifty-six, forty-one bear that they are to pass the great seal *per saltum*, but all seem to fall within the classes listed in Dallas's *Styles* as passing *per saltum*. None are grants of lands, and none appear in the Register of Privy Seal. Of those fifty-six Signatures not a single original is to be found in the Register House, but the terms of fifty are to be found in authoritative record sources — the Great Seal Register, the Privy Council Register or the Acts of Parliaments. The accuracy of fifty out of the fifty-six entries can thus be tested, and an examination suggests that they were copied from an official source, for they are accurate except for a few obvious slips in dates. It seems clear that these fifty-six writs are not copies from or represented by any one source now extant, but it is a matter for consideration whether they may not have been copies from a lost volume of the

Register of Signatures or may not even themselves comprise a draft or scroll volume of that Register. Owing to their limited scope, either they must be selections or that Register must at that date have been kept in more than one section, as the Great and Privy Seal Registers were. The facts seem consistent with the view that MS 25.3.4. is a copy (or draft) of a lost volume of the Register of Signatures, which Register was revived by the Act of 1661 cap. 60, and that this volume was one limited to writs intended to pass the Great Seal *per saltum.*

What is true of the National Library volume is true also of the volume in the Harleian MSS in the British Museum, for the character and contents of both are almost identical. They must have been copied from some official source, for Signatures, which were supposed to go to the keepers of the seals as their warrants and to be retained by them, should not survive in private hands. The London and Edinburgh volumes may have been copied from the same source, but neither was copied from the other, for there are certain differences and one or two documents are transposed. If both were copied from individual Signatures, the papers might have been displaced in the bundles, but one volume may have been taken from individual Signatures and the other from a Register.

Both McInnes and I gave evidence as to the character of those two volumes, making it quite clear that there was no possibility that the Dundee entries could have been interpolations. I said that I considered the BM version to have rather more the appearance of an official compilation than the NLS version.

This examination of those two collections was clearly the crucial point in the case. There was a dramatic conclusion to the hearing. I finished my evidence just after the lunch adjournment on 6 May. The year was 1953. After my withdrawal, McKechnie was preparing to proceed, but the Chairman checked him ('in full flight', as McKechnie said afterwards): 'I think the feeling of the Committee is that they need not trouble you any further'. Their lordships had evidently reached a decision over lunch. After a brief summing up by the Lord Advocate, the Chairman announced, 'I think I can say on behalf of my colleagues that the Committee takes a favourable view, in principle, of the case for the Petitioner', but added that judgment would not be announced for some days. McKechnie then asked, 'Does that entitle my client to prepare himself for the Coronation (as he must do) as an Earl', and the Chairman answered, 'I think he might almost safely do that.' The Coronation was due to take place on 2 June, less than four weeks later. The Petitioner was thus entitled to add strawberry leaves to his coronet and, as McKechnie said at a subsequent celebratory dinner, he came out of the hearing 'earl-ier' than he went in.

The case of the earldom of Annandale (1985) perhaps held even more interest for record scholarship than did either Dudhope or Dundee. The earldom had been dormant since 1792, when the heirs male of the body of the 1st Earl became extinct. Four times a claim had been made on behalf of an heir deriving through a female, but on each occasion (the last of them in 1879) the

Committee of Privileges gave an adverse decision. These claims had been founded on the terms of Letters Patent of 13 February 1661 which conferred the earldom of Annandale on James, Earl of Hartfell, 'and his heirs male, whom failing the eldest born of the body of the said eldest born female lawfully begotten'. This destination, beginning with heirs male general (whom it was clearly impracticable to extinguish), in effect excluded the possibility of succession of heirs through females beyond the first generation. These earlier claims had wanted to construe the 'heirs male' of the Letters Patent as meaning heirs male of the body (for otherwise the rest of the destination was unrealistic). The claim made in 1985, however, was founded on the terms of a charter of 23 April 1662 granting the lands of the earldom of Annandale, with the title, to the Earl and 'the heirs male *of his body*, whom failing to his heirs female already begotten or to be begotten of his body, and the heirs male lawfully to be begotten of the body of the eldest heir female, whom all failing the nearest heirs and assignees whomsoever'. On this destination, when the heirs male of the body of the first Earl became extinct the succession was opened to the descendants of his daughters.

Their lordships were not very ready to accept that a fresh destination, in the charter, could have followed on so soon after the former destination, in the Letters Patent, and could have in effect created a new peerage, with the same title but a different destination. It was not difficult to produce examples of two peerages going by the same name and with different destinations — Mar is only the best-known among them. The fact that the new destination followed so soon on the former one was explained by the state of the Earl's family at the time, and it was at this point that genealogical investigation made a contribution. The Earl had been married about 1650, and in 1660 he had two surviving daughters, while three other daughters had died in infancy. His only brother had died without issue in 1657, and some collateral lines had died out without male issue, so that the nearest heirs male general were distant cousins. However, a son was born to the Countess on 17 December 1660. Given the level of infant mortality at the time, it was optimistic to think that this secured the succession in the male line, and the Letters Patent of February 1661 did specify heirs male general. How long the new-born son of the Earl survived we do not know. He was baptized, when a year old, in December 1661, and we know that he was dead before the beginning of 1664, probably a considerable time before. If he did not long survive his baptism in December 1661 that could explain the terms of the charter of April 1662, opening the succession to heirs through females. Evidence was led on the state of Scottish administration in the troubled months between Oliver Cromwell's death in September 1658 and the complete restoration of governmental machinery in 1661, and also of course on the procedure for creating a peerage by Signature followed by Letters Patent or Charter. It was also necessary to explain how the Signature was accompanied by an abridgement, or docquet, designed to give the monarch some indication of the contents of the grant before he authorised it by his sign manual on the Signature.

It seemed to be a little difficult to make it clear that the Signature was in the vernacular, the Charter in Latin, and, to be fair, the terms of the Signature, especially when badly punctuated in a print, were not immediately intelligible. There were some curious exchanges. After Mr John Murray, Q.C., leading counsel for the Petitioner, had done his best to explain it all, Lord Scarman interjected, 'Does this mean that those who advised the King advised him in English, showed the King what they wanted in English and then threw it over to the Latin scribes to put it into a respectable language?' Later Lord Beswick asked, 'Is this the document which is supposed to be in English?' Scarman assured him, 'This is all in English', and the Chairman (Lord Keith of Kinkel) explained, 'You can call it Scots at this time, I think, 1662'. Much later, again, Scarman observed, 'The vernacular in the Signature is not as easy to follow to the modern mind as is the Latin. I was misled when I first looked at the Signature, and I only got the real sense when at your invitation I looked at the Latin'. Their lordships did need a good deal of guidance. Lord Scarman astonished me by asking, 'Can you explain to me the meaning of the word "procuratory"', and even after I had equated it with the English 'proxy' he had to persist, 'A clue to the meaning of it is the word "procurator"?' which did seem pretty elementary. Lord Campbell of Alloway, after an explanation of the relation between Signature and Docquet, explained, 'What does that show? I am not trying to be difficult, but I am getting very lost and am finding it difficult to follow.' Even Scarman, who on the whole showed real acuteness in getting to the root of the matter, said rather sadly, 'I have moved into a very strange world where my imagination has been put at full stretch during the last two days. I am prepared to construe that there are situations within the history of the Scottish peerage which no amount of imagination could have imagined if they had not occurred.'

Scarman, as already said, got to the root of the matter, and that was the question whether the Charter of 1662 did in fact confer a peerage title as well as lands. The document was mainly concerned with extensive lands and other subjects, which it incorporated into a territorial earldom, and then it added, quite simply, 'cum titulo stylo et dignitate comitis' (i.e., de Annandale et Hartfell). We were able to point to other instances — though not very many of them — where a peerage had been created by similar phraseology, and we thought it an important point that the title was mentioned in the docquet, where the grant was reduced to its bare bones, to indicate briefly to the king that an earldom was being conferred. However, the discussion centred largely on the extremely elementary point whether, in simple terms, *cum* with an ablative had the same force as *et* with an accusative. It was somewhat diverting to see some of the leading legal intellects of the country wrestling with this weighty problem. I was convinced that the two expressions had equally dispositive force, as I put it, but Scarman pressed me very hard on this point. 'I would', he said, 'be prepared to go this far, but I am not sure I would be prepared — unless you can persuade me — to go further: in a disposing clause, the preposition "cum" is apt, unless the context indicates otherwise, to include within the disposition the matters which the preposition introduces into the clause?' I had to ask him to repeat this, and he did so, adding, 'Would you suggest that we, construing the words of the King (i.e. of the Signature), would be entitled to leave out the words "unless the context otherwise indicates"?' My reply was, 'I find it hard to think of words in which the context would make that impossible, given the force of "cum".' And somewhat to my surprise, and certainly to my relief, he answered, 'So would I.' We had a further exchange. He repeated, showing that he had grasped the point, 'You would demur over "unless the context indicates otherwise"; you would think that there would not be any cases in which the context would?' I was not prepared to concede anything, and replied, 'Candidly, I cannot envisage one, my Lord.' His reply was, 'That is fair enough, yes. For my purposes that is enough.' That seemed to me decisive and that we had made the point that the grant of a *comitatum* of Annandale, 'cum titulo, stylo et dignitate comitis' did create an earldom of Annandale. Yet that point in the discussion was only half-way through the proceedings, which continued through Wednesday afternoon and Thursday morning, with much discussion of judgments in other peerage cases relating to more general points than the respective merits of constructions with *cum* and *et*.

When the hearing finished, we were far from confident, though we thought that we had won over Scarman and that the Chairman was not unsympathetic. Lord Templeman had all along been the most awkward of the Committee, and at one point admitted to acting as 'devil's advocate'. Thus, when the Committee, after a month, did report favourably, Templeman gave his opinion in these words: 'I defer to the views of my noble and learned friend, Lord Keith of Kinkel'. He avoided the word 'concur' and evidently he had not been personally convinced.

# 8

## *Surnames and Ancestry in Scotland*

This is the only chapter in this book which has appeared in print before. It was published privately as a leaflet, intended mainly for the use of the Scots Ancestry Research Society, which frequently has to disabuse enquirers of their misconceptions about the connections between surnames and kinship. Over the years I have personally sent many copies to people who asked me for information. Polite noises have almost invariably been forthcoming in response, but not all readers seemed to realise that the whole point of the piece is to correct the popular ideas about 'clans' which prevail in the twentieth century. There was, not surprisingly, a certain coolness from some who felt their illusions had been shattered and some who had vested interests in 'clanship'.

I enlarged on some of the thinking which lay behind the pamphlet in a Foreward I contributed to Mrs Kathleen B. Cory's excellent *Tracing your Scottish Ancestry*, where I carried through to their logical conclusions some of my ideas, deliberately exposing the folly which surrounds 'clans' and 'clan tartans'. I gratefully acknowledge the helpful suggestions I received from other scholars who read my material in draft, especially Mr William Matheson with his profound knowledge of West Highland surnames.

Many people who are interested in their ancestry think that surnames provide infallible guides to family relationships and to pedigree. This, however, is true only within certain limits, and the whole subject of surnames and their connection with kinship is surrounded by misconceptions.

Most of the more serious and prevalent errors arise from a failure to appreciate the ways in which surnames arose and the stages by which they became stabilised. There are four main sources of surnames.

Many surnames are place-names and originated with a man who lived in or came from a place, sometimes a big district like Moray (Murray) or Lothian, often a small rural community. A proprietor was particularly likely to take his name from his estate, but tenants and others also took their names from their places of residence. Clearly a number of individuals and ultimately of families could originate in the same place and take their names from it without being related to each other. Besides, the same or similar names were given to different places, and this means that individuals or families who came from different parts of the country and shared neither blood nor territorial affinity could nevertheless have the same surname. Thus anyone called Calder (or its variant Caddell) may derive from an ancestor resident in Calder in West Lothian, Calder (or Cadder) in Lanarkshire, Calder (or Cawdor) in Nairnshire or Calder in Caithness. Similarly, there is no necessary relationship among the many families called Blair, a place-name which occurs in at least a dozen different areas.

There are surnames which derive from a craft or occupation. Smith, which is the most common name in Scotland, is an outstanding example, and Wright, Baxter or Baker, Tailor, Carpenter, Mason, Shepherd, Slater, are among the many others. It would clearly be the height of absurdity to think that one single smith was the ancestor of all the people now bearing the name Smith. The same is true when a name of this type arose in the Highlands, where a designation Coinneach Gobha (Kenneth the smith) gave rise to the surname Gow. Any argument for relationship, based upon surnames of this type, must be treated with extreme reserve.

The third group is the epithet or nickname, originally descriptive of some individual, such as Little, Meikle (that is, Big), Brown, White, Gray, Black. The Gaelic *donn* (brown-haired) was one possible source of the surname Dunn; Campbell is *caimbeul* (crooked-mouthed) and Cameron is *camshron* (crooked-nosed). Grant is presumably the French *grand*, equivalent to the Scots Meikle. Once again it would be far beyond the bounds of possibility that a single 'little Richard' or Richard Little was the progenitor of all the Littles now to be found in a directory. The fact must be stressed that almost any surname could arise quite independently at different times and in different places.

The fourth group and the one which perhaps causes most misunderstanding is the surname of patronymic origin. These are the names usually represented in Lowland Scotland by the suffix '-son'; but with them must be taken the Christian names which have become surnames and are really truncated patronymics — Henry, Mitchell (for Michael) and Arthur, for instance. The development of names of this type was rather more subtle than it was in the first three categories. In a society which had genuine patronymic practice the designation changed generation by generation. Robert's son might be John Robertson, his son Andrew Johnson, his son Peter Anderson, and so on. This system was general in all the northern lands and it extended to women, with forms which would translate as, for example, Elspeth Johnsdaughter. In Denmark, Sweden and Norway the practice came to an end at varying dates between the sixteenth century and the nineteenth, but in Iceland it still continues. In Shetland it persisted in many families until the nineteenth century, so that one finds, among numerous examples, Arthur Anderson (d.

1855), son of Andrew Robertson, James Manson (d. 1875), son of Magnus
Olason, and (though this was becoming rarer) Marion Alexandersdaughter (d.
1857); illogically, women were now using the suffix '-son', as in Isabella
Johnson, daughter of John Williamson.

Throughout most of Lowland Scotland genuine patronymic practice went
out in the fifteenth and sixteenth centuries. What happened was that an
individual decided (or some authority decided for him) that he would adopt his
father's patronymic as his own surname, so that the son of John Robertson
called himself not Andrew Johnson but Andrew Robertson, and from that point
Robertson became the surname of his descendants. It was clearly a matter of
chance in which generation the patronymic was, as it were, 'frozen' to make it
a surname. In the instance just given, if the decision had been taken a generation
later the surname of the family would have been Johnson and not Robertson.
This simple fact, which is far too seldom remembered, makes nonsense of any
attempt to use such surnames of patronymic form as guides to more remote
ancestry and of any belief that there is an affinity among the holders of such a
name. Half-a-dozen Robertsons, shall we say, are probably descended from
half-a-dozen different Roberts who lived in different parts of the country at
different times and have no ground at all for claiming kinship with each other;
not only so, but it is only chance that they are called Robertson and not, shall
we say, Johnson or Anderson.

In the Highlands, where 'son of' was denoted by the prefix 'Mac-' rather
than by the suffix '-son', patronymic names were commoner than they were in
the Lowlands and seem indeed to have been the general form of designation.
The 'Mac-' could be prefixed to craft names as well as Christian names, giving,
for example, 'Mac an t-saoir', son of the joiner, which became Macintyre, and
also the group of names denoting descent from an ecclesiastic: Macnab,
Mactaggart, Macpherson and Maciver, meaning son of the abbot, the priest, the
parson and the vicar. Designations were carried into two or three stages, by the
use of 'Vic-' (mhic, the genitive of *mac*), and could represent in effect potted
pedigrees. Sixteenth-century examples are Angus MacDonald Vic Angus, son
of Donald MacAngus, and Alastair MacAllane Vic Ane Vic Coull, and there is
a splendid example in 1617: Hector MacGorrie Vic Achan Vic Allester Vic Ean
duff, son of Gorrie MacAchan Vic Allester Vic Ean duff. In women's names,
'Nean' (nighean), meaning 'daughter of', could take the place of 'Mac', giving
patronymics like Margaret nean Ean glas Vic Ilespig. Designations of this type,
recorded in official registers, were not surnames, and, while individuals so
recorded may have had surnames (as will be shown below), their surnames are
not used in the record, and identification may consequently be difficult for the
researcher. For instance, but for their territorial designation 'of Lochiel' would
anyone know that the men recorded in the mid-sixteenth century as Ewan
Allanson, John Dow, his son, and Ewan, his grandson, were in fact all
Camerons? The use of genuine patronymics in records continued well into the

eighteenth century: for example, in South Uist in 1721 we find names like John MacEwan Vic Ean Vic Charles and Murdo MacNeill Vic Ean Vic Duill. On the other hand, not only were certain Highland families recorded by surnames from a fairly early date, but the prefix 'Mac-' could mean not only 'son of' but also 'descendant of', and to that extent such a patronymic, persisting generation by generation, could be 'frozen' as a surname. An obvious example is MacDonald. Angus of the Isles, in the later thirteenth century, was the son of Donald, and his successors retained the 'style' MacDonald, perhaps not so much as a surname in the modern sense but as a mark of their descent; but (as will appear later) the vast majority of the numerous MacDonalds of later times had no kinship with the descendants of Angus or necessarily even derive from anyone called Donald at all.

The persistence of the patronymic, sometimes at unofficial level, into modern times is explained by the need to confer ready means of identification in small communities where a particular surname is common. Names indicating either parentage or place of residence are commonly given for this reason, forming the 'to-names' of the fishing communities of the north-east (a term identical with the *tilnavn* of Scandinavia) and similar names elsewhere. Perhaps the most picturesque and cryptic examples occurred in the Borders: 'John Bell called Quhitheid', 'Edward Bell called the Dansair', 'John Bell called Ranyis Johnnie', and — incredibly — 'Andrew Irvin called Tailyeour curst Geordie'.

The process by which the genuine surname took the place of personal designations which changed from generation to generation took a long time to complete, and there are instances throughout the sixteenth century, in almost any part of the country, which show that some people still had more than one designation and it may be hard to say which if any of the designations was even yet a real surname. When we find a man with a name of patronymic form and also a craft name, like 'Robertson or Pottar', it may well be that one is a genuine patronymic and the other no more than the name of his actual occupation; but with 'William Davidson or Litstar' and 'Matthew Paterson or Litstar', both of whom were priests, the 'Litstar' (i.e. dyer) is clearly a surname. And in the case of 'Andrew Wilson or Tailor, the son of Andrew Wilson', the same 'Wilson' is a genuine surname, whatever 'Tailor' may be. Even in the late sixteenth century we find an occupational name being adopted as a surname, for Andrew Strachan, who happened to be a gardener at Falkland, had a son who was styled 'John Strachan or Gardener' and a grandson who was 'George Strachan or Gardener'. We also find a surname originating in a place-name combined with a patronymic, in 'Alexander Murray or Angusson'. In Orkney and Shetland in the late sixteenth century men were still often known simply by their places of residence, e.g. John of Aywick, and, while some of them were later known by patronymics, others, especially in Orkney, adopted the place-name as their surname, e.g. Marwick and Rendall.

One very important qualification to any attempt to use surnames as guides to pedigree arises from the fact that right on to the eighteenth century at least, there was a tendency, perhaps more especially in the Highlands though not only there, for men to adopt the surname of their landlord as their own surname, and one consequence was that when a man moved from one estate to another he might change his name. In the 1750s it was related that 'John MackDonell ... was really and truly a Campbell, having changed his name to that of MacDonell upon his coming to live in the bounds and under the protection of the family of Glengary, it being the usual custom for those of a different name to take the name of the chieftain under whom they live'. The use of the landlord's name as a man's own explains why in the 1580s a servant of the Earl of Huntly was called 'Gordon or Page' — Gordon because his master, Huntly, was a Gordon and Page because he (or his ancestor) was in truth a page.

Occasionally we find a switch from one kind of designation to another: thus in the 1470s the three sons of Thomas Soutar were David, John and Thomas Thomson, and whether their descendants were Soutars or Thomsons we cannot say. There was, besides, a tendency for people to give up the more outlandish names and adopt names which were familiar or distinguished. It seems, to take a curious example, that the Scandinavian Sigurdsson, which became Shuardson in Shetland, was Scotticised as Stewartson and finished as Stewart. How true it is that not all Stewarts are 'sib' (related) to the king. And, besides, some Stewarts presumably descend from the stewards of this or that estate and not from royal Stewards, just as Baillies descend from bailies of various estates. Nor can we be certain that all the holders of that other royal name, Bruce, descend from the same ancestor. True, the name originated in a place-name in Normandy, and it is unlikely that more than one family came to Scotland from there, but, apart from the tenants of Bruces who may have adopted their laird's name, it may be suspected that some originally had the less glamorous name of Brewhouse.

Some other pitfalls may be mentioned. It was far from rare for a man to change his name on inheriting or otherwise acquiring landed property, and indeed charters sometimes laid it down that the proprietor must bear a certain name; and for similar reasons husbands sometimes took their wives' names. In each of those cases the surname ceased to be a guide to more remote ancestry.

One very elementary error is to believe that there is some significance in variant spellings of the same name, for example Clerk and Clark, Burnet and Burnett, Gray and Grey, or, in certain Highland names, the variation between Mac — and Mc — and between the use of a capital or a small letter in the second part of the name, e.g. MacLean and Maclean. The truth is that until a matter of two and a half centuries ago the spelling of proper names, as of other words, was quite arbitrary. Different scribes used different spellings, the same scribe used different spellings within the same document, an individual would spell his own name in different ways on different occasions. So no significance whatever must be attached to different spellings as indicative of ancestry or relationship. It was simply a matter of chance, as spelling did become standardised, that certain families adopted particular spellings and other families, possibly closely related to them, adopted different spellings.

On the other hand, similar spellings may confuse what are in truth totally different names. Livingston is a Lowland name, of West Lothian origin, but Livingstone is a Highland name, and there is no relation between the two. Similarly, 'Johnson' is a patronymic name, 'Johnston' derives from John's 'toun' or settlement, while 'Johnstone' might originate in the name of some landmark: there are three different names. Some Camerons — perhaps most — are Highland Camerons from Lochiel, but others must take their names from the places called Cameron in Lothian and Fife. Dewar and Shaw are other examples of names with distinct Highland and Lowland origins, and Dunn, while it may derive from Gaelic *donn*, may equally well derive from the place Dun in Angus. The distinction between a Highland and Lowland origin has often been effaced when a Gaelic name has been translated into English, so that MacNeacail becomes Nicolson and MacGille-mhoire becomes Morison — which means that they are added to the host of unrelated patronymics spanning the whole country and with no affinity among them.

We might expect that the compilers of official records would always have a consistent preference for a recognised surname over other designations, but this was not entirely so, and their practice may well have been based on no more than the purely utilitarian one of using the designation which would most clearly identify the individual. Thus some of the examples of Highland patronymics given above are from the Register of Sasines and the Register of the Privy Seal. On the other hand, there is some reason to believe that the official recording of names had a certain influence towards stabilising surnames, and in some areas the establishment of the Register of Sasines in 1617 clearly had some effect. Variation of names further declined because ministers, in their registers of baptisms, marriages and burials, preferred names which they did not think outlandish, and in the Highlands many names indicative of remote ancestry were lost because ministers had difficulty in recording Gaelic names unfamiliar to them and substituted names which had well established Anglicised forms. In so far as variation survived into the nineteenth century it was further curbed by the compulsory registration of births, marriages and deaths from 1855, because Registrars began to insist that an individual must use the same surname as his father had used.

The numerous complexities, and the many uncertainties, mean that casual assumptions or guesses about kinship and descent, based solely on surnames, are no substitute for serious research into ancestry.

# 9

## *Some Tell-Tale Christian Names*

*A Presidential address to the Scottish Record Society, 18 December 1986.*

Anyone who works over records and occasionally comes on an unusual Christian name is apt to speculate as to the reasons for its use. One does not need to look far to see Christian names which have an obvious significance as reflecting in one way or another certain attitudes and certain interests which were common at the time those names were first conferred or at the time when they became popular or fashionable. There must be a good many people now bearing the name Winston, which indicates a likely date of birth. Or, in a different field, there are the Shirleys who owe their name to the popularity of a child film-star of the mid-twentieth century.

The names of popular or renowned commanders and politicians in earlier crises, or of actors or actresses in earlier films, or probably plays, no doubt had a similar vogue at one time or another. But it is dangerous to jump hastily to conclusions. One might be apt to attribute the popularity of Gordon as a Christian name to the fame of Gordon of Khartoum a hundred years ago, and analysis might well show that the name became more popular then. But certainly Gordon was not a rare Christian name — especially, as one would expect, in Aberdeenshire — a long time before Gordon of Khartoum came on the scene. I found examples from 1748 onwards.

I have not counted how many Scottish children were christened Gladstone to keep alive the memory of the long Liberal ascendancy in the country. Stanley, which became popular in the same period as Gladstone and Gordon, commemorates a famous explorer rather than a Perthshire village. Admittedly, almost any name was more apt to be chosen if its sound was attractive, and a good many people who were famous or popular may not have been commemorated in that way simply because their names were so far from being euphonious, or were even so ugly, that even the most enthusiastic parents shirked saddling their offspring with them. However, in 1847 a radical Aberdonian who was evidently an enthusiast for the repeal of the Corn Laws had his son christened, incredibly, Cobden Bright Frost Gerrard: Cobden and Bright were leaders of the Anti-Corn Law league, a John Frost was a Chartist, and Gerrard may have commemorated a 'political martyr' of the 1790s.

It was not always the name of a person that was commemorated; it could be a place which figured in the news, perhaps a battle, that captured attention. There is the well-known case of the battle of Alma in the Crimean War in 1854, which led to the use of Alma as a girl's name. One of the first to bear it was surely the wife of the third Marquis of Breadalbane, herself of the Montrose family, born on 7 September 1854: that was actually a fortnight before the battle, but of course she would not be baptized until some time after it. I noticed two Almas in Dundee in 1854 and another in 1857. Of course Alma had an appeal as a Latin adjective meaning kindly or genial or something of that kind, familiar in the phrase *Alma mater*. This may have encouraged the continued use of the name and in any event it would, like any other, be transmitted from generation to generation in a family. 'Alma' was euphonious, and perhaps it is not surprising that I have not found Inkerman, Balaclava or Sebastopol among nineteenth-century Scottish names. However, I learned from Mrs Nan Marshall that during a later war a boy in Carnoustie was named Arras Loos after the battle in which his father had been killed, and he was always called Arras.

I think the first time that names which cropped up in records caught my attention and led me to speculate was when I was editing James Young's Protocol Book (1485-1515). I noticed that Lancelot appeared several times — at least five Lancelots in the volume. My thought immediately was, 'Ah! Malory's *Morte d'Arthur* was being read by the Scots.' But it was not as simple as that, for Malory's work was not printed (by Caxton) until 1485, and people named in consequence of it could not have been of sufficiently mature years to figure in at least the earlier volumes of Young's work. Lancelot Richardson, a chaplain, turns up as early as 1489. Malory's work, however, circulated in MS from 1470 or so, but, that apart, the appearance of Lancelot makes one wonder how far Arthurian stories might have circulated in Scotland irrespective of Malory. I also noticed a Roland in James Young: now, there was a Roland, Lord of Galloway, in the twelfth century, but it may well be that Lancelot and Roland alike, who figured in medieval romances, captured Scottish imagination much as those other English heroes, Robin Hood and Little John, did by the fifteenth century.

That was one example of the way my curiosity was mildly stirred, many years ago. But what finally stimulated me to turn my attention to some serious investigation in this field was my little book on *Sir William Fraser*. The thought did not strike me when I was writing the book, but when it had been published and I was flicking through the pages — the stage at which one all too often gets a bright idea which had not occurred when the book was in the making — my attention was caught by something on page 3. An earlier writer had suggested that the names Anne and Clementina — the names of the last Stewart Queen and of the wife of the first Stewart Pretender — might suggest Jacobite sympathies, and I had dismissed this, on the ground, as I put it, that neither of those names was altogether rare in eighteenth-century Scotland. I have since verified that Clementina was fairly popular as a name and unless it has Sobieski attached to it (which does happen) it is not significant of anything. But on this re-reading of that page of the book on Fraser I noticed in the very next sentence after the one about Anne and Clementina that Fraser's grandfather, after whom Sir William was named, was baptized William on 5 October 1746. I just wondered how many Scottish boys were being christened William at that time to indicate their parents' approval of the work of William, Duke of Cumberland, in delivering them from the threat of rule by popish pretenders. Of course I did not know — I do not know now — if the name William had appeared in the Fraser family before 1746, but even if it had, my thought ran, its use in 1746 might at least suggest that the family had no antipathy towards the Duke. It was when this thought about William Fraser struck me that I finally decided to look into the whole subject of Christian names and their significance.

I did not see how I was going to find out possible significant features except by purely random samples, or drawing on the knowledge of friends who were in the habit of working through the records for other purposes. I had recourse to the staff of the Scots Ancestry Research Society, who were able to tell me that they had occasionally noticed instances of the kind of thing I was looking for and had indeed found Cumberland used as a baptismal name — as I myself found later. Miss Alison Munro drew my attention to the fact that in the Register General's Department there are some indexes of Christian names in the old Parochial Registers and she advised me to consult those. They cover only certain parts of the country, mainly the northern half of it, but do include Aberdeen and Aberdeenshire, Glasgow and Lanarkshire, and Dundee, which seemed to offer altogether a promising field. I arranged to see these indexes of Christian names and spent two happy mornings working over them in the New Register House.

Some quite fascinating things emerged. There are of course a lot of names so common that one cannot easily make any useful deductions. No doubt if one counted the occurrences year by year over a period one could see some pattern of the rising and waning popularity of a common name and even draw interesting graphs. But it would be a tedious and laborious undertaking to do it thoroughly, and casual inspection is not very helpful. Some names — names of sovereigns for example — which are potentially of political significance are all too common in generation after generation. James had always been a common enough name. George was not unfamiliar long before the House of Hanover came on the scene, and I did not see significant fluctuations around 1714, when George I became king. The same applies to William, which had been common for centuries. There was no spurt in Williams in the aftermath of the revolution of 1689 which put William II on the Scottish throne — I hardly expected it — or in the reign of 'Silly Billy' in the 1830s. That did not mean that sovereigns' names were ignored at that time: parents in Kells parish, Kirkcudbrightshire, whose daughter was baptized on 28 June 1838, 'being the coronation day of Her Majesty Queen Victoria', gave her the Queen's name. The name of an earlier Queen, Anne, had been used for a boy, a son of the 4th Duke of Hamilton, it is said, because he wanted to curry favour with the Queen — though it has to be remembered that the boy's own grandmother had been Duchess Anne.

Dr Rosalind Marshall very kindly sent me an analysis of the names of servants at Hamilton Palace in the seventeenth century. The four most common names for males were John (seventy-four occurrences), James (fifty-eight), William (forty-eight) and Robert (thirty-nine); these would probably have been common in any setting, but the first three were the names of heads of the noble family of Hamilton and may reflect the practice whereby servants, as well as tenants, of the nobility sometimes used the name of 'the laird' — as happened, for example, with a son of tenants of the Hopetoun family who was given the rather unusual name of Adrian. (Among other names used in the Hamilton family, David occurs only ten times among the servants, Gavin only five times and Claud only once.) After the leading group of four the figures drop sharply: Thomas (nineteen), Alexander and Andrew (twelve) and George (eleven). Fourteen names score between ten and two and twenty-five occur only once. Among females, Margaret (nineteen), Elizabeth (ten), Anne or Anna (ten) and Mary (six) — all names of a Hamilton Marchioness or Duchess — rank high, but Janet (eight) and Agnes and Jean (seven) are also in the first seven, and in all twenty-eight names are represented.

So far as royal names are concerned, it is more profitable to seek political significance in names which are not among the most familiar. Stewart, for example, as a Christian name, could well be important. The earliest example I have noticed was Stewart (or Stuart) Rose, fiancée of Robert Lyon, an Episcopalian chaplain to the Jacobite army who was executed at Carlisle in 1746, and she must have been born before 1730. Stewart first seems to occur with some frequency in roughly the 1740s; there was one in Dundee in 1739 and others in 1745, 1746 and 1754; there was a small handful in Glasgow in the 1740s; in Aberdeen they do not appear until the 1770s. This would suggest a limited amount of Jacobite sentiment in the period before and after the '45, with probably an appreciable increase in sentiment after Jacobitism ceased to be of practical importance. Charles had never been common, and had found its way into the royal family only when James VI's baptismal names included it (after his uncles the king of France and Darnley's brother); it is therefore a useful indicator. The Jacobite attachment to both James and Charles is not in any doubt: in the Registers of Robert Forbes, minister of Leith, Bishop of Ross and author of *The Lyon in Mourning*, when those royal names occur they are frequently written in capital letters. (It should be kept in mind that many Jacobites, being Episcopalians, did not use the Parish Registers for their baptisms.) In both Glasgow and Aberdeenshire there had been a good crop of Charleses at the Restoration, roughly 1660-62, but they become rather thin thereafter and there seems to be a distinct slump in the 1690s; there was an increase in 1713-4, when perhaps there was hope of a Stewart successor to Anne. Then Glasgow does not show a single Charles in 1745 — which is what one would expect in a city which was doing very nicely under the Hanoverians and did not want to see things upset by the Stewarts; but Charleses pick up in 1747, after the rebellion was over and Charlie could be my darling without dire consequences. Charles Grant, a future Director of the East India Company, born in March 1746, was named after the Pretender under whom his father was serving at the time. I am told that Charles Edward does crop up, but I did not myself note one. Going back to an earlier generation, I did not notice a Henrietta in the reign of Charles I and Henrietta Maria (who was, however, prayed for as 'Queen Mary'), though the name became popular in later times.

Still in the Jacobite — or anti-Jacobite — context, the question was raised earlier of the incidence of Williams in 1746, but William was such a common name, generation by generation, that it would require elaborate calculation to discover whether it was any more or less popular in that year. It was far more significant that, as already mentioned, Cumberland was used as a Christian name in 1746. There were two in Aberdeen, one on 1 March and the other on 22 April — Culloden was fought on 16 April; there were five in Dundee, on 5 and 23 March, 6 and 30 May and 20 July; and one in Glasgow, on 13 April. This name, too, was transmitted and could even pass to females, for there was a Cumberland Ann Garden in Kincardine on 21 October 1817. One can compare this very positive evidence of the welcome given to Cumberland — of which there is any amount of evidence of other kinds — with some negative evidence. It did not surprise me to find that there had been no crop of Olivers in the 1650s, and I found not one Cromwell, though I seem to recall a Cromwell Swinton, named by a father who was an enthusiastic Cromwellian. Clearly attitudes to Cromwell, reviled as a conqueror, were very different from attitudes to Cumberland, cherished as a liberator.

There is no doubt at all in my mind that we have in those Christian names a possible source of information about the attitudes and opinions that were current at various points, and at a particularly personal level. If parents could not express their own views in naming their children, where could they do so? It was not a field in which politicians or theologians were likely to dictate the choice (though we cannot discount the possibility that a priest or a minister might have a voice, if only in giving advice to check the exuberance of some parents). I am told that Herr Hitler recommended or ordered that no German boys should be given the name Adolf, presumably because he did not want to share it with anyone, but that was surely an exceptional piece of megalomania.

Theologians might not dictate the names given in baptism, but Christian names can tell us something about the faith as well as the politics of the people,

even if only in a negative kind of way. It is well known that in the sixteenth and
seventeenth centuries English puritans went in for two categories of names:
personal names from Scripture, including some obscure ones, and, secondly,
names of abstract qualities or virtues like mercy, charity, faith and so on. This
did not happen so much in Scotland, as far as I can see, and I deduce that,
however 'distracted' Scottish ecclesiastical views were in the seventeenth
century, that particular eccentricity did not much affect them. Certain scriptural names were indeed always fairly or even very popular in Scotland, like
Daniel and Samuel for men and Sara for women, but there was certainly no
flood of such names in that period. Rachel and Rebecca, it seems, actually
became more common *after* the seventeenth century, and Esther was fairly
common. As to the 'virtuous' names, if one can call them so, I do not find
Mercy, Patience, Prudence or Faith at all. And among scriptural names one
looks in vain for Seth and Silas, which turn up in England. There was a stray
Reuben in Aberdeenshire, and my attention has been drawn to a Naomi and a
Magdalene. It has been suggested that some of the Christian names given by
Scott to characters in *Old Mortality*— Silas, Gabriel, Ephraim and Habakkuk
— derive from English plays written in derision of the puritans. The Scots were
certainly not addicted to such names, but we do find Nathaniel, Ezekiel and
Elisha. One must beware of assuming that dwellers in Scotland who had
unusual names were native Scots: Dr Marshall has identified an Abraham, a
Benjamin, a Nathaniel and a Rebecca as persons of English origin. Oddly
enough, one of the most conspicuous and unusual scriptural names, Habakkuk,
was introduced to Scotland not by any puritan but by Mary, Queen of Scots.
She had a caterer called Bisset who came to her one day and asked her to give
a name to his newborn son. Mary, in a hurry to attend mass, said she would give
him 'the first name she cast up', presumably in a book of devotions she was
carrying, and the name happened to be 'the prophet Abacuke' — which, spelt
without an 'h', would be first in an alphabetical list or index.[1] That reminds one
of a character in a novel, I think one of Thomas Hardy's, who was unhappily
called Cain because his mother wrongly identified Abel, and not Cain, as the
murderer.

One does not, then, see much sign of the influence of either the first
reformers or their more extreme successors. Someone may say, 'What about
John Knox? Didn't he call his sons Nathaniel and Eleazar?' He did, but that just
shows how untypical and how un-Scottish Knox was. It seems reasonable to
argue that in this as in so much else he revealed his anglicised outlook and was
following the example of English puritans, with whom he shared certain
opinions although he had little sympathy with them when they defied authority. Knox's boys may have been named by their mother the first Mrs Knox, who
was of course an Englishwoman. One wonders how far Knox, who blasted so

[1]H. Bisset, *Rolment of Courtis* (Scottish Text Society, Edinburgh, 1920-21), i, p. vii.

loudly against the monstrous regiment of women, was hen-pecked at home. After all he called one of his daughters Elizabeth, surely a token of respect to the Queen whom he told the English puritans to obey but whom he derided as 'neither good protestant nor yet resolute papist'. The daughter Elizabeth, however, was the child of Knox's second, Scottish, wife. (Eleazar Knox was not unique, for there was an Eleazar Downie in Leith in the seventeenth century.)

Yet the whole question of those religious names does raise some speculation. The reformers were so imitative of the English in other respects, taking over from them the Prayer Book, the Book of Common Order, the Metrical Psalms, and Book of Homilies — and evidence has recently come to light that the Prayer Book Catechism was reprinted for Scottish use, with Scotticised spelling (Dundee Archive and Record Centre: Town Clerk Protocol Book fragments). And yet they did not imitate the English in this trivial particular of naming their children. Similarly, the Covenanters took over the English Confession of Faith, Form of Church Government and Catechisms and yet, once more, did not imitate the English in naming their children. Very odd.

References at the beginning of this article to names like Winston, Gordon, Gladstone and Cobden Bright indicated that Christian names might be some index of Scottish interest in British wars and British politics. It occurred to me to apply this in the eighteenth century, when, as I have remarked several times, Scots were not much interested in Britain's wars. So far as my searches went the indications were indeed rather negative. I hardly thought it worth while to look for signs of interest in the wars at the beginning of the eighteenth century. There might indeed have been Johns named after John Churchill, Duke of Marlborough, but if they existed they are lost among the unnumbered hundreds of other Johns. Curiously enough, however, I did find in Dundee in 1721 the baptism of a 'Eugine', who may have owed his unusual name to a desire to commemorate Marlborough's ally Prince Eugen or Eugène, who was still engaging in campaigns in 1733 and did not die until 1736. I did look to see whether any of the great commanders of the Seven Years' War period turned up — Clive, for example (which did later become a Christian name), but I did not find them. At the very end of the century Nelson seemed a possibility, and although I did not find it I did find Horatio: it does not appear until 1830, and then again in 1854, which would suggest that the individuals then so named were not the earliest members of their families to bear a name which had presumably first been given in the previous generation, in Nelson's own day. I also found Horatia, the female version which was the name of Nelson's daughter; it appears in 1826 and 1828. Nelson's contemporary, Admiral Rodney, who died in 1792, was commemorated in the baptism of a boy in Aberdeen in 1793.

On the whole, so far as the evidence goes for this subject, the indications are that it was only with the Napoleonic wars that Scots first began to feel concerned with Britain's wars. I have pointed out in another chapter in this book, on 'The

Anglicisation of Scotland',[2] the similar indications given by street-names and memorials. Names of lesser distinction can sometimes indicate more subtle ways in which English influence was extending in Scotland. For example, Dr Marshall has pointed out that a Duchess of Hamilton had an English uncle called Basil, after whom she named her sixth son. This Lord Basil Hamilton died young, and after his death his sister called her next son by his name. Then that sister, as Duchess of Atholl, lived in Dunkeld, where in the Old Parish Register the name of 'Basil' suddenly appears among the children of local shopkeepers and farmers.

One other possibility I kept in view was in the cultural field, in line with my speculation about the influence of Arthurian legends in the fifteenth century, and that was the Ossianic phase in the late eighteenth century. I kept my eyes open for Oscar (which became a name of Swedish kings) but I did not find one.

Clearly all one can do is to suggest that the evidence of Christian names is not to be lightly dismissed and might well be worth pursuing on a systematic and extended, rather than desultory and spasmodic, basis. Pending something of that kind one can only note unusual names which one comes across and any particular concentrations of certain names at certain times and places.

[2]See below, p. 118.

# 10

## Reflections on the Royal Succession

*An expanded version of a lecture given in the
Scottish National Portrait Gallery on 10 October 1990*

Not many subjects recur to my mind as often as the succession to the Scottish throne, and I doubt if there is any subject on which my views have so often changed. My concern with it started when Professor Dickinson and I were compiling the *Source Book of Scottish History*, vol. i, the first edition of which was published in 1952. Professor Dickinson had thought a lot about the royal succession already, and I fell in with his views. In that volume there is a chapter with the title 'Kingship and Succession to the Throne' and there is a genealogical table which has the title 'The Rule of the Throne'. In that table, out of the sixteen kings who reigned before 1100 no less than eleven are coolly noted as having been killed, usually by or in favour of a successor. This should have made me 'smell a rat', for to give the word 'Rule' to such sanguinary ongoings seems a misuse of language. Perhaps it was a rule that kings should be killed.

However, I came on suggestions that these proceedings could be rationally explained. There were, some said, two branches of the royal house, from each of which the king was chosen alternately; but if that was a *rule*, why were the murders necessary? Others spoke of a system called 'tanistry', but so far as I could make out tanistry meant designating a successor in the lifetime of a monarch in order to avoid a disputed succession. That would have made sense of murdering tanists, but not of murdering kings. Others had discovered in Anglo-Saxon England something called fraternal or horizontal, as opposed to filial or perpendicular, succession, and that might have applied in Scotland. Others again babbled that the succession was open to anyone whose great-grandfather had been king and that the throne went to the eldest or ablest individual within that group. This seemed to me to make more sense, for one obvious way to prove that you were the ablest was to defeat your rivals in battle or otherwise dispose of them by violence. This began to look more like a free for all, or at any rate a free for all within a certain group of kinsmen, and there was some rationality about that,

# TABLE 1

## 'THE RULE OF THE THRONE'

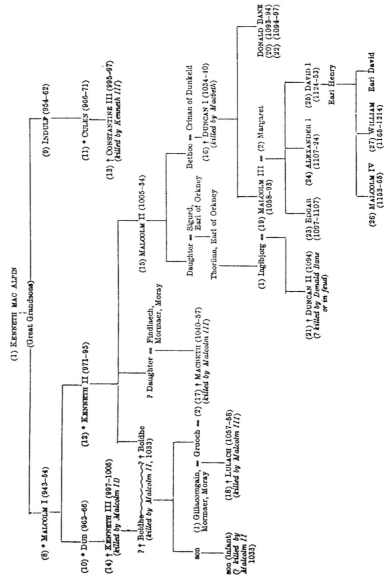

(1) Kenneth mac Alfin

(Great Grandsons)

(8) • Malcolm I (943–54)

(9) Indulf (954–62)

(10) • Dub (962–66)

(11) • Culen (966–71)

(12) • Kenneth II (971–95)

(13) † Constantine III (995–97) *(killed by Kenneth III)*

(14) † Kenneth III (997–1005) *(killed by Malcolm II)*

? Daughter = Findlaech, Mormaer, Moray

(15) Malcolm II (1005–34)

Bethoc = Crinan of Dunkeld

Daughter = Sigurd, Earl of Orkney

Thorfinn, Earl of Orkney

(16) † Duncan I (1034–10) *(killed by Macbeth!)*

Donald Bane (20) (1093–94) (22) (1094–97)

?† Boldhe ~~~~~~? † Boldhe *(killed by Malcolm II, 1033)*

son

son (Infant) (? killed by Malcolm II 1033)

(1) Gillacomgain, = Gruoch = (2) (17) † Macbeth (1040–57) Mormaer, Moray            *(killed by Malcolm III)*

(18) † Lulach (1057–58) *(killed by Malcolm III)*

(1) Ingibjorg = (19) Malcolm III = (2) Margaret (1058–93)

(21) † Duncan II (1094) (? killed by Donald Bane or in feud)

(23) Edgar (1097–1107)

(24) Alexander I (1107–24)

(25) David I (1124–53)

Earl Henry

Earl David

(26) Malcolm IV (1153–65)

(27) William (1165–1214)

• Killed in feud, possibly in favour of his successor

† Killed by his successor

though hardly what one would call a rule.

However, while such irregularities were usual before 1000, I fell in with the idea that in the eleventh century there began what has come to be regarded as the norm — primogeniture in the male line and so on. I fell in with the idea that the succession of Duncan I to his grandfather Malcolm II in 1034 represented the introduction from the south of the practice which was eventually to prevail and then that Macbeth, by disposing of Duncan, represented a native reaction against such an innovation. When Macbeth in turn was put out by Malcolm Canmore that was the southern practice asserting itself, and when, after tussles with Donald Bane and Duncan II, the Margaretsons established themselves, Scotland had finally come into line with southern, general European, ways, and everything in the garden was lovely.

In my innocence I just accepted all that. And — God forgive me, I suppose I should say now — that is what I taught to generations of students and even what I put into print, before I saw the light. I began to have some glimmerings of the light when I realised, not for the first or the last time, the validity of the question 'What do they know of Scotland who only Scotland know?' and began to look at what happened in other countries. I noted that among the twenty-three Visigothic kings of Spain seven were murdered by their successors and only eight times did a son succeed a father. In Denmark, over a period of a century, not one king was the son of his predecessor, and in England during the ten reigns in the hundred years before the Norman Conquest there was hardly a succession that was not disputed and only twice did a son succeed a father. When you look at the royal succession in other lands you see that Scotland was not so peculiar.

Look at England again, this time after the Norman Conquest. William I, the Conqueror, was succeeded in England not by his eldest son, Robert, to whom was allotted the family's older inheritance of Normandy, but by his second son, William Rufus. Then when Rufus was killed, so suddenly and so mysteriously, in the New Forest, he was succeeded not by his elder brother Robert but by his younger brother Henry, apparently for no better reason than that Henry got off his mark first and lost no time in reaching Winchester, the site of the royal treasury and a traditional royal seat. Henry left only a daughter, Matilda, who was challenged successfully by her cousin Stephen, himself a male but one whose claim came through a female, for his mother was the daughter of the Conqueror. And, although Matilda was not acceptable as a queen regnant, she likewise could transmit the succession, for her son, Henry II, followed Stephen, whose own son had died. Henry was succeeded by his eldest surviving son, Richard. On the death of the childless Richard, his brother John took the throne but had to secure himself by killing Arthur, son of John's elder brother Geoffrey — a murder which would have been typical in Scotland a century earlier. So it had been a troubled century for England after the conquest.

Thereafter the English succession went smoothly with Henry III, the first three Edwards and Richard II. The deposition of Richard II, however, in the interest of his cousin Henry IV, contained the seed of the Wars of the Roses, when the competition of York and Lancaster bore some resemblance to what had been happening in Scotland about four centuries earlier. However, there was one very significant novelty: when, in 1460, the Duke of York formally made a claim to the crown then worn by Henry VI, on the ground that York was descended through a senior line from Edward III, we can say that what became known as legitimism — the supposed foundation of Jacobitism — was born. And the Wars of the Roses ended with a curious episode. Henry VII, who somewhat tenuously represented Lancaster and ousted the Yorkist Richard III, owed his place in the succession to his mother, Margaret Beaufort, who was still alive and indeed outlived him. Thus once again we have transmission through a female who was not herself acceptable as queen.

Enlightened by the example of England from the twelfth century to the fifteenth, let us return to Scotland in the eleventh. When Malcolm II died in 1034 he left no sons. One of his daughters, Bethoc, had married Crinan, Abbot of Dunkeld, and they had a son, Duncan; a second daughter, whose name is not known, was the mother of Thorfinn, Earl of Orkney. Transmission of succession through females was apt to lead to disputes, partly because, while there was a presumption in favour of an elder son over a younger son, it was not so certain that such a presumption applied to daughters. It would not have been surprising, therefore, if Duncan and his cousin Thorfinn had been rivals. There was a third claimant, Macbeth, around whom fantasies have been woven by writers of fiction among whom William Shakespeare was neither the first nor the last. Dorothy Dunnett based her novel *King Hereafter* on the idea that Macbeth and Thorfinn were one and the same — a startling theory on which W. F. Skene had almost stumbled a century earlier when he observed that 'our authorities for the history of Macbeth know nothing of Earl Thorfinn and his conquests. On the other hand, the sagas equally ignore Macbeth and his doings'.

Some historians would have it that Macbeth's claim to the throne was in right of his wife, who must indeed have had a place in the dynasty (no doubt as a granddaughter of a previous king) and a right to transmit a claim, for her son Lulach — Macbeth's stepson — was king briefly after Macbeth's death. But even had she been a *daughter* and not merely a granddaughter of a previous king that would not have given her husband a right to the throne, any more than Crinan's marriage to Bethoc gave him a right. The most likely source of Macbeth's claim was through his mother, who may have been a daughter of a king, possibly even of Malcolm II. There may thus have been three cousins — Duncan, Thorfinn and Macbeth — who all considered themselves entitled to the throne when Malcolm II died in 1034. Duncan became king, possibly because he was the eldest or ablest, but just as likely because, on Malcolm's death, he managed to beat his rivals to the scene of royal inaugurations at Scone, much as in England Henry I beat his brother Robert to Winchester.

It would be understandable if Duncan's two cousins, Thorfinn and Macbeth, then ganged up against him, put him out of the way and partitioned the kingdom between them (1040). Macbeth got the royal title, but Thorfinn, we are told, held nine Scottish earldoms, which by any reckoning looks like a generous share. A continuing alliance between the two might explain why they both went on pilgrimage to Rome; even if they were not one man under two names, Thorfinn and Macbeth may have been fellow-travellers.

After a reign of seventeen years, Macbeth was defeated and killed by Malcolm III (Malcolm Canmore), elder son of the deceased Duncan. The Saga says that Malcolm took as his first wife Ingibjorg, Thorfinn's widow, but it is much more plausible that Malcolm, eager to ensure the succession after he had overthrown Macbeth in 1057, lost no time in coming to terms with Macbeth's ally Thorfinn and marrying Thorfinn's daughter, who may well have had the same name as her mother.

Malcolm III, who overthrew Macbeth, was the son of Duncan I by a Northumbrian wife; he was thus half-English before he spent his formative years, during Macbeth's reign, in the England of the half-Norman Edward the Confessor, and, after the termination of his marriage to Ingibjorg (whether by her death or by a dissolution on the ground of their relationship as second cousins), he married Margaret, the Confessor's grand-niece. Margaret's brother, Edgar the Atheling, had in 1066 been the native candidate for the English throne, which William the Conqueror had seized. When Margaret gave her first four sons the names of English kings — Edward, Edmund, Ethelred, Edgar — did she see them as potential pretenders to challenge the Normans? She certainly meant to emphasise their place in English rather than Scottish society.

In 1093 Malcolm was killed in an invasion of England. The throne was seized, to the exclusion of the sons of Margaret, by Malcolm's brother Donald Bane, who seems to have been brought up during Macbeth's reign not, like Malcolm, in England but in the western isles, where he learned Norse (or possibly Celtic) ways. He was soon confronted by a Norman element, in the person of Duncan, eldest son of Malcolm (by his first, Norse, wife) and grandson of Earl Thorfinn. Duncan, who had been a hostage at the court of the Conqueror and his son Rufus for twenty years, now came north with help from Rufus to oust his uncle Donald and reign briefly as Duncan II.

That first attempt at a Norman conquest of Scotland failed, for Donald soon returned and Duncan was killed. Only three years later, however, Edgar, the eldest surviving son of Malcolm and Margaret, arrived, as Duncan had done, with an army supplied by Rufus. An unnamed battle in 1097, when Edgar and his Normans defeated Donald, was the Scottish equivalent of Hastings, and Edgar ruled the country — or part of it — as an Anglo-Norman vassal. He may have been acceptable enough in the south, whose inhabitants had probably had enough of Donald and his islanders, but a king called Edgar would not appeal to elements which had supported Donald or even Duncan II, and north of the Tay he had to be content with a toehold at Invergowrie, whence he could make a quick getaway by sea. The line which came in with Edgar retained the throne and continued in the male line for nearly two centuries, until Alexander III.

Curiously enough, there has been no consensus on a suitable label for this dynasty. Normal practice has been to style a ruling line from the family name or the place of origin of its male progenitor: Plantagenet or Angevin, Tudor, Stewart, Hanover, Coburg, Hohenzollern, Hapsburg and so on. The male progenitor of the dynasty to which Edgar belonged had been Crinan, Abbot of Dunkeld, who married a daughter of Malcolm II, and one would therefore expect the style to derive from him — perhaps 'the House of Crinan' (or possibly 'the MacCrinans') or (which sounds better and which I long ago adopted) 'the House of Dunkeld'. However, when Scots cannot succeed in making themselves ridiculous they do their best to make themselves seem quaint or peculiar, and much use has been made of 'the House of Canmore', although 'Canmore' was a mere nickname of one individual and not a family name and although Malcolm Canmore was neither the male progenitor nor the first of the line to reign. 'The House of Duncan' or 'Duncansons' would be slightly more defensible. It might make sense to name the dynasty from the first of the line with whose accession the unbroken tenure of the throne began, namely Edgar, but he should be ruled out since he had no heirs of the body. A recent product of the determination to make Scotland quaint has been 'the MacMalcolms'.[1] This is open to objections which apply to 'Canmore', for Malcolm III was neither the progenitor nor the first king of the line, but open also to the objection that it is a transparent attempt to veil the alien nature of this dynasty. Edgar, the first to reign, was no more than one quarter native and as time passed the proportion of native blood was halved in each generation. 'MacMalcolm' may thus be dismissed as a bogus product of Celtomania. I have sometimes called these intruders 'the Margaretsons', which suggests right away the fact that they represented external, southern influence. Men bearing names like Edward, Edmund, Ethelred and Edgar reflect the parentage of Margaret rather than Malcolm, and their mother clearly thought them an offshoot of the House of Wessex. To call the dynasty 'MacMalcolms' is at best like calling the Tudors Hendersons or calling the Stewarts Robertsons or perhaps Jamiesons. In any event, if there were true 'MacMalcolms' they were the descendants of Malcolm Canmore by his first wife, beginning with Duncan II, continuing with a series of 'Pretenders' who made trouble for the reigning line for over a century and now represented, it seems, by Lord FitzWalter.

Although the 'Margaretsons' reigned not by right of blood but by armed conquest, and for more than a century were challenged by descendants of the senior, 'legitimist' descendants of Malcolm III, yet the Margaretson succession

---

[1] M. Lynch, *Scotland A New History* (London, 1991), p. 74.

went on remarkably smoothly. This has given the impression that somehow a new principle of stability now prevailed, and this was how I saw it in my own unenlightened days. I realise now that this illusion arose from the simple fact that within the Margaretson line there were hardly any alternative heirs — partly, I think, because the family had little taste for matrimony and were influenced by the contemporary emphasis on the superior merits of celibacy. Such distaste for matrimony, peculiar in a royal family, has obvious dangers from the point of view of securing the succession, and yet at the time it affected Edward the Confessor (d. 1066) and Earl Magnus of Orkney (d. 1116). The really important change that came with the Margaretsons was that there was in Scotland no more succession by murder, but of course when there were few heirs there were fewer possible victims of murder.

There were indeed few alternative heirs. There was the succession of the three brothers, Edgar, Alexander I and David; then David had only one son who reached adult years, Henry, and when Henry predeceased his father there was no challenger to Henry's eldest son, Malcolm, although he was only twelve. To Malcolm his next brother, William, was the only possible heir. When William died his son, Alexander II, was already sixteen and clearly a candidate preferable to William's brother David, who had retired to England and whose only son was childless. When Alexander II died there was no alternative to his son, the eight-year-old Alexander III.

Even in such circumstances, primogeniture was not a foregone conclusion. David I, to ensure, as he hoped, that his son Henry would succeed, caused Henry to be styled 'Rex designatus' and when Henry died before his father Henry's son Malcolm was conducted round the country to be shown to his future subjects. This may look like the tanist or designated successor, but it was widely paralleled in other lands. In Anglo-Saxon England, where Alfred had no brother, his elder son was styled *Rex* in his father's lifetime. In Norman England, Henry II took the same step in the hope of avoiding trouble among brothers. Such a practice was common in the Empire. Charlemagne had crowned his son Louis in his own lifetime and it became usual for the imperial heir to be crowned King of the Romans. In France, Hugh, son of Robert I, was crowned in his father's lifetime but predeceased him (1026), and more than a century later Philip Augustus was crowned king in his father's lifetime. The practice spread to Norway, where in 1257 Haakon Haakonsson appointed his son and heir Magnus as king.

Possibly the concept of the designated successor, even though the person designated was the heir apparent, may have suggested that a successor could be designated when there was no one first in line, no obvious successor. In France an infant was passed over in favour of his uncle in 888, and on the death of Charles IV in 1328 the 'council of peers' designated Philip of Valois as the preferred successor — preferred, that is, to the king of England among others. In Spain in 1284 Alfonso X left two infant grandsons, but 'according to the old

Visigothic law, the second son of the king, if of age, was recognised as heir, in preference to any infant child of the eldest son' and the Cortes recognised Alfonso's eldest surviving son, Sancho, as king, to the exclusion of the grandsons. No doubt other examples could be found, even without going to places like Bohemia where there was quasi-elective kingship. Some element of choice was very widespread.

William the Lion did not marry until he was about forty-three and his heir was not born until twelve years later. It must have looked for a time as if William was not going to have a son, and it is said that in 1195 he proposed to designate one of his daughters as his successor but that the magnates argued that his brother David should be preferred. Alexander II married when he was twenty-three but had no children by his first marriage, which lasted for seventeen years, and when his first wife died, in 1238, there must again have been despair about a direct heir. To make matters worse, Alexander's male cousin, John the Scot, son of Earl David, had died childless in the previous year. Therefore, so it was alleged, a Scottish council declared that if Alexander II died without a son he should be succeeded by Robert Bruce, Lord of Annandale, the nearest male (though inheriting through a female), to the exclusion of females. The crisis was ended by the second marriage of Alexander II and the birth of Alexander III.

It would seem that the apparent regularity of the succession in the Margaretson line had been almost accidental, that the Scots were not unfamiliar with occasional anxieties, if not crises, about the succession, and that the practice of determining the succession by a formal act was not unknown. In other words, the concept of something like what we may call a statutory succession was already there in the thirteenth century. It need not surprise us that when the next crises after that of 1238 arose the council was ready to take a decision. Alexander III's last surviving child, his elder son Alexander, died in 1284 and within days a council met to nominate an heir. They boldly selected the three-year-old Margaret, 'Maid of Norway', daughter of Alexander III's daughter Margaret by King Erik of Norway — a female deriving from a female.

When, only two years later, Alexander III was killed, the Maid was accepted, though with some evident reluctance, for there were adult males who thought themselves better suited than she to the responsibilities of kingship. During the four years of her nominal reign no attempt was made to define the succession further, probably less because of any confidence that the child would survive and have issue than because there would have been no agreement among conflicting claimants. Then, when the Maid died in 1290 and the Scots were so far from agreeing among themselves that there was a risk of civil war, Edward I of England undertook to adjudicate and he decided in favour of John Balliol, who had the best claim by primogeniture. When, in 1296, Balliol was deposed (after military defeat by Edward) there was another interregnum, lasting for ten years, before Robert Bruce became king.

At this point it is appropriate to assess some of the factors which shaped the problems of the succession in the recurring 'competition for the throne'. Alexander III, who had died on 19 March 1296, is often called 'the last of Scotland's Celtic kings' or 'the last of Scotland's native kings'. This is nonsense, for out of his thirty-two great-great-great-grandparents no more than two or three could be regarded as in any sense native. The great majority were English or Norman or Anglo-Norman, because generation by generation Scottish kings had been marrying ladies from England or France. Alexander III himself had married a sister of a king of England, his father had married a sister of a king of England, his grandfather had married a Frenchwoman (and he had been known by *her* name as Guillaume de Warenne), and so on. There had not been a native queen of Scotland for at least seven generations. In each generation the proportion of native blood in the reigning sovereign's veins had been halved, so that by Alexander III's time there was hardly any left.

As contemporaries realised, these kings were French rather than anything else in their blood, outlook and way of life, and it was the rebels who resisted them who had the better claim to be called 'native'. Scotland was then what would now be called a multi-racial and multi-lingual society, not unlike what we now know as 'the former Yugoslavia'. There were — in modern terms — French and English and Welsh, Irish and Norwegians and Flemings, sometimes settled in substantial blocs, sometimes intermingled in small groups. Each ethnic element had its own language, and the official languages — the languages of legal deeds and official records — were to some extent French, which was the tongue of the ruling class, but mainly Latin, which was much used by clergy and other professional men. Thus no less than seven languages were spoken, and one must ponder the problems of communication in the polyglot hosts which William Wallace and Robert Bruce led against the English.

Besides such ethnic and linguistic divisions, there was another complication, which is better known. It was still largely true that what may be called the horizontal division into classes was more potent than the vertical division into nations. A Scottish baron, shall we say, had more in common with an English or a French baron than he had with his native tenants or vassals in Scotland; and a burgess of Perth or Stirling or Berwick had more in common with a burgess of Newcastle or a burgess of Hamburg than he had with a herdsman from the Highland glens or the Border hills. The international, cosmopolitan character of society was not least notable at the higher levels, whence leadership had to come. It was not until very much later — not until the second half of the seventeenth century — that the lower orders in Scotland showed any sign of taking the initiative and acting without the traditional leadership of the barons.

And at this stage the barons hardly looked like the people to give leadership in a national cause, for it would be hard to see why they should feel any national sentiment. Some of them had lands in France and England as well as in Scotland and, members of an aristocracy which straddled the Border and the English Channel alike, were equally at home in all three countries. I suspect that if you had asked one of them 'Are you English or Scottish?' he would hardly have known what you meant. If you had varied the question to 'Are you a subject of the king of Scotland?' the answer might well have been, 'Yes, but I'm a subject of the king of England as well', and he might have added for good measure that he was also a subject of the king of France. Some historians of this period have written a lot about 'the community of the realm', and it is true that people did think a lot in terms of communities at both local and national level. But being a member of 'the community of the realm of Scotland' did not preclude Anglo-Franco-Scottish nobles from membership of other communities as well. Thus the issue of loyalty, whatever its basis, was not straightforwardly founded on nationality, and this meant that there were enormous difficulties in organising a resistance movement based on the concept of the nation and providing leaders for it.

In a sense, the crunch was bound to come when there was war, because that would make it impossible to profess dual nationality or a dual loyalty to two kings. There had been Anglo-Scottish wars before, and people had become aware of the difficulties. At the battle of the Standard, when David I invaded England in 1138, the Anglo-Norman Lord of Annandale, Robert Bruce, harangued David on the folly of enlisting a motley crew, including even Galwegians, to lead against an army composed largely of Anglo-Normans, the very people on whom David's dynasty relied for its elevation to and its maintenance on the Scottish throne. The Lord of Annandale declined to follow the Scottish king and instead joined 'his own countrymen' from the south. It is, however, eloquent of the problems of cosmopolitan magnates — and of one way of solving them — that Annandale's younger son fought in the Scottish army. Clearly, at that stage and perhaps even later, the issue between 'Scotland' and 'England' was no more clear-cut than it had been when the scribe who wrote the early part of the Chronicle of Melrose described the English historian Bede as 'the ornament and glory of our nation' or when Adam of Dryburgh, a native of Berwickshire in the twelfth century, described himself as being at work 'in the land of the English and the kingdom of the Scots'.

It would seem hardly possible that there was enough national emotion to generate enthusiasm for military operations. Yet in time what were regarded as external threats caused men to think the vertical division into nations more important than the horizontal division into classes. The fading away of 'class' as determining loyalty almost makes one think of the fatuous belief of socialists in 1914 that the working classes of the European nations would not fight against each other. One of the familiar themes of the 'war of independence' which Robert Bruce waged against England was the way that the struggle 'forged a nation', and Bruce himself has even been given the credit for 'forging a nation'. To put it differently, Edward I has been called 'the Hammer of the Scots', and a hammer, in the blacksmith's forge, is a constructive implement.

The issue took a long time to crystallise as a clear-cut one between national independence and submission to England. There was not only the question of leadership, which meant the attitude of the barons, but the question of loyalty to a king. A baron who had been loyal to the king of Scots and loyal to the king of England found it hard to choose, and the people who were going to follow him might well have found it harder to choose — if they had been at liberty to choose. Could patriotism or national sentiment be distinguished from preference for one leader over another, for one dynasty over another? And if one claimant to the throne declared for resistance, then the supporters of his rival were apt to declare for England.

## TABLE 2

## THE HOUSE OF DUNKELD

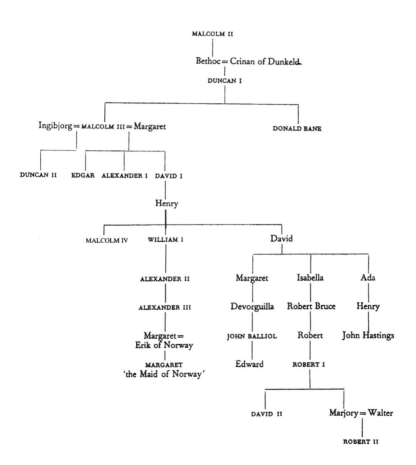

William Wallace was fighting for the lawful king, John Balliol, whom the English had ousted, but there were other claimants, especially Robert Bruce. Division went so deep that Balliol supporters thought it better to support the English than to support Bruce, and Bruce supporters thought it better to support the English than to support Wallace and Balliol. I have already alluded to some similarity between the racial situation in Scotland and that in Yugoslavia, and another parallel can be drawn. During the Second World War, when the Germans invaded that country there were two national factions. General Mihajlovic led armies who supported the Yugoslav king; but the Communists, led by Tito, challenged them. And some of the royalists were so opposed to the Communists that they preferred to collaborate with the German invaders. When this parallel came to my mind in 1992, as I was thinking of what I might say at the Wallace monument above Dryburgh, I thought it was a new idea, but I happened to look at the review I had written six years before of Andrew Fisher's book on Wallace and I found that I wrote there: 'Wallace hardly seems cast for the part of an unsuccessful Tito, nor Bruce for that of a successful Mihajlovic, but there was the same hostility between resistance and collaboration'. It was claimed that Wallace had the higher moral ground, for unlike Bruce he was not seeking a crown for himself.

But if the Balliol cause was dynastic rather than national, the Bruce cause was also dynastic rather than national. Besides, Bruce could not, any more than Balliol, be regarded as what we might call a national candidate. Both were of Norman-French extraction, both were vassals of Edward in respect of English estates. They can hardly have thought it would make much difference if they became his vassals for a kingdom as well; they may even have thought it would greatly simplify matters. Presumably both of them conversed most freely in French, and if John Balliol gave his son the English name Edward, Robert Bruce had a brother who bore the English name Edward — a fact which Robert may have found faintly embarrassing. However, while their male ancestry was Norman, Bruce's mother had been Countess of Carrick in her own right and her ancestry had a strong native element in it; Balliol, similarly, was a grandson of a lord of Galloway and that gave him a partially native ancestry. If neither was plainly more 'native' than Alexander III had been, together they represented the racial make-up of Scotland better than he had done.

When Bruce was crowned in 1306 the country was so deeply divided and disunity so permeated it that he had civil wars on his hands as well as campaigns against the English. In north and south, east and west, he had to deal with Balliol's supporters — the Comyn party in Buchan, the MacDougals of Lorne, the Macnabs in central Perthshire and the MacDowells in Galloway. Bruce was thought by his enemies to be at best an usurper, for Balliol was still alive and, even if his renunciation of the throne, made under duress, had been valid, he had a son who was unquestionably the lawful heir by primogeniture. Balliol's kingship, moreover, had the additional sanction that he had been inaugurated on the sacred Stone at Scone, which Bruce never was. He retired to his French estates and when he died in 1313 his son Edward inherited his rights.

In short, Bruce was in the same position as the Hanoverian kings four centuries later in that he had a rival in 'a king over the water', and an Old Pretender and a Young Pretender challenged his claim. It was all very well to justify his claim in battle by defeating supporters of his rivals and defeating the English, but no number of battles could give him legal rights. His kingship, like that of the Hanoverians later, could be justified only by what we should now call a statutory title; it could be validated in law only by retrospective legalisation of his action in dispossessing the senior line of Balliol. Thus Bruce needed not only war but propaganda. His case was advanced on various grounds. It was alleged that the Scots had always preferred the Bruce line and that Balliol had been forced on them by Edward I. It was alleged that Bruce had the best claim by right of blood and also because he had been selected by the people. Now, the assertion that he had the best claim by right of blood was a singularly doubtful proposition, which had exercised the best legal minds between 1290 and 1292 after the death of the Maid of Norway — and the decision then had been against it; the more convincing claim could have been that he had been chosen by the people — but what proof was there of this? Besides, it always seems to me that to combine the two grounds — hereditary right and choice by the people — while it may have made good propaganda, was poor logic: if he had the hereditary right he did not need choice and if he had choice he did not need the hereditary right.

A declaration in Bruce's favour issued by the clergy in 1310 claimed that the Bruces had always had the support of the people — a quasi-statutory claim — and that the present Bruce had been chosen and made king by them. The Declaration of Arbroath in 1320 stated that Bruce had become king by the right of succession, by the laws of the kingdom and by the consent and assent of the people. This was even more like statutory succession, for by that time a Scots parliament had twice over defined the succession, in 1315 in favour of the king's brother, Edward, in preference to his daughter Marjory, and in 1318 in favour of Marjory's son, Robert, who thus (though not automatically) inherited through his mother. The great novelty of the Declaration of Arbroath was its firm proclamation that, should Robert Bruce abandon the struggle against England, the Scots would find a substitute to continue the fight. Thus the nation had found constitutional expression as something independent of and superior to the claims of one royal family or another. Bruce had indeed won the hearts of a people and he had won them for his own leadership: with him, they said, a faithful people would live and die. But he had also won their hearts for the cause of national independence, irrespective of the leadership of his family.

On three more occasions within the century there was a statutory definition of the succession. King Robert's queen had a son in 1324, and there must have been a statute in his favour cancelling the earlier decision in favour of Robert

Stewart. In 1371 there was a kind of ratification in favour of Robert Stewart when he became king as Robert II, and in 1373 there was something tantamount to an entail of the crown on the several sons of Robert II, successively, and the male heirs of each.

Scottish acceptance of statutory succession may have been the more ready as other countries followed the same practice. In Norway about 1260 there had been a law of succession debarring females, but in 1302 it was decided that a daughter could inherit; within less than a century a woman did accede to the throne (through marriage); and in 1389 Norwegian councillors decided that Erik III was the lawful sovereign. Statutory succession became common in England a little later, because there had been no need for it earlier. Henry VIII was acknowledged as king by statute in 1485, but he claimed by hereditary right — through a woman, as we saw. Statute came on the scene in strength under Henry VIII: thanks largely to his matrimonial adventures, which broke all the rules, the succession was three times defined by act of parliament. And on Elizabeth's accession it was declared treasonable to deny that the sovereign, with consent of parliament, could define the succession. But Henry VIII's final decision had been against the Scottish line, so that James VI succeeded to England in defiance of statute law.

The Scottish statute of 1373, which defined several lines of male succession, to the exclusion of females, provided that should all such lines fall, then 'the true and lawful heirs of the royal blood and kin shall henceforward succeed to the kingdom and the right of reigning'. But who was to determine who should have that right? Experience showed that a further statutory definition would have been required. Yet this did not happen. When James V died in 1542 all the lines specified by the 1373 statute became extinct. Yet so far as we know there was no debate, and there was certainly no statute. Instead a week-old female infant — the late king's daughter Mary — succeeded without challenge.

This brings me to my conclusion and — is it surprising? — another change of mind. For years I had been preaching that there was never anything so illogical or irrational as Jacobitism. Why? Because the Stewart title to the Scottish crown was a statutory title. On Jacobite principles, legitimist principles, the Stewarts would never have been on the throne at all. Balliol had a better claim than Bruce, through whom the Stewarts derived their royal descent. Not only so, but, going farther back, the descendants of Malcolm Canmore's first wife had a better claim than the whole brood of the Margaretsons. In short, as I have put it, the Stewarts, with their statutory title, were no better placed than the Hanoverians, and the struggle in the eighteenth century was not one of statute against divine right but of one statute against another. James V said in 1542 'It cam' wi' a lass and it will pass wi' a lass'; but James VII, in 1689, might have exclaimed, 'It cam wi' a statute and it will pass wi' a statute'.

All very well, but the last things we have learned were that in 1542 Mary's succession in Scotland was at best doubtfully valid by statute and, which is even more telling, that in 1603 James VI's accession to England was plainly in defiance of statute. Are we thus driven to the conclusion that the later Stewarts did after all reign by divine right and not by statute? I begin to think that it would not after all require extraordinary ingenuity to make a case for Jacobitism. But whether any Jacobites had recourse to the involved arguments I have brought is another matter.

Robert I could not have foreseen, though he may have feared, that his male line would die with his son. Still less could he have foreseen that the time would come when the country would dispense with the senior heirs of him and his descendants and adopt another line by statute, precisely as (so he alleged) the nation had adopted him in preference to Balliol. The Bruce dynasty and the Stewart dynasty would alike in turn pass away, but a nation had been established which would outlive them both.

# 11

# The Anglicisation of Scotland

Most of this lecture served in many years as a kind of final entertainment for my Ordinary Class but was rarely delivered on any other occasions. The stimulus to printing it in this volume arose in January 1992. I then received a letter from a 'Student Action Committee' in the University of Edinburgh's Scottish History Department, inviting me to support an appeal to the University to except the Chair of Scottish History from the University's general policy of temporarily postponing appointments to vacant Chairs. It seemed to me improper that the University should capitulate to external political pressure and surrender academic freedom. However, what most astonished me in the letter was faulty history — an allusion to 'the anglicisation of Scotland which began in 1603'.

Anglicisation of the country we now call Scotland started in the sixth century, almost contemporaneously with the beginning of its Scotticisation or Hibernicisation, for Angles settled in what is now south-east Scotland within less than a century of the arrival in Argyll of Irish 'Scots'. Scots and Angles alike expanded at the expense of the earlier inhabitants, the Picts and Britons.

Anglicisation can be detected more clearly in the late seventh century, when in 681 the Angles of Northumbria established a bishopric at Abercorn on the Firth of Forth 'for the Pictish province which was subject to the Angles'. Four years later, at the battle of Nechtansmere, the Northumbrians lost the war against the Picts, but in less than thirty years they won the peace by accepting an invitation from the Pictish king to send Northumbrian clergy to instruct his people in southern ways and a Northumbrian architect to build a church of Northumbrian type. Anglicisation went on century by century thereafter, with peak periods in the eleventh, twelfth and thirteenth centuries and in the Reformation era. I dealt at some length with the developments of the later middle ages and the sixteenth century in an article on 'Foundations of Anglo-Scottish Union' which was reprinted in my *Scottish Church History* (1985). The events of 1603 and 1707, while they did create additional opportunities for the mingling of the two peoples, also created certain tensions which arose from their close association, and it is in the interplay of attraction and repulsion that the interest of the period since 1603 lies.

The first manifestation of Scottish penetration into England after 1603 was one not too creditable to the Scots. It soon became notorious that Scots of all conditions flocked to England to enjoy the benefits of the dynastic union and the common nationality which ensued:

> Bonny Scot, we all witness can
> That England hath made thee a gentleman.
> Thy blue bonnet, when thou came hither,
> Could scarce keep out the wind and weather;
> But now it is turned to a hat and a feather:
> Thy bonnet is blown — the devil knows whither,
> Thy shoes on thy feet, when thou comest from plough,
> Were made of the hide of an old Scotch cow;
> But now they are turned to a rare Spanish leather,
> And decked with roses altogether.
> Thy sword at thy back was a great black blade,
> With a great basket hilt of iron made;
> But now a long rapier doth hang by his side,
> And huffingly doth this bonny Scot ride.

There had to be a proclamation against 'the daily resort of great numbers of idle persons, men and women, of base sort and condition, without any trade or calling, going from Scotland to the court, by sea and land', to the annoyance of His Majesty, who was importuned by their suits and begging, and to the disgrace of their country, since it was slandered as if there were no Scots of good rank, comeliness or credit; and emigration without licence of the council was forbidden. Thomas Ross, son of John Ross of Craigie, affixed to the door of St Mary's Church, Oxford, ten propositions that all Scotsmen except the king, his sons and a very few others should be debarred from the court of England; he expressed surprise that the English should suffer such an unprofitable and pernicious multitude, the very offscourings of the people, to domineer within their territories.

There was, however, the more honourable resort to London of nobles, politicians, scholars and merchants, on their various lawful occasions. There was, too, as much contact as ever between English and Scottish clerics of both persuasions. Before the Reformation Scottish clergy had learned — and it is a thing they have never since forgotten — that good livings were to be had south of the Border. Scottish ministers continued to find benefices in the south. Some of them, indeed, were men who had not come up to the rather exacting standards required in their own country; Paul Methven, for example, minister of Jedburgh, was deposed for adultery but went south, where he attained preferment, and he is known to the *Peerage* writers as the eminently respectable prebendary of Wells who was ancestor of the noble family of Methuen.

In the early seventeenth century, however, Scots of high calibre were attaining eminent offices in the Church of England and filling them worthily. Walter Balcanquhal became dean of Durham; John Young was dean of Winchester and was designated by Charles I as Laud's successor at Canterbury. Two centuries later a Scottish bishop was still reminding his priests that they should expect their reward in a better country than England and from a King whose kingdom is not of this world.

On their visits to Scotland in 1617 and 1633 James VI and Charles I were accompanied by English visitors, some of whom made friends in the north and returned privately. Ben Jonson visited Scotland in 1618, coming on foot and having to buy a new pair of shoes at Durham. He spent six months in Scotland, mainly in or near Edinburgh and including two or three weeks with his fellow-poet William Drummond at Hawthorndean.

The Commonwealth period brought nine years of English occupation which, not in the most pleasant way, contributed to anglicisation. There were English officials in Scotland, there were English garrisons. Some of the English soldiers married Scots women, and it is commonly said that the people of the Inverness area learned their English from the nearby Cromwellian garrison. In the Restoration period, the Duke of Monmouth (illegitimate son of Charles II and husband of the heiress of Buccleuch), as military commander, and Charles II's brother the Duke of York (the future James VII), as commissioner, brought their English trains to Holyroodhouse. The Duke of York's following included his younger daughter, the future Queen Anne, and some of his company of players. According to John Dryden they were not the most accomplished of its members:

> Our brethren are from Thames to Tweed departed,
> And of our sisters all the tender-hearted
> To Edenborough gone, or coached, or carted;
> With bonny blewcap there they act all night
> For Scotch half-crown, in English threepence hight.
> Our trusty doorkeepers of former time
> There strut and swagger in heroic rhyme.

The comments of English visitors on what they found in Scotland range from the flattering to the scurrilous. Some had evidently learned to appreciate the scenic beauties of the country, and perhaps to discover some of its attractions from the point of view of 'huntin', shootin' and fishin''. Thus, Richard Franck, who visited Scotland in 1658: 'You are to consider that the whole tract of Scotland is but one single series of admirable delights, notwithstanding the prejudicate reports of some men that represent it otherwise.... Scotland is ... a legible fair draught of the beautiful creation, dressed up with polished rocks, pleasant savannahs, flourishing dales, deep and torpid lakes, with shady firwoods, immerged with rivers and gliding rivulets, where every fountain o'erflows a valley and every ford superabounds with fish.... Every field is filled with corn and every swamp swarms with fowl'. But Franck was an enthusiastic angler; he was, moreover, a very young man, who today would have lived in Youth Hostels and did not expect five-star accommodation.

Other Englishmen objected to Scottish standards of cleanliness. Sir Anthony Weldon (1617) was particularly hostile. He remarked that in Scotland 'the air might be wholesome but for the stinking people that inhabit it', and went on: 'Their beasts be generally small, women only excepted, of which sort there are none greater in the whole world. There is great store of fowl, too, as foul houses, foul sheets, foul linen, foul dishes and pots, foul trenchers and napkins'. He also criticised Scottish methods of preparing food. If Weldon stood alone he could be discounted, but other Englishmen, who were in general more friendly, alluded to the same points. Sir William Brereton, in 1636: 'Edinburgh ... were a most healthful place to live in, were not the inhabitants most sluttish, nasty and slothful people. I could never pass through the hall but I was constrained to hold my nose'. He refers again to 'the sluttishness and nastiness of this people' and adds: 'Their pewter, I am confident, is never scoured; they are afraid it should too much wear and consume thereby; only sometimes, and that but seldom, they do slightly rub them over with a filthy dish-clout, dipped in most sluttish greasy water'. Both Brereton and John Ray, who followed him in 1662, criticised the ineffective efforts of the Scots to wash their linen, which they did by trampling it in a tub, and when supposedly clean it looked as English linen did when it was thought ready to go to the laundry. The same two travellers, like Weldon, also complained of the Scottish methods of preparing food. Some Englishmen thought the Scots lazy. Brereton said that it was because of sloth that Edinburgh people fetched fresh water only every second day, and Ray noted as a sign of laziness that men might frequently be seen wearing their cloaks when ploughing. Samuel Pepys, it may be added, remarked that 'There is so universal a rooted nastiness hangs about the person of every Scot (man and woman) that renders the finest show they can make nauseous, even among those of the first quality'.

The most scurrilous of the seventeenth-century accounts came from Thomas Kirke, in 1679: 'The country is full of lakes and loughs and well stocked with islands, so that a map thereof looks like a pillory coat bespattered all over with dirt and rotten eggs.... The people are proud, arrogant and vainglorious boasters, bloody, barbarous and inhuman butchers. They show their pride in exalting themselves and depressing their neighbours'. It is hard to know what interpretation to put on his curious remark that in Scotland 'The women dislike Englishmen because they have no legs'.

There were from almost all English visitors adverse comments on Scottish modes of worship. Weldon, in 1617, summed it up: 'They christen without the cross, marry without the ring, receive the sacrament without reverence, die without repentance and bury without divine service'. When William Laud came to Scotland he was scathing about that curious structure the parish church of Burntisland: 'When I passed over at the Firth I took it at first sight for a large square pigeon house, so free was it from all suspicion of being so much as built like an ancient church'. Yet Christopher Lowther (1629) was very complimentary to Scottish churches. Leith, he said, had 'two fairer churches for in-work than any I saw in London'. At Selkirk there was 'a very pretty church' and at Galashiels 'there was the finest seats I have seen anywhere, and the orderliest church'.

The more hostile of those critics called forth rejoinders. It was this type of Englishman who was rebuked by Sir George Mackenzie: 'I say not this to asperse the English — they are a nation I honour — but to reprove the petulance and malice of some among them, who think they do their country good service when they reproach ours'. Mackenzie was a moderate man. Some Scots could be bitter. Away back in 1609 there had been a Scots act against 'pasquilis, libellis, rymis, cokalanis, comedies and siclyk' against the English. Robert Baillie, the Covenanting leader, said of the English: 'The humour of this people is very various and inclinable to singularities, to differ from all the world, and from one another, and shortly from themselves. No people had such need of a presbytery'. He might have reflected that the Scots had precisely the same faults, which no presbytery had done anything to cure. In 1671, when relations between the two countries were strained by a trade war, an English observer described the Scots as 'perfect English haters'. And if Englishmen were contemptuous, Scots were proud: 'The Scots', said John Ray, 'cannot endure to hear their country or countrymen spoken against'.

Plainly, the personal union had not brought the two nations into real friendship or understanding. Yet numerous contacts, in their diverse ways and at various levels, had been making further contributions to the anglicising of Scotland. Some of the leading reformers in Scotland had been Englishmen or anglicised Scots — facts which their adversaries did not allow them to forget — and an English Bible, an English Prayer Book, an English Book of Common Order, an English Psalter all came in. Thus the Reformation had been a great milestone so far as language was concerned, and by the early seventeenth century English had become the literary language. In the mid-seventeenth century the Covenanters were as much under English influence as the reformers had been: George Gillespie, like John Knox, sojourned in England and associated so much with Englishmen that he developed a strong English accent, and another batch of English formulae were introduced — Confession of Faith, Directory of Church Worship, Form of Church Government and Catechisms (above all the Shorter Catechism, which remained a standard channel of instruction in Scottish schools into the twentieth century). Linguistic changes can be discerned even before 1600: the Scottish 'quh-' yields to the English 'wh-', the Scottish '-is' to the English '-s', '-it' to '-ed', 'and' to '-ing' and so on. By 1660, after the short sharp shock of the Cromwellian episode, variation between the written languages of the two countries was hardly noticeable. The same period saw a rapid development in the substitution of the vernacular for Latin in legal deeds and records, and no doubt it was felt that for such purposes English had more dignity than the everyday spoken tongue. The adoption of English ecclesiastical terminology progressed with the triumph of the Covenanters and their English puritan allies: 'kirk' gave way to 'church' in official usage, and whereas the 1637 Prayer Book had carefully preserved the Scottish 'Pasch' and 'Yule' as alternatives to Easter and Christmas — and 'Yule' retained official sanction until the Yule Vacance Act of 1712 — we find 'Christmas' used in Glasgow in 1655. Even the hostile visitor of 1679 had to admit that 'the Lowland language may be well enough understood by an Englishman', and the difference was already becoming one of what we should call accent rather than speech. Thomas Morer, a visitor in 1689 who was on the whole friendly, wrote: 'They (the Scots) are great critics in pronunciation and often upbraid us for not giving every word its due sound.... Wherein, however, they are as faulty themselves, as I showed them.... They have an unhappy tone, which the gentry and nobles cannot overcome, though educated in our schools, or never so conversant with us; so that we can discover a Scotchman as soon as we hear him speak.'

From 1707 the coming and going between the two peoples increased enormously. Freedom of trade meant ever-growing commercial contacts, and in several of the industrial enterprises of the eighteenth century there was plenty of Anglo-Scottish co-operation. English capital and English technical skill came north to exploit Scottish natural resources in minerals and water-power; Scottish inventors went to England. Scottish legislators, both peers and commoners, were necessarily much in London; Scottish administration — limited in scale as it was — was for a long time centred in London. There was not only the penetration of Scotland by English ideas; there was also the penetration of Scots into England and there was to that extent a two-way traffic. But the Scot in England, as was apparent as far back as David I, who was 'polished from his boyhood by his intercourse and friendship with us' was an adaptable Scot; unlike the leaven which leavens the lump, he makes no attempt to Scotticise England, but is himself receptive and adaptable and becomes merely another instrument in the anglicisation of his own country. The 'adaptable' Scot made his appearance not long after the Union. The artist Allan Ramsay, who had as an early patron Clerk of Penicuik, who had helped to frame the Union and never regretted it, had no reluctance about being called an Englishman. Later examples of such adaptable — one might almost say denationalised — Scots were Gladstone, Ruskin, Carlyle, J. S. Mill, T. B. Macaulay and Norman Lamont.

A direct instrument of anglicisation was provided in education. Long ago the Great Schism, when England and Scotland supported rival popes, had first driven Scottish students from English universities and then led to the foundation of the first native university, at St Andrews, followed by others. Scottish lawyers and medical men long continued to complete their education on the continent; in the case of the lawyers there was the special reason for preferring the continent to England that they had to learn Roman law, which was of little use in England but central in Scotland as in Holland and elsewhere. Medicals and lawyers apart, however, Oxford and Cambridge had attracted many Scots even in the sixteenth century. But after 1707 England became an educational centre for Scots in a way it had not done for centuries. Lawyers, indeed, now more often contented themselves with studying at home, while medical men now had the best medical school in Europe in their own capital city; but for literary men and for general education England became the goal. It is true that Oxford and Cambridge were closed to the more conscientious presbyterians until the nineteenth century, but this was not a serious obstacle. There were, in any case, excellent colleges and academies conducted in England by Dissenters, and to them went many Scots.

On the other hand, from about the middle of the eighteenth century Scottish universities became more attractive than before to Englishmen, not least nonconformists, and drew them away from such German universities as Göttingen, Brunswick, Freisburg, Clausthal, Dresden and Frankfurt am Main, all founded on new models. In Scotland eminent professors lectured in the vernacular, class-distinctions were far less marked than in England, there was no serious religious bar and expenses were modest. Glasgow offered such teachers as Hutcheson, Leechman, Simpson and Adam Smith, as well as the great Joseph Black, and it maintained close links with the English dissenting academies. Edinburgh was the mecca for medical students, and to it Joseph Black migrated, to spend thirty-one years in a chair. In the Royal Society of Edinburgh geology was being carefully explored by James Hutton, John Playfair and Sir James Hall. It has been remarked that 'not without reason did such men as Lord Palmerston, Lord John Russell and Lord Brougham find in such universities the mental stimulus for which their natures were so suited'. Meantime distinguished English nonconformist divines who could not receive degrees from English universities got doctorates in divinity in Scotland. There was again a two-way traffic.

English education for Scots began to mean not only English universities but also English schools. This was no novelty either, for John Knox had sent his sons to school in England, but the attraction increased as adult Scots made more acquaintances among Englishmen of their own social standing. Clerk of Penicuik, one of the commissioners for the Union, sent his son to an English school. He brought his boy home to Edinburgh University, but others did not imitate him. The Scot wholly educated in England became a more common phenomenon, and his contribution to his own country was not only its further anglicisation but also the introduction of a class distinction hitherto unknown. The Scottish attempt to compete with the English 'public' schools, when it came in the nineteenth century, took the direction not of strengthening the traditional Scottish grammar schools but of establishing schools on the English model which only carried anglicisation and class divisions further.

Meantime the Union and the contacts which followed it opened to Scots careers south of the Border on a scale hitherto undreamed of. From quite an early stage Scottish medicals, trained at home, achieved prominence in England. In 1778 there was a club in London, composed of Scottish physicians, meeting weekly in a coffee-house. One of the members, John Clephane, is credited with the invention of the toast, 'May no English nobleman venture out of the world without a Scottish physician, as I am sure there are none who venture in'. A recent Scottish writer — himself trained in medicine — remarked that 'the descendants of men who had fought at Inverlochy or Culloden had put away their claymores and were bleeding their English neighbours more profitably than anyone since the Black Douglas'.

The great series of Scottish contributions to English literature had begun in the seventeenth century, when Scottish poets abandoned Scots for English, and in the eighteenth century it extended into prose as well. James Thomson, author of *The Seasons*, spoke Scots but wrote in an acquired English; then there was David Malloch, who in deference to the English changed his name to Mallet; and James Beattie, author of *The Minstrel*. Among prose writers one of the earliest to attain fame was Tobias Smollett.

The penetration of the Scots into the British diplomatic service was worked out by the late Professor D. B. Horn. Scots started from scratch at the Union, for of the twelve leading diplomats at the beginning of the reign of Queen Anne in 1702 not one had been a Scot. But already by the end of Anne's reign in 1714 they were conspicuous: Argyll was ambassador in Spain, Sir James Wishart was on a mission in Holland and two other Scots represented British interests in Poland, Saxony and Russia. This wave expanded in the early years of George I, with Stair as ambassador in France and other Scots in Denmark, Russia, German states and Venice. In the 1720s there was a decline, but after 1741 the trickle became a broad stream. In 1760 Scots were in charge of British relations with Russia, Prussia, Portugal, Sardinia and Saxony-Poland. The position became really extraordinary. About 1770 Lord Stormont was at Vienna, Sir Andrew Mitchell at Berlin, Lord Cathcart at St Petersburg, Sir Robert M. Keith at Warsaw, Sir William Hamilton at Naples. Later there were Scots at Paris, Constantinople and Stockholm. To show the development in perspective it may be said that under Anne one appointment in every eighteen was of a Scot, under George III the ratio had risen to one in seven.

Why this success? In the first place, the diplomatic service was then a career open to talents, not an exclusive, aristocratic body; entrance and promotion did not depend on social status or kinship and many successful careers started from inconspicuous origins and without the support of powerful patrons. But this merely moves the question one stage farther back. If the career was open to talents, how did the Scots come to have the talents?

One factor was Scottish education. A very high proportion of the successful diplomats had been students at the University of Edinburgh, where they were trained in habits of industry and a taste for study. When 'Jupiter' Carlyle was in the Logic class, the students were 'carefully examined three times in the week'. Sir Robert Liston wrote: 'We certainly applied to our studies with great attention and assiduity ... without the relief of much exercise, unless it be the going backwards and forwards to the college ... and walking to and from the parish of Kirkliston, where we were born, at the end of every week if the weather was good; we used to study for fifteen hours a day, and sometimes more, with little or no intermission.' The contrast between this regime and life at an English university was obvious: a Scot who went to one of them remarked that the undergraduates were much idler than he could have conceived. And the same contrast was made by the English Captain Topham, who in 1774-75 wrote of Edinburgh: 'There are few places where a polite education can be better acquired than in this city.'

The Scots also had the advantage of being good linguists. They were apt at learning foreign languages, and some of them, even now, had had the advantage of studying at a continental university such as Leyden. Unlike English diplomats, who were usually content with French, Scots were prepared to take the trouble to acquire other tongues, and this is sometimes stated to have been a reason for their advancement. Moreover, when at a loss in respect of a modern language and compelled to have recourse to Latin, the Scots — again unlike the English — used a pronunciation which foreigners could understand. James Boswell was 'entertained' when he heard the Westminster boys speak Latin in the English manner.

The penetration of Scots into other professions has not been explored as it has been for the diplomatic service. In the eighteenth century they did not as yet possess anything like the importance which they came to possess in the later nineteenth and twentieth centuries, when, according to the story, they monopolised headships of departments. And the time was still far distant when — to mention only the two highest positions in church and state — out of ten successive Prime Ministers six were Scots (Gladstone, Rosebery, Balfour, Campbell-Bannerman, Bonar Law and Ramsay Macdonald) and out of five successive Archbishops of Canterbury three were Scots (Tait, Davidson and Lang). Scots have sometimes been heard, in the present reign, to complain that Scots have no part in a coronation, and need to be reminded that both the late king and his father were crowned by Scotsmen, taking their proper place in a British coronation. But already, in the late eighteenth century, Scots were sufficiently prominent in public life to be remarked. The Earl of Bute was Prime Minister. From 1756 the Lord Chief Justice was Lord Mansfield (who, however, had been educated in England and illustrates the truth of Dr Johnson's remark that 'much may be made of a Scotsman if he be caught young'). Alexander Wedderburn, first of all Solicitor General, became Chief

Justice of the Common Pleas and then the first of several Scots to hold the highest judicial office of all, that of Lord Chancellor. Hay Drummond was Archbishop of York. Two Scots were Lords of the Treasury. One was the Queen's private secretary. Allan Ramsay was the painter and Robert Adam the architect most in favour at court. Scots were prominent in the army and navy as well: Lord Loudoun was Commander-in-Chief in America in 1756 and second-in-command in Portugal in 1762; James Murray succeeded to Wolfe's command when the latter was killed on the Heights of Abraham, and became first civil governor of Canada; Hector Monro won the battle of Buxar in 1764.

The path to promotion in almost every vocation was then generally through 'patronage', which, all else apart, was one feature in the 'management' of parliamentary elections. Scots had exceptional opportunities because Henry Dundas, 1st Viscount Melville (1742-1811), himself held office at one time or another as Lord Advocate, President of the Board of Control for India, Treasurer of the Navy, Home Secretary and Secretary for War; and those offices gave him patronage through which he was able to control the elections in 36 of the 45 Scottish constituencies. Opportunities in colonial administration, though beginning to expand, were still limited, but John Macpherson was Governor General of India in 1785, and later Walter Scott was able to refer to the India Board as 'the corn chest for Scotland, where poor gentry must send our younger sons as we send our black cattle to the south'. At home, at the centre of the British government, from 1707 until 1789 Scotland provided only three cabinet ministers; from 1789 to 1832 it provided ten.

When Scottish penetration had first become marked, in the 1760s, it had aroused strong criticism. The first Scot to achieve front rank in the United Kingdom was John, Earl of Bute, as no less than Prime Minister. He was personally unpopular — 'a mushroom minister bearing the odious name of Stuart and unexpectedly elevated to the premiership by royal favour', and he was blamed for the prominence attained by his fellow-countrymen:

> Nothing with gentle George's nose will suit
> But burrs and thistles from the Isle of Bute.

That was unfair, for the Scots were making their way before Bute came on the scene, and the unpopularity of 'Jack Boot' might just as likely have had an adverse effect on the prospects of his compatriots. But it was the age of Wilkes and *The North Briton*, when Englishmen were inflamed until they saw signs everywhere of a conspiracy of Scots headed by Bute. A pamphlet of 1766 read: 'The Scots have poured in upon us like swarms of locusts, into every quarter and every scene of life. The army abounds with them.... Divinity is not without them.... And even the law, which used to be pretty clear of them, begins to abound with their dissonant notes and ragged quality. Physic has them plentifully likewise. And where there is anything to be got, you may be sure to find a number of Scotchmen convened, like hounds over a carrion or flies in a shambles.... It would be happier for this country if it were to become a province of France, rather than to continue in subjection to Scottish men. Who would not sooner be a slave to a gentleman than to a blackguard?' Horace Walpole wrote in 1773: 'Colonial governments and embassies were showered on the Scotch, while officers and private men of that nation crowded, or were crowded, into the army and navy.' At the same time a letter in the *Public Advertiser* asked: 'Tell me if we are not a ruined and insulted people, if the black whirlpool of the north has not borne down all before it.' On the other hand, the sober writer of a pamphlet of 1778 called *Scotch modesty display'd* went to the trouble of going through the Royal Kalendar to analyse the numbers of Scots in positions in the royal household and in the army and navy, and he proved to his own satisfaction that they were not in truth heavily represented.

It is not difficult to detect some reasons for the unpopularity of the Scots, even leaving aside the fact that Bute's own position tended to distort attitudes. The Scottish members of parliament had a reputation, whether deserved or not, for being unduly subservient and venial. Scots were sneered at for their speech and their ecclesiastical idiosyncrasies. Englishmen who had seen their own country invaded in 1745 by a small and mobile army which came from Scotland felt humiliated and did not stop to consider either that in 1745 there had been more Scots in arms on the government side than on the rebels' side or that the great majority of Scots, especially Lowlanders and Presbyterians, had welcomed the Duke of Cumberland. One Englishman declared that 'A Scot is a natural, hereditary Jacobite' and it was useless for General Douglas, writing from London a fortnight after Culloden, to protest that 'disaffection has been most unjustly and indiscriminately imputed to the whole nation.... We are in general looked on as a rebel people'. But perhaps the chief reason for the Scots' unpopularity was simply their manifest success as careerists. Smollett's *Roderick Random* gives a certain picture of the Scots in England in that period.

English visitors to Scotland, however, do not seem to have been much influenced by the prejudices which affected those who did not leave the deep south, and on the whole they regarded the country with a more kindly eye than their predecessors in the seventeenth century. None of them are severely critical, at least of Lowland Scotland. Bishop Pococke, in 1760, was almost consistently laudatory. I think he only once complains even about the weather. He thought the road between Perth and Edinburgh was 'the finest turnpike road in Britain'. Of Edinburgh he wrote: 'The streets of Edinburgh are finely paved like St James's Square, with a gutter on each side near the walking place, which (the gutter) is cut in a semicircular form in hewn stone about eight inches broad, through which the water runs that overflows the reservoir towards the Castle (i.e. on Castlehill, at the foot of the esplanade), which is supplied by water brought from the Pentland Hills by pipes; and is kept full for use in case of fires. There are flagstones for foot people on each side of the street, with stones set up to keep off the carriages, which is a late improvement.' No doubt cleanliness still left much to be desired, but English visitors were now looking not for features to criticise but for features to praise. Their approval did not extend to the Highlanders, who had not yet acquired a romantic and glamorous image. One visitor described how in the summer, when the tenants and their cattle migrated to the hill grazings, the women milked the cows and made butter and cheese while the men mostly idled — 'stretched in crowds basking in the sunbeams, or else in the whisky house'. Bishop Pococke remarked, 'By the sea they have plenty of fish in summer, and yet they will hardly be at the pains of catching it but in very fine weather'. There were, moreover, some Englishmen who continued to be prejudiced against Scots because of their success in England. Thus William Cobbett, who had expressed his hearty dislike long before he visited Scotland in 1832: 'The Navy will, like India, soon be a Scotch thing altogether.... This miserable Northern corner of the island, the whole of which is not worth so much as the county of Kent and does not pay so much clear into the King's Exchequer, is fast getting possession of ... all the good things of the English Navy.... I look upon the cormorant Scotch ... as being far less my countrymen than the Yankees are.'

Scottish visitors to England were sometimes less satisfied with what they saw there. Mrs Calderwood of Polton, who travelled in England in 1755, took a poor view of the inns on the Dover road, and of London, with its brick houses; she thought the capital looked all too much alike, so that if she saw one part she saw the whole. She thought the English in general parochial and narrow in their outlook. And she was not impressed by the leading politicians: 'those who know and see our ministers every day see there is no wisdom in them, and that they are a parcel of old, ignorant, senseless, bodies, who mind nothing but eating and drinking and walking about in Hyde Park'. Boswell, too, tells us that his respect for the House of Commons 'was greatly abated by seeing that it was such a tumultuous scene' — something which has not changed in more than two centuries. Scots who settled in England, and had come to know the English, were more favourable. A Scots gardener — one of many employed in England at that time — remarked that 'though God had not given the English overmuch wit or sense, yet they were braw bodies to live with'.

The principal casualty in Scotland was of course the vernacular. As late as 1740, when a Scottish judge made a speech in the House of Lords, a brother judge commented that the English understood not one word. Yet less than a generation later Johnson wrote: 'The conversation of the Scots grows every day less unpleasing to the English; their peculiarities wear fast away; their dialect is likely to become in half a century provincial and rustick, even to themselves. The great, the learned, the ambitious and the vain, all cultivate the English phrase and the English pronunciation, and in splendid companies Scotch is not much heard except now and then from an old lady'. Johnson's hint that the cultivation of English was deliberate is perfectly true. One reason for seeking education in England was the desire to learn to speak in a way intelligible to southerners. When Fergusson of Kilkerran sent his son to England he decided not to send a Scots servant with him because 'as I hope for a great improvement in his language, which in this country is wretchedly bad, I am afraid a Scots servant might do him harm that way'. And in writing to his son he remarks, rather pathetically, that one of his objects had been to 'send you among strangers who speak a language I could not teach you'. In 1761, Thomas Sheridan, father of the famous Richard Brinsley Sheridan, delivered a lecture on the English language (in St Paul's Chapel, Carrubbers Close, Edinburgh) to three hundred noblemen and gentlemen, including James Boswell. This led to the formation of a society for speaking and reading correctly — of which that sturdy old Jacobite, Sir Stuart Threipland, was, rather oddly, a member. When Boswell went to London, we find him deliberately cultivating southern speech. Although his Scots blood could 'boil' on occasion, he had not been long in the metropolis when it pained him to meet Scots fresh from Scotland. 'The Fife tongue and the Niddry's Wynd address were quite hideous', he tells us at one point. Again, 'I ought not to keep too much company with Scotch people because I am kept from acquiring propriety of English speaking'; and 'Mrs Miller's abominable Glasgow tongue excruciates me. I resolved never again to dine where a Scotchwoman from the West was allowed to feed with us'.

The vernacular was a long time a-dying. About 1840 Cockburn suggested that the change was then spreading down the social scale. 'The sphere of the Scotch language is speedily and rapidly abridging. The lower orders still speak Scotch, but even among them its flavour is not so fresh and natural as fifty years ago, particularly in the towns. This is the necessary consequence of the increased habit of reading English books and of listening to English discourses, and of greatly increased English intercourse. When I was a boy, no Englishman could have addressed the Edinburgh populace without making them stare and probably laugh. Scotch is pretty deeply engrained into the people, but among the gentry it is receding shockingly.... We lose ourselves. Instead of being what we are, we become a poor part of England.' But, on the other hand, it must be admitted that it had been precisely when denationalising had been gaining momentum that Scottish cultural and intellectual achievement had reached unprecedented heights.

Among the factors which extended English influence improvements in transport and communications have been the most powerful. Scott noticed this nearly two centuries ago: 'The mail-coach and the Berwick smacks [which, designed for conveying Tweed salmon speedily to London, offered passengers a shorter journey than was then possible by land] have done more than the Union in altering our national character, sometimes for the better and sometimes for the worse.' And Scott did not live to see a railway service, still less an air-service. Later factors aiding assimilation have been the cinema, broadcasting and the press. Much of the newspaper market is held by popular dailies originating in the south, but even so-called 'national' newspapers bear clear marks of being written partly by English people or anglicised Scots who direct readers to go to the Public Record Office in London to see Scottish Census records and refer to a treaty between 'Britain' and the Netherlands in 1528.

There were other factors, less obvious but very potent. One was the acceptance in Scotland of English literature and English history. For three centuries and more the two countries have shared an ever-growing body of English literature — much of it, it is true, written by Scots and some of it by Irishmen, but still literature which reflects English society and culture. This heritage has given an English slant to education as conducted even in purely Scottish schools. Equally, the study of English history and the neglect of Scottish history have been influential in Scottish universities as well as Scottish schools. Scottish children were apt to learn more about Magna Carta than about the Declaration of Arbroath, about the Petition of Right than about the National Covenant and perhaps even about Alfred and the Cakes than about Bruce and the Spider. The idea has been widely insinuated that the two countries share the same historic heritage, which is not altogether true. The victory has not been complete, for I doubt if Scotland has taken over the heroes of English history and made them her own; I suspect that Ralegh, Drake, perhaps even Nelson, probably still seem somewhat remote, if not alien, in Scottish eyes. Anyone who lectures on Scottish history knows that one way to raise a giggle or a snigger is to mention John Knox, who is regarded as the embodiment of ideas which never crossed his mind. When you tell people that Knox had no objection in principle to a Prayer Book, that he was in some ways less puritanical than contemporary popes were and that he did not disapprove of bishops, the shutters visibly go up. People will not believe you. It is the same with the Covenanters; 'It is news to me that the Covenanters massacred women and children. I refuse to believe it'. I sometimes wonder if, when Knox declared that God of His providence and mercy had erected the archbishops as principals in ecclesiastical jurisdiction in England, he was rebuking the Almighty for not extending similar providence and mercy to Scotland.

Then the industrial revolution and subsequent economic developments, with the great social changes which accompanied them, intensified class divisions. The horizontal division into classes seemed again — as had been true in the thirteenth century — more important than the vertical division into nations. Not only could the Scottish 'worker' be persuaded that his interest and that of the English 'worker' were one, but the unity of some industries throughout Britain increased the sense of solidarity. The entire Trade Union Movement and Socialism generally were based on such concepts. Scotland is still a more egalitarian country than England (where men are divided into those who say 'Sir' and those to whom 'Sir' is said), but the class consciousness which came to prevail in Britain as a whole was more in keeping with English tradition than Scots.

A factor often overlooked is the result of the immigration of English people into Scotland. Much was made a century ago of Irish immigration, but recent figures show that in Scotland there are now far more people of English than of Irish birth. Not all the immigrants are eager to come, and indeed some schemes for dispersing civil servants from England to Scotland encountered strenuous opposition. And anyone can notice that some Englishmen who come north for employment regard their sojourn in Scotland as a disagreeable exile or interlude from which they escape as soon as they are free to do so. Others, however, not only find Scotland tolerable but even enjoy their new homes and choose to remain in Scotland when they retire. They succeed in a quite unaffected manner in identifying themselves with their adopted country, and their neighbours and colleagues cease to think of them as English. Others again, not content with such quiet assimilation, try to make themselves more Scottish than the Scots. An Englishman who is sensitive about his position may feel that the best way to secure acceptance is to wave the ScotNat flag a bit. I recall remarking in my Inaugural Lecture that 'among my predecessors it was Professor Dickinson alone, a Yorkshireman, who sometimes gave what might be called a nationalist interpretation to the history of his adopted country, and he wrote with considerably more emotion than either Hume Brown or Hannay had done'. Of course, one cannot fail to see that an Englishman holding a Chair of Scottish History in the capital of Scotland could hardly afford to be other than rampantly Scottish, if only to escape the SNP slogan, 'English go home' — a cry which sometimes raised serious apprehension. Plainly, the irritation which many Scots feel about Englishmen occupying prominent positions in Scotland is by no means generally justified. Yet some of the incomers seem peculiarly insensitive, to the extent of declining to learn the correct pronunciation of Scottish names. It is disagreeable to sit through a graduation ceremony in Edinburgh and hear a Dean, presenting the candidates, saying Wadd*ell* or La*mont* or *Mun*ro or *Dun*lop or making Louttit rhyme with cow-tit. Are they arrogant, or have they simply no ear?

This is not the place to enter into the very important factor of the Scottish contribution to the British Empire, for I could say nothing I did not write in a book called *The Scots Overseas*. Scotland populated and administered the Empire to an extent far out of proportion to her population; and her substantial share in this field enormously increased the sense of unity with England.

I come finally to a factor which is not often enough stressed — namely the gradual penetration into Scotland of a sense of sharing in British foreign policy and British wars. The many wars of the eighteenth century did not make much impression on the Scots. Days of thanksgiving or fasting for national victories or defeats were duly observed but aroused little enthusiasm. The Border minister Ridpath, in his Diary, for instance, does refer to the great battles of the Seven Years' War, but as a rule in only a word or two. The delay in receiving news, especially of events on the other side of the Atlantic or in the far East, was probably a good reason for the coolness of Scottish interest. In April 1758

Ridpath was reading *The Scots Magazine* for February, which contained an account of the Black Hole of Calcutta in June 1756. There was even the danger that more recent events had cancelled the rejoicing or mourning which for the moment seemed appropriate: it was said that one minister, who had announced a victory one Sunday and learned before the next Sunday of a subsequent defeat, had to admit, 'My brethren, it was a' lees I telt ye last Sabbath'. The later acceleration of the news services must have contributed to the sense of sharing. But, in any event, the long French wars of 1793-1815, during which Britain was at times in very grave danger, consolidated national feeling as British. Attention has often been drawn to the way in which those wars were the first to be commemorated in monuments and street names in Scotland, and it was for those wars that the Scots for the first time planned a national monument, the unfinished structure of which stands as twelve pillars on the Calton Hill.

The change in public opinion can be traced in the popular attitude to the armed forces. Scotland can hardly be said to have had a standing army before the Revolution of 1689, though the Scots Guards are dated from 1662, the Royal Scots Fusiliers from 1678 and the Scots Greys from 1681. The disturbed conditions at and after the Revolution led to the embodying of the Cameronians and the Earl of Leven's (or Edinburgh) regiment, which became the King's Own Scottish Borderers. In the circumstances of the personal union, when Scotland had in effect no independent foreign policy, the forces of the king could be called on for any campaigns, and some Scottish regiments fought with English and allied forces in the wars of Marlborough. After the Union of 1707 nearly a generation elapsed before any more Scottish regiments were raised, now under British auspices. Then nine appeared during the War of the Austrian Succession and the Seven Years' War, all but three of them under the inspiration of William Pitt, who said, with reference to a decision in 1757: 'I have no local attachments; it is indifferent to me whether a man was rocked in his cradle on this side or that side of the Tweed. I sought for merit wherever it was to be found. I found it in the mountains of the north. I drew it into your service, a hardy and intrepid race of men.' By 1763, then, there were sixteen Scottish regiments, and most of those which had been raised under British auspices were from the Highlands. For the American War of Independence and the French wars which followed no less than another thirteen regiments of foot were raised in Scotland, five of them in the Highlands. In addition, regiments for home defence, called 'Fencibles', were organised.

Throughout most of the country — the Highlands were a partial exception, and some Lowlanders of good social standing were glad to serve as officers — there was an inveterate prejudice against the regular army, and most of the regiments stationed in Scotland seem to have been mainly, if not wholly, composed of Englishmen. The day when there would be pride in the achievements of Scottish regiments was yet remote. If a son enlisted it was a family disgrace and to get him out was a matter of family honour. One minister remarked that in nineteen years in his parish only one person had been banished for theft and only one had enlisted as a soldier; and he adds the quaint comment that 'having been got out of the army he has ever since lived an industrious labouring man'. It should be added that, while a kind of smear was attached to volunteering, ministers showed no sign of disapproving of the powers of the government to call men up for the defence of the realm: the Rev. John Mill, a Shetland minister, supported the government's demand for soldiers and approved of conscription for the navy.

There was even less hesitation about the part-time service of militia and volunteers. The rejection of a proposal for a militia in Scotland during the Seven Years' War was displeasing to many Scots, and during the American War there was something of an outcry about the undefended state of the country. When war with France started again in 1793 the question was raised once more, and in 1794 there came the Volunteers. Initially their object was police as much as defence, in a period when there was apprehension lest Scotland might follow the example of revolutionary France, so persons willing to co-operate in the maintenance of 'internal tranquillity' were invited to enrol. By 1796 there were companies in forty-one districts, and the membership was not confined to the middle and upper classes, but had become more broadly based socially; some thought such an extension was dangerous, but Volunteers were used success-fully against rioters in Edinburgh in 1800.

Scotland at length got a compulsory militia for home service in 1797, when the Militia Act provided for the selection of 6,000 men aged 18-23. There was resentment at the exemption from such service of men who were members of the Volunteers, which continued alongside the militia and changed from a police force to a defence force. They were at their most energetic in 1804-5, during the height of the invasion scare. They did plenty of drilling and manoeuvring, and certainly had the enthusiasm, if they had not the skill and experience, which would have made them a match for Boney's regulars. They took themselves very seriously. Cockburn wrote: 'We are all soldiers. Professors wheeled in the College area; the side arms and the uniform peeped from behind the gown at the bar and even on the bench; and the parade and the review formed the staple of men's talk and thoughts.' Patriotism had done a lot to absorb the Scottish attitudes into those of a United Kingdom. After all, it had been a Scotsman, James Thomson, who had written 'Rule, Britannia' in 1740, and it was another Scotsman, Thomas Campbell, who wrote 'Ye mariners of England', 'Hohenlinde' and 'The Battle of the Baltic'.

The Edinburgh volunteers received instructions from their commander that they must not go on active service without a worsted or flannel nightcap, two flannel undervests and two pairs of flannel drawers, and no gentleman was to lie down to sleep while warm or with wet feet. Moreover: 'In case of being very wet, it is highly useful to rub the body and limbs with spirits, warm if possible, taking at the same time a mouthful, and not more, inwardly, diluted with warm water, if to be had.' These precautions were to ensure that they should escape the fate, commemorated on a gravestone in the precincts of Winchester Cathedral, of a grenadier in the Hants Militia who died of a violent fever by drinking small beer, when hot, on 12 May 1764, aged twenty-five years:

> Here sleeps in peace a Hampshire Grenadier
> Who caught his death by drinking cold small beer:
> Soldiers, be wise from his untimely fall
> And when ye're hot drink strong or none at all.

# 12

## Presenting Scotland's Historic Heritage

*A slightly modified version of the St Leonard's Lecture,*
*delivered at St Andrews University on 16 November 1984*

My approach to the topic of presenting Scotland's historic heritage is shaped by the fact that I have been in some sense a practitioner in presenting it for half a century. During that time both my interpretation of 'heritage' and my own techniques in presenting it have widened.

I began my professional career as an archivist. I sometimes say that at heart I am still an archivist, but, unlike some archivists, I considered my function as not simply to preserve and administer archives but also to present them. At any rate, I remain very much a documents man, a records man, to the extent at least that few things give me greater pleasure than settling down with a record volume or unfolding a crisp parchment.

I therefore yield to the temptation of giving first place to our archival heritage. It is being presented better than ever before. The central administration of the Record Office in Edinburgh has been expanded out of all knowing, in staff, in premises and in operations — all to meet an enormously growing demand. I don't recall figures for the numbers of readers who came to the Historical Department before the War, but I am sure the total in a year never exceeded 200; recently it has been over 2000. The demand occasionally exceeds the supply, for there have been occasions when there were not enough desks and seats for all the intending readers. And the archives are being presented to a public far wider and larger than the enquiries who apply for permits to use the Search Room. The late Sir James Fergusson, when he was Keeper, initiated special exhibitions, and now there seems nearly always to be at least one, usually with a topical theme, in progress. In addition, there has been the occasional 'Open Day', which can bring over 1,000 people into the Register House.

The great revolution of recent years has been the reversal of the policy of centralisation which long dominated Scottish record policy, and the creation for the first time of something like a system of record offices outside Edinburgh. I say 'something like' a system because there are formally constituted record offices in only five of the nine regions, in four districts and in the island authorities of Orkney and Shetland, but elsewhere various agencies serve as repositories for local archives. Not only are local records thus being retained in local custody, but some local material, transmitted in earlier years to Edinburgh, is now being sent back to the localities. I was always an advocate of such decentralisation, and I recall at one stage holding out as a rough yardstick that anyone should be able to see his local records without having to be away from home overnight.

The other outstanding archival development has been the work of the National Register of Archives (Scotland), whose purpose is to examine and list the archives of private families, semi-public bodies, business firms and other organisations. When it started, in I think 1946, with modest aims, the idea was that it would be a two-year exercise, with inspections of archives being carried out largely by unpaid part-timers. After nearly fifty years, with a vastly extended scope, it has acquired a substantial full-time staff.

There may be a price to pay for the widening scope and aims of the presentation of the archival heritage, in that the central archive authority, in extending its service to the general public, may risk sacrificing its service to scholars. No doubt I may be accused of élitism when I say that. What is happening is that lightweight handlists and finding-aids proliferate, to meet the needs of casual genealogists or even of schoolchildren, while the great stream of published records, as we have known them for over a century, has come to an end. It is also noticeable — and no doubt laudable — that the appointments to the Scottish Records Advisory Council now extend far beyond the circle of academics, legal dignitaries and local authority officials of whom it was made up in the past.

The survey of our archival heritage being undertaken by the National Register of Archives is in some ways parallel to what has been done for our architectural heritage by the Royal Commission on the Ancient and Historical Monuments. The Commission started in 1908 with, it is said, the same modest kind of programme as the Register of Archives: it was all to be done in two years by one man on a bicycle. After eighty years it had not yet covered half the country, despite expanded staff and the facilities provided by modern technology, though, to be fair, the scope and scale of its work and the splendour of its published *Inventories* had come to be in a totally different class from the modest efforts of its earlier years. The Commission finally capitulated and abandoned the splendid *Inventories* which had so long proceeded imperturbably with a serene disregard for changing conditions. It decided, rather like the record authority, to go down-market with a much more lightweight series called *Exploring Scotland's Heritage*, intended to have a wider appeal and to be easier on the pocket. Private — and semi-private — enterprises have also made and are making contributions to supplement the prestigious *Inventories*. *The Buildings of Scotland* series of volumes, which look like a very serviceable 'poor man's *Inventories*', makes progress but it might be reckless to be confident that it will be any more successful than the Commission in covering the whole country. Meantime the Royal Incorporation of Architects in Scotland has produced a series of 'Illustrated Architectural Guides' which compress comprehensive information and abundant illustrations into modest and inexpensive books. Such efforts — and other more private ones — can enjoy certain support from The National Monuments Record (a dependency of the Commission), a collection of photographs, drawings and plans of buildings throughout the length and breadth of the country.

Governmental agencies, then, have taken substantial responsibility for surveying two segments of our heritage — manuscripts and buildings. The emphasis of their labours has been heavily on recording, but recording is a necessary preliminary to presenting.

The manuscripts recorded by the Register of Archives and the buildings recorded by the Royal Commission are closely associated with each other, for what is often called 'the charter chest' of a family — which usually means not a single box but the contents of one or more sizeable apartments — is as much a part of the heritage of the family as the furniture or the family portraits. But quite often the house in which the family and the family archives alike had their home has been demolished or has ceased to be a residence, and even when the house is still occupied by the family it is seldom satisfactory to leave the archives there, especially if historians are to have access to them, unless — which can seldom happen — there is a resident archivist. Too often the only solution is removal — though in my view preferably to a local repository (which may well be the family's own preference) rather than to Edinburgh. When the family muniments are thus transferred to a repository, while furnishings and portraits remain in the house, the unity of the heritage is broken, but we do not need to remind ourselves that the charter chest and house belong to each other and some means should be found of linking the presentation of the two. The archivist may be too ready to get his hands on the muniments and ignore their home.

In my own emphasis on the relative importance of archives and other material objects, especially buildings, I — though an ex-archivist — underwent something like a conversion, for my views and my practice changed. In my teaching I was still presenting the heritage — institutions, economy, society — but I was interpreting it more widely. One conspicuous change was my increasing use of other visual aids besides blackboard, maps and the occasional handout of a genealogical table or a list of economic statistics. I was able to draw on the great stock of facsimiles of documents which had happily been preserved in my department — some of them residual plates from the *Acts of the Parliaments* and other record publications, a greater number of them plates from Sir William Fraser's volumes which had presumably been surplus to requirements when publication took place — and I was able to circulate multiple copies, so that each student could have in his hands a facsimile of some document which I wanted to expound. This was, however, a bit cumbersome, and I turned to the flexibility afforded by slides of the facsimiles, though that did not give the students the tactual intimacy of the facsimiles.

But I also began to use slides to supplement documentary material. It did occur to me that, however intelligent a man may be, he may see little to interest him in a document which he is unable to read because of the handwriting or the language or both, and that more impact is made by the most tangible and visible evidence everyone has of the past, namely material objects, especially buildings, which, unlike minor artefacts, reflect a whole way of life and even something of the nature of society. I believe my appreciation of buildings was stimulated by the visits our Ordinary Class used to pay to old castles and churches, initially under the leadership of the late Dr J. S. Richardson, one time Inspector of Ancient Monuments. Richardson would assemble us in front of some piece of building which had a significant feature that was not immediately obvious and would exhort us to use our eyes. And after one of those excursions was over he would remark, reflectively, 'What I'm trying to teach them is to use their eyes'. When Richardson was no longer able to lead our expeditions I continued them myself, literally as well as metaphorically following in his footsteps — and giving some of his anecdotes a further airing. But I began to realise that for teaching purposes slides (although they replaced reality by photography) might be more profitable. After all, one could visit at best two or three sites in an afternoon, whereas with slides one could cover dozens of sites and put them in their context. Slides also liberated us from the hazards of weather: I recall once reaching the pier at Aberdour but being unable to cross to Inchcolm in the teeth of a south-wester, and another occasion I returned home from an East Lothian tour so thoroughly chilled that I promptly took a hot bath and went to bed with a hot-water bottle.

It would now be unthinkable for me to attempt to present the reorganisation of Scotland in the twelfth century, shall we say, without showing examples of motte-and-bailey castles and some Norman churches. And not only Scottish examples. How can one demonstrate the extent to which Scotland was then integrated into the culture of western Europe? No amount of words or documents can equal the conviction one carries on a subject like that by showing pictures to illustrate how people could then have moved throughout western Europe, including Scotland, without being aware of any differences in material culture. 'The face of Scotland' becomes at once apparent and is not significantly different from the face of England, France and countries even farther away.

This increasing interest in buildings as a vehicle of instruction brought me closer to the problems surrounding the presentation of our material heritage and the conservation of that heritage. I was in any event to some extent involved, as a member of the Royal Commission for eighteen years and as a member of the Council and Executive of the National Trust for five years. As properties of one kind and another came before the Trust for consideration I was stimulated to ponder points of principle as well as of detail relating to the presentation of Scotland's heritage.

The Trust is only one of many agencies in the fields of conservation and presentation. There are numerous structures all up and down the country which are the responsibility of what is now called Historic Scotland, the successor, by many stages removed, of the Office of Works. That body has enormously improved its standards of presentation of some of the great historic buildings which are in its care. Some of them used to look rather dowdy, but that cannot be said now. One thinks, for example, of the refurbishment of Stirling Castle, especially the Great Hall, the restoration of which has been such an enormous and time-consuming task that the exterior showed little change between 1977 and 1984. If Historic Scotland is to be criticised, it must be said that its publicity lays too much stress on blood and violence and that its resources are heavily concentrated on the great show-places, while lesser buildings get less attention and may even be relinquished to the tender mercies of local authorities.

Museums, displaying artefacts, have proliferated so much that a recent survey shows that there are over 300 galleries and museums up and down the country. Many of them, of interest for the general history of an area, are long established. More recently there has been increasing emphasis on the specialist museum, like the Maritime Museum in Aberdeen, the Fisheries Museum at Anstruther and the Agricultural Museum at Ingliston. There has been a change in the emphasis of their exhibits too. One used to see mainly prehistoric or at best medieval artefacts, but now one sees the artefacts of yesterday. Indeed it is a little startling for anyone of my generation to see in a museum implements which he himself has used.

I wrote 'galleries and museums', and the two form, from the historian's point of view, a single category. To the historian portraits and many other paintings are a species of documents, but any painting or sculpture is, like architecture, part of our cultural heritage. The museum, as I see it, involves the removal of objects from their context, or one might almost say their habitat, and their display usually with other objects of the same or a similar type and not with other objects with which they were originally associated. I would not go so far as to say that the museum is a necessary evil or even a second-best, for it manifestly has its uses to facilitate comparative study. But the alternative, of preserving objects in their natural habitats, has its value too. I suppose similar alternatives exist for plants and animals — safari parks as opposed to cages — but the zoo and the botanical garden are probably as unavoidable as the museum. It seems to me that one of the great merits of the National Trust's approach is that it is not dominated by a museum concept. It tries instead to preserve furnishings, tools and utensils in their natural settings, frequently in the very premises in which they were used and perhaps are even still being used. We therefore have a presentation not of one facet of the life of a period, but of its whole way of life.

Perhaps the best-known and most appreciated aspect of the Trust's work has been its presentation of great houses and castles, most of them taken over as in effect going concerns, sometimes with the present representatives of the historic owners still in residence almost as part of the plenishing, occasionally even with the muniments still remaining *in situ*, to keep the heritage intact. But how the heritage is to be put before the public in one of those houses is a less simple issue than might at first appear.

A house may have existed for centuries and have undergone many changes not only in its fabric but in its furnishings and in the style of life that has been lived in it. Over the generations possessions accumulated and those that passed out of fashion were not always discarded, but might be retained, so one rarely finds a house that is furnished consistently in the style of one period. The house has passed through various phases, but we have in our hands the place as it took shape in its latest phase. Thus a sense of the earlier periods is hard to find. One is apt to say that the Trust has few Victorian or Edwardian houses in its possession — that is, Victorian or Edwardian in design and construction — but almost all of its properties are Victorian or Edwardian in the sense that they reflect the way of life of those eras — Dun, Kellie and Haddo are examples. How can we present the life of an earlier era?

It would be an inconceivable stroke of luck to find a house which had been, as it were, frozen in one of its earlier phases. We can hardly put the clock back by discarding the accretions of generations. The best solution might be to start with an unoccupied tower of the fifteenth or sixteenth century and furnish it in the manner of the period of its origin. There might be a touch of the museum about this, but it might be the best we could do. Failing that, when I am in a medieval hall I might rather have it empty or at best sparingly furnished, rather than filled with anachronistic plenishing, however comfortable. I noticed in *The Scotsman* of 27 April 1991 an article by Brian Pendreigh heavily critical of the introduction of tableaux of wax figures, audio-visual displays and even fake furniture. He went on: 'The public would prefer to see rooms left bare than filled with furniture from elsewhere in an attempt to create a sense of atmosphere. It leaves much more to the imagination.'

The Trust is not, however, interested only in 'stately homes', castles and great houses. A few years ago it broke new ground by the acquisition of a tenement house in Glasgow — an almost unbelievable opportunity to take over a typical Glasgow dwelling with all its furnishings and artefacts as they had been a hundred years before. Looking at it one realises how much urban interiors have changed in a century — and, incidentally, how the standard of living has risen. The same is perhaps even more true of rural cottages. Sir Steven Runciman remarked in the Trust's *Guide* that 'the interior of the crofter's cottage now looks much the same as the interior of a small villa in a London suburb', and this has become even more true since he wrote in 1976. It is, however, only right to add that the occupant of such a cottage may now be a crofter only in name, for he is as likely as not simply enjoying the privileges of crofting tenure without laying a hand on the croft, which he has turned over to sheep or perhaps let out to caravanners — whence, possibly, his ability to furnish the house like a London villa.

The Trust has its lower-middle class tenement house and it has two or three working-class dwellings, preserved as showplaces primarily because they were the birthplaces of famous men like James Barrie, Thomas Carlyle and Hugh Miller. It rejected an upper-middle class residence when it had the opportunity to acquire Cardy House in Lower Largo, which was as remarkable a case as the tenement house was of a dwelling which, after a century, retained its character and its plenishing.

The presentation of smaller houses poses some of the same problems as do the big houses, but they have their own special problems. Because of lack of space, they do not lend themselves to the shepherding through them of regiments of visitors — 'trampers and gawkers', as I heard them described, not too civilly, by the owner of one stately home. Then a small house is less likely than a big one to come ready furnished, and it is more likely to require to be fitted out and furnished with a selection of artefacts appropriate to its character as a memorial to a famous man. The result is that it looks more like a museum. Ideally, any house, large or small, should be presented as a home. We all know the difference between visiting a castle or mansion as the private guest of the owner and visiting it as one of the 'trampers and gawkers'. But, while it is practicable to continue to live in a stately home, in the midst of its splendour (archaic though it may be), to ask anyone to live in an unaltered, unimproved crofter's cottage is asking him to become himself a museum piece, and no one could do it unless uncommonly dedicated. Not every one would be content to live in even a fair-sized Victorian house if unimproved. The preservation, as homes, of small houses and cottages in un-modernised condition is not practicable, and we may have to settle for their presentation mainly as museums commemorative of distinguished former residents. Once the museum concept is accepted, there is the option of reconstructions of interiors in museum settings, as in the Farming Museum at Ingliston and the Fisheries Museum at Anstruther.

The divergence between the museum pattern and the contrary concept of presenting a living entity applies not only to furnishings but also to structures. The main agency in the care of old buildings, the government department now known as Historic Scotland, has always set its face against any restoration, and considers its function to stop at conservation. As a result there are buildings which stand almost complete to the wallheads and need only a roof to make them serviceable — examples are the Earl's Palace in Kirkwall, Scalloway Castle and Linlithgow Palace. While the department may do conservation work which is beyond praise, it has not been so daring as to put a roof on. The corresponding agencies in other lands seem to think along different lines, and that is why Britain appears to have far more ruins to the square mile than most continental countries. On deciding whether or not to restore, one consideration might very well be: what do we intend this building to recall or represent? Linlithgow Palace, as it stands, is not, as it might be, a presentation of the court of James V, but a presentation of the destruction wrought by Hawley's dragoons in January 1746.

It is undeniable that there may be a case for leaving ruins untouched if they have particular significance as ruins. Coventry Cathedral may be a case in point. Continental examples provide contrasting situations. There is the Marienkirche in Lübeck, where the bells which crashed to the base of the tower during air attack in the Second War have been left in a crumpled heap to form a singularly moving War Memorial. On the other hand, in Bergen, Haakonshallen might have been kept a ruin to commemorate the destruction caused when an ammunition ship blew up in the harbour during the war, but it has been restored as a reminder of the culture of mid-thirteenth century Norway.

It is amusing, too, to reflect that one of Historic Scotland's recent acquisitions, Doune Castle, where I was present to see the keys being handed over by Lord Moray to the Secretary of State in 1985, had been a roofless ruin until it was re-roofed a hundred years ago by the private owner. So Historic Scotland has the building with a roof which that organisation itself would never have put in place.

Other roofs were put on by private enterprise, as Lord Moray did at Doune. It has happened with churches like St Fillan's at Aberdour, which had been abandoned for generations until it was restored in 1926. Until a few years ago St Mary's Church in Haddington, with its roofless choir and transepts, was a memorial — a singularly elegant one — to the work of English invaders in the 1540s. Now re-roofed, it is a memorial to the prosperity and piety of late medieval burgesses and a monument to the culture of twentieth-century East Lothian.

Again rather oddly, while the government refuses to put on roofs, it gives grants which enable others to do so. The Historic Buildings Council has helped to save and maintain a good many properties, largely in private hands. More recently, in 1980 there came along the National Heritage Memorial Fund, set up to give financial assistance for 'the acquisition, maintenance and preservation of land, buildings and objects of historical or other importance to the national heritage'. Other more modest funds can sometimes help and it is not unknown for local authorities to be generous. Such grants may have a merit of flexibility, for they usually leave some latitude to owners and their architects, and they help private owners, great and small, instead of taking over the properties for the state or some impersonal authority, and this means that houses are more likely to be presented as homes.

One of the beneficiaries of the National Heritage Memorial Fund has been the National Trust for Scotland. It has not, so far as I recall, embarked on an ambitious scheme for restoration of the roofless ruin of a major building such as a great house or castle — or that standing reproach, Balmerino Abbey. But its work in restoring properties large and small is well known, and during the last hundred years or more many private owners, aided partly from sources already mentioned and partly by local authority housing and improvement grants, have rescued 'castles' once roofless and ruinous and have made them habitable: Barcaldine, Duart, Kisimul, Stalker, Breachacha in Coll, Fawside near Tranent and Niddrie near Winchburgh. More modest structures have likewise been restored by private owners, with grants to assist them; there are two in the Shetland island of Yell.

There has been a transformation in cities as well, led by something of a change of policy. About the middle of the twentieth century the only answer to the problem of tenements which had decayed (largely because taxation and rent restriction had made it impossible for landlords to maintain them) was demolition: 'It's auld, ca' it doon' was the cry. But in the last thirty years or so such properties have been lovingly restored, with the assistance of various grants. There was not always a change of heart on the part of local authorities: Burntisland Burgh Council reiterated its determination to demolish Rossend Castle, and the building was rescued by private enterprise. Yet even in official hearts a change can take place. For generations the two sides of the Shore of Leith, and much of the Dock area, were bordered by a uniform arrangement of elegant cast-iron columns and chains. Then, in what I can only call a total eclipse of reason, and in the face of strong protests, Edinburgh Corporation decided to replace one section of the old arrangement with the kind of conventional crash-barriers familiar on motorways. After some years of this eyesore I learned to my astonished delight that the crash-barriers had been superseded by restored pillars and chains. Even a local authority can be educated.

The remit of the National Trust is the 'permanent preservation for the benefit of the nation of lands and buildings of historic or national interest or natural beauty'. Possibly those who drafted the phrase were thinking of land of natural beauty and buildings of historic interest, but that was not what they said. They specified lands as well as buildings of historic interest. This authorised the Trust to acquire a number of historic sites — Bannockburn, Killiecrankie, Culloden, Glenfinnan, Glencoe and Iona. Most of those sites were places of natural beauty as well, but each offered an opportunity to present an aspect of the historic heritage. There could, unhappily, be no mistaking where the emphasis was going to lie: three of the six were battlefields, one the scene of the raising of a standard of rebellion, one best known as the scene of a massacre. Iona as well as Glencoe was once the scene of a massacre, but while tears are shed for the 38 thievish MacDonalds who were killed in Glencoe in 1692, not one is to spare for the 68 blameless monks who were killed in Iona in 806. It is extraordinary how stereotypes are fixed. Yet, among those six sites, Iona alone stands mainly for something other than the blood-and-thunder side of Scottish history. And, of the seven Trust properties which lead in the popularity stakes, blood-and-thunder sites take second, fourth, fifth and seventh places. No doubt there is something to be said for giving the public what they want and catering for 'greeting patriots'.

It so happened that, as I was on the Trust's Executive when both Bannockburn and Culloden came up for review, I had plenty of opportunity to ponder the problem of presenting battles. Personally, I believe battles are over-rated. perhaps the one lesson to be drawn from all the centuries of warfare is the sad one of the futility of it all. Think of all England's medieval wars: centuries of expenditure of blood and treasure in attempts to conquer Scotland and France, and the only thing that England gained at the end of it all was the single town of Berwick-upon-Tweed. Who will say it was worth it? But, apart from the outcome of the wars, peaceful pursuits continued during them. I often recall that on 3 September 1939, when Neville Chamberlain announced that Britain was at war with Germany, he reminded us that the life of the nation must go on. And over the centuries, through all the wars, it has gone on. (I alluded to this topic in the context of Culloden in the Introduction to this book and in the context of Flodden in the chapter on 'Archives and the Historian', but it is the former which is relevant to assessment of the work of the National Trust.) Less than 5,000 Highlanders were in the Jacobite army at Culloden — about the average size of a miners' picket in the strike of 1984-5 — and I remember saying many years ago 'Let's hear less about the 5,000 or so Highlanders who were at Culloden on 16 April 1746 and more about the quarter of a million or so Highlanders who were nowhere near Culloden, some of them at home industriously weaving linen'. One may suggest, similarly, that the really important thing about the battle of Prestonpans was not that a small army of rebels routed a small army of regulars but that it was the first battle in history in which a railway line figured — the old wagonway from the Tranent pits to Cockenzie harbour.

The presentation of Prestonpans is a particularly interesting case, for the place — never mind the battle — has a lot to offer, in a remarkable concentration of monuments from around the reign of James VI. Preston Tower itself is of fifteenth-century origin, but it has a significant early seventeenth-century addition at the top. Hamilton House is 1628, Northfield House bears the date 1611. Nearby is the superb Mercat Cross, of 1617, and not far away the later, once-elegant, Bankton House. There is a beehive-shaped doocot behind Northfield as well as a lectern-shaped doocot in the grounds of the Tower. These illustrations of Scottish culture are far more important than the battle: in short, Prestonpans should be presented not as Jacobite but as Jacobean.

But battles are picturesque, battles are exciting, and each is a famous victory — for one side or the other:

> 'Now tell us all about the war
> And what they fought each other for?'
> But what they fought each other for
> I could not well make out.
> 'But what good came of it at last?'
> Quoth little Peterkin.
> 'Why, that I cannot tell,' said he,
> 'But 'twas a famous victory'.

Little Peterkin's intelligent questions are seldom asked by those who flock to Bannockburn and Culloden. And when they are asked the wrong answer is usually given. Bannockburn, we are told, was a decisive battle which secured Scottish independence. But Bannockburn was no decisive battle: within twenty years Scotland was overrun again and once more an English vassal sat on the Scottish throne. One might say, a little cynically, that as the Scots generally lost their battles against the English it does no harm to let them celebrate this victory, and it is profoundly true that Bannockburn did demonstrate that the English could be defeated.

There are more serious criticisms than that of the presentation of Bannockburn. It is not usually seen in its European context or even in the context of the art of war. In a socio-political context Bannockburn fits in with Courtrai in 1302 and Morgarten in 1315, two other battles in which a force consisting largely or mainly of peasant infantry defeated mailed knights. Not only so, but in terms of tactics Bannockburn was no more than a precise re-run of Courtrai. King Philip of France had declared Flanders annexed to his crown, had garrisoned Flemish towns and appointed French officials to administer the country. Then in May 1302 a Flemish insurrection drove the French out of most of Flanders, and the insurgents besieged Courtrai, which was soon believed to be on the point of surrender. To relieve it Robert, Count of Artois, led the feudal levies of the north of France, with ample cavalry. The Flemish army, which lacked full support from the local nobility, was mainly an infantry force, composed of townsfolk and peasants, armed with pikes and spiked clubs and clad in heavy tunics of quilted cloth or leather, and steel hats. Count Robert came on the Flemings drawn up before Courtrai in a position well protected by a stream running through bogs and pools to join the river Lys. They were posted athwart the road from Menin to Courtrai, with the Lys on their left and ditches running into the city moat on their right, and they strengthened their position further by digging 'pots' in front of their line. The difference from Bannockburn was that they did not have a Torwood in the rear as a possible refuge in the event of suffering a reverse. They were in one body of about 10,000 men, with a small reserve behind the centre and a force to block the exits from the castle lest the garrison should sally out and take them in the rear. After an initial attack on

them by crossbowmen the Flemings retired, whereupon Count Robert withdrew his light infantry and launched his cavalry, who got mixed up with the
retiring crossbowmen and got stuck in the marshy ground and the 'pots' and
lost their impetus, whereupon the Flemings took the offensive and did
enormous destruction among the French. Sir Thomas Gray, author of the
*Scalachronica*, whose father was taken prisoner at Bannockburn, wrote: 'the
Scots had taken a lesson from the Flemings, who had at Courtrai defeated the
power of France'. Morgarten, in 1315, when the Swiss defeated their enemies,
was more like Stirling Bridge, with a narrow road running between a mountain
side and a lake in place of the bridge.

But to say that Bruce was merely imitating the Flemish commander of eleven
years earlier (of whose exploit he must have known) would detract from the
fame of The Good King Robert. That apart, however, I confess it had not
occurred to me to see much wrong with the presentation of Bannockburn until
two things happened. One was that a local authority in the north of England
brought forward plans for what I suppose they called the 'development' of the
field of Flodden. This raised an outcry among Scots, who said that the place was
essentially a war grave, appropriately marked by a simple memorial inscribed
'To the brave of both nations', and it should not be desecrated by car-parks, ice-
cream kiosks, public conveniences and a children's playground. But this
brought a retort from the English: 'Why should we not commemorate our
victory over a foreign invading army?' That was exactly what the Scots were
doing at Bannockburn, and it seemed hard to deny the English the right to do
the same at Flodden. But the site of Bannockburn, too, is a graveyard, and what
might be considered the desecration by the Trust's display is hardly palliated by
the fact that not many casualties occurred on that spot, as most of the fighting
took place more than half a mile away.

Nor had it occurred to those who planned the display at Bannockburn that
little sympathy was shown for the English, who presumably suffered far more
than did the Scots. The English, fortunately, are a tolerant people and I recall
only one complaint, which led us to remind visitors that Scotland and England
have long been united under monarchs descended from both the commanders
at Bannockburn and that the brave of both nations have many times fought side
by side in the cause of a wider liberty. We should have been alerted to this hazard
because, many years ago, there was an outcry in Scotland when an English
society proposed to erect at Dunbar a memorial to Cromwell's victory over the
Scots in 1650. We thought that insensitive, but was it any more insensitive than
what we do at Bannockburn or what the English proposed for Flodden? (I may
say that I visited Flodden again in 1992 and found that all that had happened
was a modest and discreet car park — with only four cars in it and a prohibition
of buses, caravans and camping — a litter bin with an unobtrusive notice,
'Please take your litter home' and a path leading up to the monument, while a
plough was peacefully at work in an adjoining field. I had forgotten how steep

the slope is, and I realised afresh as I came down what a tremendous momentum the Scottish phalanx must have gathered as it moved down that hillside. I could hardly check my footsteps. One would never get a comparable impression at Bannockburn. I suppose that at Flodden there is less to distract the imagination.) At the lowest, I have more sympathy with the English view of Flodden than with the people who want to rename Waterloo Station: has it really come to this that we are ashamed of the fact that our ancestors ever won a battle?

And how is Culloden presented? That was a battle which can properly be claimed as decisive, in that it finally extinguished all possibility of a Stewart restoration. It is not, however, presented, as it might be, as a victory by a British government supported by the great majority of the people of Scotland and England alike — a victory which secured the throne to the dynasty to which we are almost one hundred per cent loyal today. Culloden could in fact be presented as a close parallel to Bannockburn, and not only because in both battles there were Scots on both sides. Bruce, like the Hanoverians, had a rival in 'a king over the water' in the person of John Balliol and then his son Edward, whose hereditary right, like that of the Stewarts, was the stronger. Bruce, like George II, could plead only a statutory title or something like it. Thus Bruce was not cast for the part of a successful Bonnie Prince Charlie but for the part of the successful George II. Odd.

As most Scots were in a sense on the winning side at both Culloden and Bannockburn each battle deserves to be acclaimed as a famous victory. In the presentation at Culloden it is emphasised that the battle was not an Anglo-Scottish encounter but a battle in a civil war in which even the Highlands were far from being of one mind. I remember suggesting that we might have a register of the names of all persons known to have been in the armies on both sides, so that visitors could see whether persons of their name had taken part. That did not go down very well, for the people who flock to Culloden are not in general going to commemorate a famous victory but believe that their ancestors supported 'that messianic prince' who 'is still one of the cherished components of Highland nationalism', to quote a recent writer. And, as it happens, a book which went on sale at Culloden lists the men in the rebel army, leaving the government soldiers anonymous. To put it at the lowest, over-emphasis on the Jacobite army is offensive to people whose ancestors were on the other side. And of course the divisions among the Highlanders make it nonsense to refer to 'The defeat of the Gaels' at Culloden. But the 'civil-war' character of Culloden could be brought out more emphatically. Why not display an extract from the Address to the Duke of Cumberland by the General Assembly of the Church of Scotland which met a month after the battle?

> That the General Assembly of the Church of Scotland has met at this
> time in a state of peace and security exceeding our greatest hopes, is,
> under God, owing to his Majesty's wisdom and goodness in sending
> your Royal Highness, and to your generous resolution in coming to be

the deliverer of this Church and nation....

The Church of Scotland are under peculiar obligations to offer their most thankful acknowledgments to Almighty God, who has raised you up to be the brave defender of your Royal Father's throne, the happy restorer of our peace and, at this time, guardian of all our secular and civil interests....

That the Lord of Hosts, who has hitherto covered your head in bloody battles, may still guard your precious life amidst those dangers to which you may be yet exposed, in leading armies against the common invaders of the liberties of Europe, and crown you with the same glorious success over our enemies abroad which you have obtained over traitors at home ... shall be the prayers of ... the ministers and elders met in a General Assembly of the Church of Scotland.

Two days later ministers and kirk sessions were instructed to censure those who had taken part in the 'late unnatural rebellion'. I do not believe that Culloden had far-reaching significance at all, or that the history of Scotland (and even of the Highlands) would have been substantially different had the battle never been fought or if the '45 had never taken place. It is a landmark to the extent that never again did a Highland army threaten the Lowlands (as had happened in 1644-5, 1689 and 1715); but would such a threat have occurred again without the '45? The '45 may have had some effect in accelerating social and agrarian changes in the Highlands which had started and would have taken place in any event. For one thing, landlords who were forfeited and exiled lost their connection with their tenants. True, they mostly got their estates back after forty years, but habits had been broken on both sides. Further, the Forfeited (or rather Annexed) Estates were maintained and administered by commissioners who encouraged agrarian improvements and modified land tenure. Admittedly, these conditions applied only in limited areas, but example might have been influential elsewhere.

Culloden is still presented, in one word or at any rate in two hyphenated words, as a tear-jerker. We are reminded of the atrocities after the battle. But we hear nothing of the atrocities after Bannockburn. After Culloden we hear of the cruel treatment of prisoners; after Bannockburn we do not hear of prisoners at all. I suggested at a meeting of the Trust's Executive that after Bannockburn prisoners who were not worth ransoming simply had their throats cut, and Sir Steven Runciman, who knows about medieval warfare, concurred.

Culloden, which was laid out, not much more than a hundred years ago, with its neat rows of 'Graves of the Clans', is presented as a graveyard. But when does a battlefield become a graveyard, or when does it cease to be a graveyard? There is a time element. The battlefields of this century are thought of primarily as war graves, but this concept recedes as we move back in time, though it is not a steady or consistent recession: Flodden is remembered as a war grave, but the comparable Scottish disaster of Pinkie, thirty-four years later, is not, and the site is not even marked except, rather oddly, by a stone on the ground where the English camped the night before the engagement.

Reflection on the subject suggests that the presentation of battles is apt to be full of paradox or plain illogicality. I remarked earlier that two things happened to give me second thoughts about Bannockburn and that one was the English attitude to Flodden. The other was the war in the Falkland Islands. War, even though remote geographically and small in scale, was suddenly brought home to us and, owing to television, we realised both the fervour war aroused and the suffering it caused. This reinforced my doubts about setting up funfairs on battlefields. And my doubts might have been sharpened had Britain lost that war. Not long ago I was speaking to a group of Americans and somehow the matter of attitudes to battlefields was raised. I mentioned the Falklands War, and went on, 'But you too have had experience of war since World War II. You had Vietnam'. The difference was at once pointed out to me: 'You won', someone said. All in all I conclude that the sensitive and appropriate presentation of battlegrounds gives rise to enormous problems.

I was led on to the subject of battlefields by reflecting on the National Trust's holdings of lands as well as buildings — and not only or even mainly historic lands, but the heritage in topography and landscape, flora and fauna, the natural as opposed to the man-made inheritance. It is impossible to enlarge on this topic, except to say that the interests of the natural and the man-made can conflict. Obviously the demands of naturalists in relation to Sites of Special Scientific Interest can conflict acutely with the interests of farmers. It would be interesting to have a debate between John Prebble, who thinks that the Highlands, as a result of the 'Clearances', have too much wilderness already, and the conservationists, who are all for more wildernesses. The conflict was sometimes exacerbated by extravagant statements. Farmers on Lochtayside expressed fears that they were going to be compelled to clear their sheep from Ben Lawers, and pointed out, not unreasonably, that if the sheep had had any appetite for the precious Alpine plants the Alpine plants would have vanished long ago. It was startling, too, to read that in Fetlar 'damaging reseeding and reclamation operations are being carried out by crofters on breeding grounds of whimbrel, snowy owls and arctic skuas'. 'Damaging reclamation operations' indeed, at a time when it was still thought desirable to extend agriculture and when, whatever the over-production in Europe, there are food shortages throughout the world. And that statement was made at least ten years after the snowy owls had ceased to breed in Fetlar. Such pre-eminent claims of ornithology reminded one of the bogus roseate terns in *Rockets Galore*. The area of Fetlar from which the public were to be excluded in the interests of snowy owls and other birds bore a close resemblance to the area which was cleared of its tenants for the sake of sheep in the last century. The naturalists seem to be saying 'Hurrah for the Clearances', a sentiment with which Mr Prebble would hardly agree.

However, conservation of the natural heritage (since April 1992 vested in Scottish Natural Heritage) can sometimes be combined with conservation of historic heritage. In Lanarkshire the great natural beauties of Clydesdale are presented as joint attractions with the industrial archaeology of New Lanark and the architectural grace of Châtelherault. Perhaps the naturalists' interest in Ben Lawers might ensure the preservation of that nearby feature, the old settlement of Lawers down by the Loch, perhaps Scotland's best example of a deserted village. In the island of Rum the primary interest of the Nature Conservancy is wild life, but that monument of Edwardian grandiosity Kinloch Castle, which might otherwise have been abandoned, was preserved by that authority's own resources, to the tune of about half a million, with only token assistance from the National Heritage Memorial Fund. On the other hand, conflict can arise when restrictions in the interests of nature are placed on access to sites of historical interest: access to the island in Loch Leven with the remains of St Serf's Priory, a prime historical site, is barred in the interests of the birds.

Mentioning access brings me to another point. There are a good many sites and structures which are difficult of access and which seem to have become more difficult of access despite 'progress'. That remarkable book by T. S. Muir, *Ecclesiological Notes on some of the Islands of Scotland*, published in 1885, was based on personal visits to some very out-of-the-way places. While Muir meticulously dates his visits, he is reticent about how he made them except when he occasionally alludes to 'engaging a boat'. The same phrase occurs many times in Tudor's *The Orkneys and Shetland* (1883): 'engage a boat', writes Tudor airily. It cannot be done so readily now and there is little chance of seeing some of our historic heritage unless, like the MacNeils at the Flood, you have a boat of your own. If I had not had a boat of my own I would never have been at Glensanda Castle or the castle on Shuna of Appin or the chapel on Bernera, off Lismore, not to mention some places in Shetland. And if I had not had friends with boats of their own I would never have been on Eilean Munde in Loch Leven or seen the beehive cells on Eileach a Naoimh in the Garvelloch Islands. Official persons now make use of helicopters.

In that context, the National Trust has done invaluable service with its cruises. I suspect that in the last forty years more people have visited St Kilda than had been there in all the previous centuries. Sometimes I wish the Trust or some other agency would turn its attention to places which are not remote and yet are difficult of access, like the islands in the Firth of Forth. It always seems odd that Historic Scotland, which runs a boat to its priory of Inchmahome, does not do as much for its abbey of Inchcolm (though it is now otherwise served). And how many have viewed the remains of the sixteenth-century fortifications on Inchkeith and its lighthouse, now nearly two hundred years old? I would never have viewed them but for the co-operation of Dr Marcus Merriman of Lancaster University, who regularly conducts his students to such exciting places and is enterprising enough on occasion to 'engage a boat' as Muir and Tudor used to do.

Small islands can attract visitors, if facilities are available. In one recent year Inchcolm recorded 17,700. A few years ago, on a foray across the Border I reached the Farne Islands, where I learned that the premises of the English National Trust there had 40,000 visitors in a year, which puts them almost on the level of Falkland Palace and far ahead of places like Culross or Craigievar. I wondered why so many people are attracted to the Farne Islands, except possibly by the pleasure of having a boat trip. The historical associations are not great, the scenery is trivial by our standards and I see a greater variety of birds from my windows at home.

A whole new field for presenting the heritage has been opened up with industrial archaeology. And there are whole categories of buildings which used to be at the very core of the life of the nation. As Professor Smout observed in the *National Trust Guide*, churches and schools are not being presented by the Trust. It is not strictly true that the Trust has no churches among its properties, for, besides the unmentionable Balmerino Abbey, it does have a church with a roof on — the church on St Kilda, where I once attended a service when on a cruise. Churches, however, on the whole fare quite well at the hands of other agencies. As to schools, I would just observe that in recent years two very notable buildings in Edinburgh have ceased to be used as schools — the Royal High School and John Watson's — and as far as I know the opportunity was missed to preserve a specimen of an historic classroom.

It is true that the Scots were often all too ready to replace old buildings which had become inconvenient with new structures. Or, perhaps especially with churches, when preserving an ancient church they chose to give it treatment which was designed to disguise — and which often did disguise all too successfully — its medieval character.

I recall an incident when I lived in Prestonpans and was one day walking up to my home in the shadow of the old Tower. I overtook a man and woman and, I suppose, their teenage daughter, who said, 'I wonder what they'll do with that old tower.' 'Pu' it doon and build hooses', said one parent. 'Blaw it up', said the other. The girl entered a mild protest, 'Is it not historic?' to which the retort was 'To hang wi' history.'

# Index